Mary Berry

Cooks the Perfect

STEP BY STEP

Mary Berry

Cooks the Perfect

STEP BY STEP

Penguin Random House

Senior Editor Polly Boyd
Senior Art Editor Karen Constanti
Managing Editor Dawn Henderson
Managing Art Editor Christine Keilty
Senior Jacket Creative Nicola Powling
Designer Miranda Harvey
Editorial Assistant Elizabeth Clinton
Producer, Pre-Production Rob Dunn
Senior Producer Stephanie McConnell
Creative Technical Support Sonia Charbonnier
Art Directors Peter Luff and Maxine Pedliham
Publishing Director Mary-Clare Jerram
Recipe consultation Angela Nilsen and Jeni Wright
Recipe photography William Reavell and Stuart West
Author photography Georgia Glynn Smith

NOTE: The author and publisher advocate sustainable food choices, and every effort has been made to include only sustainable food in this book. Food sustainability is, however, a shifting landscape, and so we encourage readers to keep up to date with advice on this subject, so that they are equipped to make their own ethical choices.

First published in Great Britain in 2014
This edition published in Great Britain in 2016 by
Dorling Kindersley Limited
80 Strand, London WC2R 0RL

A CIP catalogue record for this book is avaliable from the British Library.
ISBN 978-0-2412-8286-1

Printed and bound in China

A WORLD OF IDEAS:
SEE ALL THERE IS TO KNOW

www.dk.com

Contents

Introduction

Welcome. I'm very excited about this recipe collection. All of the recipes are brand new – some are my tried-and-tested favourites given a refreshing twist; others contain a selection of new ingredients or flavour combinations. I have included a variety of recipes for the whole family to enjoy, quick suppers for you to rustle up after work, and impressive dishes for when you're entertaining. I'm sure you'll find much to tempt you.

One of the most exciting things about this book is that it's given me the opportunity to crystallize the knowledge and experience I've gained over so many years of cooking for my own family and friends, and to pass them on to you in a way I hope you'll find useful.

For each recipe, I identify the "key to perfection" – that is, the crucial part that you need to get right to guarantee excellent results. Sometimes it's a case of preparing some of the ingredients correctly, or you might need to be aware of a technical step during the cooking process or learn to recognize when a dish is done. Whatever it is, the step-by-step photographs and guidance make it easy to understand what you need to do to get the recipe perfect. Imagine I'm in the kitchen, cooking alongside you. I might just gently say in your ear, "Ah, watch out for this bit" or "Keep an eye on that". Well, that's what I'm doing here, while sharing with you a host of techniques that I've honed over the years. Some of the recipes may look a little longer than my usual ones – but it's not that they're complicated, it's just that I'm giving you more detailed information than I ever have before.

The more you cook these recipes and master the keys to perfection, the more they will become second nature. And who knows, perhaps *you* will then become the one whispering gentle advice into the ear of a less experienced cook! Just read through the recipe and keys carefully, and cook with care, and you, too, will achieve perfect results – time and time again.

Wishing you happy cooking.

Soups

Pea and Ham Soup with Mustard Croûtes

Soup is one of my favourite weekday lunches, and this one is quick and nutritious. I buy ham from the deli, as you can have it cut thickly and it has a good flavour, or use leftover roast ham.

 Serves 4   560 calories per serving

INGREDIENTS

- 50g (1¾oz) butter
- 1 onion, coarsely chopped
- 1 celery stick, coarsely chopped
- 750ml (1¼ pints) chicken stock
- 500g (1lb 2oz) frozen peas
- 2 tbsp snipped fresh chives
- 200g (7oz) roast ham off the bone, excess fat removed
- salt and freshly ground black pepper

FOR THE CROÛTES

- 25g (scant 1oz) butter (room temperature)
- 1½ tsp Dijon mustard
- 16 slices from a baguette loaf, cut about 1cm (½in) thick

1 Melt the butter in a large pan. Add the onion and celery and fry for 8–10 minutes over a medium heat, stirring often, until softened but not browned. Pour in the stock and bring to the boil over a high heat. Stir in the peas and quickly bring back to the boil, then reduce the heat and simmer for 3 minutes or until they are just cooked (see below, Bright green colour).

2 Using a blender or food processor, purée the soup with the chives until smooth. Return the soup to the pan.

3 Shred the ham into small pieces (see below, Bite-sized pieces of ham) and drop it into the soup. Set aside.

4 Make the croûtes: preheat the grill to its highest setting. Beat the butter and mustard together with a palette knife or spoon. Lay the baguette slices on a baking sheet and toast on both sides under the grill until golden. Spread the mustard butter on one side of each slice of toasted bread. (See below, Crispy croûtes.)

5 Reheat the soup briefly over a low heat. Season with salt and pepper, then serve with the mustard croûtes on the side.

KEYS TO PERFECTION

Bright green colour

Add the peas to the boiling stock and start to time the cooking once the stock has returned to the boil. Fast cooking makes the peas soft enough to purée easily without losing colour.

Bite-sized pieces of ham

You are aiming for bite-sized pieces of ham for this soup. Use two forks to shred the meat – one to hold the ham steady and the other to pull it apart.

Crispy croûtes

Watch the slices of bread carefully during grilling to ensure they don't burn. Spread the mustard butter on the bread while it's still slightly warm, so it soaks in.

Roasted Tomato Soup

I've made many versions of tomato soup, but roasting the tomatoes really brings out their rich, sweet flavour. Add the cheese at the last minute, so it doesn't melt too quickly.

 Serves 4    180 calories per serving

INGREDIENTS

- 800g (1¾lb) small, ripe vine tomatoes
- ½ small red onion, coarsely chopped
- 3 garlic cloves, sliced
- 2 tbsp olive oil
- freshly ground black pepper
- ½ tsp caster sugar
- 400ml (14fl oz) vegetable stock or chicken stock
- 1 tbsp tomato purée
- small handful of fresh basil leaves, plus extra small leaves to serve
- salt (optional)
- 125g (4½oz) ball Italian mozzarella cheese, torn into small pieces

1 Preheat the oven to 200°C (fan 180°C/400°F/Gas 6). Scatter the whole tomatoes, onion, and garlic into a large, shallow roasting tin. Pour over the oil and toss all together. Season with pepper and sprinkle the tomatoes with the sugar. Roast for 30–35 minutes (see below, Sweet, soft tomatoes).

2 Remove the roasting tin from the oven and add the stock, tomato purée, and the handful of basil leaves, stirring gently to combine them with the syrupy juices in the tin.

3 Transfer the mixture to a blender or food processor and purée until smooth, then press it through a sieve (see below, Really smooth texture).

4 Pour the soup into a pan to reheat. Check the seasoning (you may not need salt), then ladle into warmed bowls. Scatter some of the mozzarella, a few small basil leaves, and a grinding of pepper on top of each serving.

KEYS TO PERFECTION

Sweet, soft tomatoes

1 A sprinkling of caster sugar over the tomatoes before roasting helps to draw out their sweetness and make the flavour of the soup more intense.

2 You will know the tomatoes are fully roasted when they are soft, starting to burst, and turning brown at the edges. They will have produced tasty, syrupy juices.

Really smooth texture

Sieving the soup gives it a smooth texture and bright colour. Set a fine sieve over a bowl and press the soup through, a little at a time, using the back of a wooden spoon.

Salmon and Prawn Chowder

When served with warm, crusty bread, this makes a perfect main meal soup. It's a combination of two types of chowder – fish and shellfish – gently simmered in a creamy, fragrant broth.

 Serves 4   493 calories per serving

INGREDIENTS

- 25g (scant 1oz) butter
- 1 celery stick, thinly sliced
- 8 spring onions, trimmed: 6 thinly sliced, 2 finely chopped
- 1 tsp chopped fresh thyme, plus extra to garnish
- 1 bay leaf
- 2 tbsp plain flour
- 600ml (1 pint) fish stock
- 90ml (3fl oz) white wine
- 350g (12oz) fluffy potatoes, such as King Edward, peeled and cut into 2.5cm (1in) cubes
- 350g (12oz) salmon fillet, skinned and cut into slices 2.5cm (1in) thick
- salt and freshly ground black pepper
- 100ml (3½fl oz) double cream
- 100g (3½ oz) cooked, peeled king prawns

1 Melt the butter in a large pan. Add the celery, sliced spring onions, thyme, and bay leaf and cook gently over a medium heat for 2 minutes, stirring, until softened but not browned. Stir in the flour and cook for 1–2 minutes.

2 Gradually blend in the stock, then add the wine and potatoes. Bring to the boil over a high heat, still stirring, and cook until the liquid has slightly thickened, then reduce the heat to medium and simmer for 10 minutes or until the potatoes are just tender.

3 Season the salmon with salt and pepper, then carefully slide the slices into the pan. Reduce the heat and simmer very gently, covered, for about 4 minutes or until almost cooked. Remove from the heat, pour in the cream, and scatter the prawns over the top. Cover again and leave to sit for 5 minutes. (See below, Tender salmon and prawns.)

4 Remove the bay leaf and, if necessary, heat the chowder through gently but very briefly, for no more than 1 minute. Ladle the chowder into warmed bowls. Scatter over the chopped spring onions and extra thyme, plus a grinding of pepper if you wish.

KEYS TO PERFECTION

Tender salmon and prawns

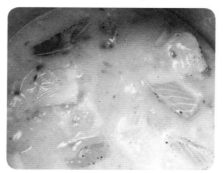

1 After adding the fish to the pan, don't stir the chowder. The salmon will cook better if left undisturbed and won't break into smaller pieces that could become overcooked.

2 As you add the cream, swirl the soup around so it mixes in; don't stir. Leaving the pan off the heat enables the salmon to finish cooking gently and the prawns to warm through.

Mary's
TOP TIPS
1

Read the recipe

Read through a recipe carefully a couple of times: first to check you have the ingredients and equipment, and identify what you need to buy, then again before you start so you're familiar with the order of work.

Summer Vegetable Soup

Early summer offers so many different vegetables and herbs, and this soup is a great way to make use of them. Brief cooking of the beans and asparagus keeps the soup looking and tasting fresh.

 Serves 4    200 calories per serving

INGREDIENTS

- 250g (9oz) podded fresh or frozen broad beans
- 50g (1¾oz) butter
- 125g (4½oz) shallots, finely chopped
- 3 garlic cloves, finely chopped
- 1 large courgette, about 200g (7oz)
- 200g (7oz) small new potatoes, such as Charlotte, scrubbed, halved lengthways, and sliced thinly across
- 900ml (1½ pints) vegetable stock or chicken stock
- 125g (4½oz) fine asparagus, sliced into 5cm (2in) lengths
- salt and freshly ground black pepper
- chopped fresh tarragon, to garnish
- chopped fresh flat-leaf parsley, to garnish

1 Cook the broad beans in a small pan of simmering water for 3 minutes (or up to 5 minutes if using large, fresh beans), then drain and rinse under cold running water. Skin the beans and set aside (see below, Skin the beans).

2 Heat the butter in a large pan. Add the shallots and garlic and fry over a low heat for about 10 minutes, stirring occasionally, until well softened but still quite pale. Meanwhile, grate the courgette down its length to create long strands (see below, Grate the courgette).

3 Add the potatoes to the pan and cook for 3–4 minutes, stirring often, without letting them brown. Increase the heat, then tip in the grated courgette and stir for about 1 minute to start to let it soften and take on the buttery juices. Pour in 750ml (1¼ pints) of the stock and simmer for about 8 minutes or until the potatoes are tender.

4 Add the asparagus and the remaining stock, or less if you like a slightly thicker soup, then simmer for 2–3 minutes or until just tender. Stir in the skinned broad beans to warm them through. Season with salt and pepper.

5 Ladle the soup into wide, warmed bowls and serve sprinkled with tarragon and parsley.

KEYS TO PERFECTION

Skin the beans

1 Very brief simmering ensures the broad beans retain their colour and flavour. As soon as the beans are cooked, drain them in a sieve under cold running water. This will cool them quickly, making them easier to handle.

2 Squeeze one end of each bean so it pops out of its skin. Removing the skins from the podded beans may seem rather labour-intensive, but it shows off their bright colour and accentuates their tender texture.

Grate the courgette

Grating the courgette gives variety of texture. Run the courgette down the coarse side of a box grater for long strands. Using the coarse side ensures the courgette won't disintegrate easily once added to the soup.

Dolcelatte and Leek Soup with Parmesan Crisps

This is a rich version of a popular classic – leek and potato soup. The accompanying Parmesan crisps are easy to make and add a special touch for a smart occasion.

 Serves 4    475 calories per serving   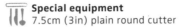 **Special equipment**
7.5cm (3in) plain round cutter

INGREDIENTS

- 600ml (1 pint) full-fat or semi-skimmed milk
- 2 bay leaves
- 2 sprigs of fresh thyme
- ¼ tsp grated nutmeg
- salt and freshly ground black pepper
- 45g (1½oz) butter
- 1 large fluffy potato, such as King Edward, about 300g (10oz), peeled and cut into 2.5cm (1in) cubes
- 2 large leeks, trimmed and finely sliced
- 400ml (14fl oz) vegetable stock or chicken stock
- 85g (3oz) Dolcelatte cheese, cut into small cubes
- double cream, to serve

FOR THE PARMESAN CRISPS

- 50g (1¾oz) Parmesan cheese, coarsely grated

KEYS TO PERFECTION (see overleaf)
Infuse the milk; Gently simmer the vegetables; Add the finishing touches; Make golden brown Parmesan crisps

1 Pour the milk into a small pan and add the bay leaves, thyme, nutmeg, and a grinding of pepper. Bring just to the boil, until you see tiny bubbles appear around the edge of the pan. Remove from the heat and set aside to infuse for 20 minutes. (See p22, Infuse the milk.)

2 While the milk is infusing, make the Parmesan crisps: preheat the grill on its highest setting. Line a baking sheet with baking parchment. Make 8 circles from the grated Parmesan, each about 6cm (2½in) in diameter, on the baking parchment. Place the cutter over each Parmesan circle and spread out the cheese so it fills the cutter. Place the baking sheet under the grill and cook for about 4 minutes or until the cheese is melted and pale golden. Transfer the crisps to a wire rack to cool. (See p23, Make golden brown Parmesan crisps.)

3 Melt 25g (scant 1oz) of the butter in a large pan, add the potato cubes, and cook over a very low heat for 5 minutes or until starting to soften but not turn brown.

4 Increase the heat, add the rest of the butter and the leeks, and cook for 3–4 minutes, stirring often, until almost tender. Pour in the stock and strain the infused milk into the pan. Bring the liquid to the boil, then simmer for 8–10 minutes to finish cooking the vegetables. (See p22, Gently simmer the vegetables.)

5 Using a blender or food processor, purée the soup until smooth. Pour it back into the pan.

6 Reheat the soup and stir in the cubes of Dolcelatte. Remove from the heat and season to taste. (See p22, Add the finishing touches.) Serve topped with a drizzle of cream, with the Parmesan crisps on the side.

KEYS TO PERFECTION

Infuse the milk

Infusing the milk with herbs and spices gives the soup a lovely subtle flavour and aroma. It's important to use full-fat or semi-skimmed milk rather than skimmed, which doesn't have the required strength of flavour and richness. You will need to strain the milk before adding it to the soup in order to remove the flavourings.

Gently simmer the vegetables

Sautéing the leeks briefly over a high heat initially enables them to soften and take on the flavour of the butter without losing their colour. As soon as the leeks have wilted down, stir in the stock and milk. Reduce the heat as soon as they have come to the boil. The soup should simmer gently. If it boils vigorously, it will become too thick and the vegetables will overcook, which will impair the flavour.

Add the finishing touches

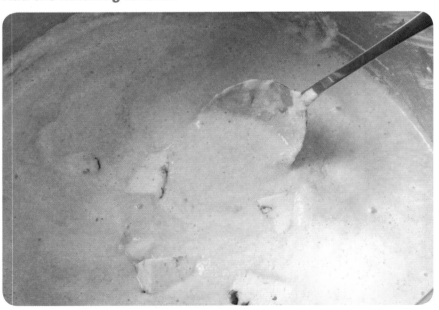

After puréeing the soup, reheat and stir in the cubes of Dolcelatte cheese over a very low heat. As soon as they start to melt, remove the pan from the heat. If the cheese is melted over too high a heat or left over the heat for too long, it will overcook and spoil the texture of the soup. Taste the soup before seasoning with salt; with the stock and cheese, which are both salty, you may not need much.

About Dolcelatte cheese

Dolcelatte is a blue-veined soft cheese that is ideal for this soup, as it has a smooth, creamy texture, mild, slightly sweet taste, and it melts easily. If you can't find Dolcelatte, the texture and taste of Gorgonzola makes it the best substitute, or you could also use Stilton.

Make golden brown Parmesan crisps

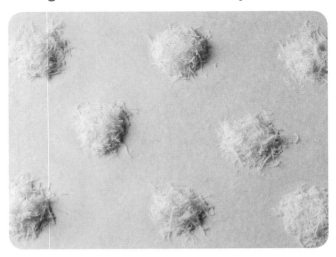

1 It's important to line the baking sheet with baking parchment, because it will prevent the crisps from sticking while they bake. When making the Parmesan circles, you don't have to make them really neat initially: just ensure they're all roughly the same size and that they're far enough apart that they won't touch when grilled.

2 After laying out all the Parmesan circles, place the cutter over each and spread the cheese out as level as possible within the cutter. The cutter will help to make the crisps neater and more uniform in size and shape so they cook evenly. After you've neatened the circles, put the baking sheet under the grill.

Watch the crisps closely!

When grilling the Parmesan crisps, watch very closely, as they can quickly become too brown. The baking sheet should be about 7.5cm (3in) from the heat. If it's too close to the element, the cheese will burn; if too far away, it won't brown well enough to turn crisp. Grill until the cheese has melted and turned pale golden, about 4 minutes.

3 When the crisps are golden, remove the baking sheet from the grill and let the Parmesan crisps sit for 1 minute on the sheet. Lift them off with a palette knife and place them on a wire rack to become completely cold – they will crisp up as they cool. It's best to eat the crisps while they're fresh, as they soften if stored for too long.

Curried Lentil and Spinach Soup

This is one of those really warm, comforting soups made with just enough spice to add interest without being overpowering. To complement the flavours, serve it with warm Indian bread.

 Serves 4    100 calories per serving

INGREDIENTS

- 2 tbsp sunflower oil
- 1 onion, finely chopped
- 2 carrots, diced
- 2 garlic cloves, crushed
- 1½ tsp peeled and grated fresh root ginger
- ¼ tsp ground turmeric
- 2 tsp garam masala (see below, box) or mild curry powder
- 140g (5oz) dried red lentils
- 900ml (1½ pints) chicken or vegetable stock
- 150ml (5fl oz) tomato juice
- salt and freshly ground black pepper
- 50g (1¾oz) fresh spinach, finely chopped
- plain, full-fat yogurt, to serve

1 Heat the oil in a large pan. Add the onion and carrots and fry gently over a medium heat for 8–10 minutes, stirring occasionally, until the onion is very lightly coloured. Increase the heat to medium–high, add the garlic and ginger to the pan, and fry for 1 minute more. Stir in the turmeric and garam masala.

2 Tip in the lentils and pour in the stock and tomato juice. Bring to the boil over a high heat, then reduce the heat and simmer gently for 15–20 minutes or until the lentils and carrots are tender (see below, Al dente lentils). If the soup looks like it is thickening too quickly, pour in a little more stock. Season with salt and pepper.

3 Remove the pan from the heat. Immediately before serving, stir most of the spinach into the soup (it should just start to wilt). Ladle the soup into warmed bowls, top with a scattering of the reserved spinach, and swirl a dollop of plain yogurt into each bowl.

KEYS TO PERFECTION

Al dente lentils

About garam masala

Garam masala, a blend of aromatic spices used in Indian cooking, is really handy to have in the store cupboard. It instantly adds an authentic Indian flavour without the need for buying and storing lots of different spices.

1 While the lentils are cooking, taste them occasionally to see if they're tender. They should be soft but still retain their shape and bite. Overcooking breaks up the lentils and makes the soup too sloppy.

2 After 15–20 minutes, when the lentils and carrots are cooked (and not before), season the soup with salt and pepper. If salt is added too early in the cooking process, it can make the lentils tough.

First Courses

Chicken Caesar Salad Crostini

These crostini are creamy, crisp, salty, and crunchy – all in one delightful mouthful. For informal occasions, you can pass them around with drinks rather than serving them at the table.

 Serves 6  300 calories per serving

INGREDIENTS

- 12 diagonal slices from 1 long white baguette, cut about 1cm (½in) thick
- 3 tbsp extra virgin olive oil
- 85g (3oz) mayonnaise
- 1 garlic clove, crushed
- ½ tsp Dijon mustard
- 1 tsp lemon juice
- freshly ground black pepper
- 115g (4oz) cooked chicken breast
- 8 leaves from a Romaine lettuce, root ends trimmed
- 4–5 canned anchovies, drained and chopped
- 1½ tbsp finely grated Parmesan cheese

1 Preheat the oven to 190°C (fan 170°C/375°F/Gas 5). Brush both sides of the bread with the oil and place the slices on a large baking sheet. Bake for 10 minutes. Turn the bread over and bake for a further 4–5 minutes (see below, Crunchy bread). The bread can be baked up to 1 day ahead and will keep crisp if wrapped in foil or stored in an airtight container.

2 Meanwhile, in a small bowl, stir together the mayonnaise, garlic, mustard, and lemon juice, and season with pepper. Set aside. Finely shred the chicken into small pieces using two forks – one to hold the meat, the other to pull it apart. If it does not shred easily, cut it into fine strips.

3 Just before serving, finely shred the lettuce leaves (see below, Crisp lettuce) and put in a bowl with the chicken and anchovies.

4 Spread just a little of the mayonnaise mixture over one side of each slice of bread. Lightly stir the rest of the mayonnaise into the chicken, anchovy, and lettuce mixture in the bowl. Season with pepper. Pile up a little lettuce, chicken, and anchovy mix on each slice of bread, then sprinkle some Parmesan over the top (see below, Perfect timing). Serve immediately.

KEYS TO PERFECTION

Crunchy bread

Turn the bread over when it's just starting to turn golden. This gives a wonderful crispy texture to complement the topping. Keep a close eye on the crostini, as they can quickly become too brown.

Crisp lettuce

Roll up each lettuce leaf like a cigar and slice it across into fine shreds. Don't do this too early, or the lettuce may wilt, and stir in the mayonnaise at the last minute, otherwise the lettuce will lose its crunch.

Perfect timing

Spread each crostini with the mayonnaise mixture and spoon over the lettuce, chicken, and anchovy topping just before serving. If assembled too far ahead, the crostini will lose its crispness. Finally, sprinkle with Parmesan.

Mango, Parma Ham, and Mozzarella Platter

This is a very easy first course that doesn't require any cooking, just assembling lovely fresh ingredients. If you don't have time to marinate the wraps, simply put it all together at the last minute.

 Serves 4   237 calories per serving

INGREDIENTS

- 125g (4½oz) ball Italian mozzarella cheese
- 6 slices Parma ham
- salt and freshly ground black pepper
- 12 fresh basil leaves
- 1 ripe mango (see below, box)

FOR THE MARINADE

- 2 tbsp extra virgin olive oil
- 2 tsp lime juice
- 1 small garlic clove, crushed
- 2 tsp chopped fresh flat-leaf parsley

FOR THE DRESSING

- 150g carton plain, full-fat yogurt
- 2 tsp runny honey
- finely grated rind and juice of ½ lime

1 Cut the mozzarella into 6 slices, then cut each slice in half lengthways. Cut each slice of Parma ham in half lengthways. You should have 12 slices of mozzarella and 12 of ham. Season each slice of mozzarella with pepper and lay a basil leaf on top. Wrap a strip of the ham around each piece of mozzarella and basil.

2 Make the marinade: mix together the olive oil, lime juice, garlic, and parsley, then season with salt and pepper. Pour this into a shallow dish. Put the mozzarella wraps in the dish and turn to coat well. Set aside for 1–2 hours, but no longer as the Parma ham can soften and lose its brightness.

3 Make the dressing: spoon the yogurt into a small bowl and stir in the honey, lime rind, and lime juice. Set aside.

4 Remove the stone and peel from the mango and cut the flesh into thin slices (see below, Attractive mango slices). To serve, arrange the mango slices on a platter. Sit the mozzarella wraps on top, with the join underneath, and drizzle over the marinade. Serve with the dressing on the side.

KEYS TO PERFECTION

Attractive mango slices

1 The stone runs flat through the centre of the mango, so using a sharp chef's knife cut the fruit vertically down either side of the stone to give you two mango "cheeks". Peel the mango cheeks and remaining mango.

2 Put a mango cheek on a board, flat-side down, and cut it lengthways into thin slices. Repeat with the other half. Finally, slice off any bits of flesh clinging to the stone into neat wedge shapes.

Buying and using mangoes

Choose a mango that is fully ripe, as that will give the best flavour, colour, texture, and shape. To test for ripeness, press the fruit at the tip of the stalk end; it should have a bit of give. Also, it should have a perfumed aroma.

Aubergine, Butter Bean, and Chorizo Tapa

Spicy and colourful, this Spanish-style appetizer can be served hot or at room temperature. If you're preparing it ahead, keep the butter bean mixture moist by drizzling over a little olive oil.

 Serves 4  215 calories per serving  **Special equipment**
Ridged cast-iron chargrill pan

INGREDIENTS

- 2 tbsp olive oil, plus extra for drizzling and frying
- 1 tbsp lemon juice
- 1 aubergine, sliced into rounds 5mm (¼in) thick
- salt and freshly ground black pepper
- 115g (4oz) firm Spanish chorizo
- 1 onion, halved lengthways and thinly sliced
- 1 red pepper, deseeded and cut into small pieces
- 2 garlic cloves, finely chopped
- 115g (4oz) cherry tomatoes, cut into small pieces
- 400g can butter beans, drained and rinsed
- 2 tbsp chopped fresh flat-leaf parsley

1 Mix the oil and lemon juice in a bowl. Preheat the chargrill pan over a high heat for 5–10 minutes. Brush one side of the aubergine slices with half the oil mixture. Chargrill for about 3 minutes. Oil the other side and grill for 2 minutes (see below, Soft, chargrilled aubergines). Transfer to a large, shallow dish, season, and drizzle over some olive oil. Set aside.

2 Slice the chorizo very finely (see below, Crisp chorizo shavings). Heat a large, non-stick frying pan and add the chorizo slices. Fry for 2–3 minutes over a high heat, turning often, until crisp. Using a slotted spoon, transfer the chorizo to kitchen paper to drain. Leave the oil from the chorizo in the pan.

3 Reduce the heat to medium–high and add the onion, red pepper, and garlic. Fry for 6–8 minutes or until softened and starting to brown, adding extra olive oil as needed. Increase the heat to high, add the tomatoes, and cook until softened. Stir in a few tablespoons of water, then add the butter beans to warm through. Season well with salt and pepper, remove from the heat, and stir in the parsley.

4 Spoon the butter bean mixture onto 4 plates, top with folded slices of aubergine, and scatter over the crisp chorizo shavings.

KEYS TO PERFECTION

Soft, chargrilled aubergines

Crisp chorizo shavings

1 When you add the aubergine, the pan must be very hot and the slices must fit in a single layer. Place the slices oiled-side down and chargrill for 3 minutes or until soft. While grilling, brush the tops with the remaining oil.

2 When the undersides of the aubergines are starting to look soft and juicy, and the markings from the ridged pan have become a dark golden colour, turn the slices over. Cook for a further 2 minutes or until soft.

Slice the chorizo using a very sharp knife, as thinly as possible on the diagonal. The thinner the slices are, the more the chorizo will create interesting curly shapes and become crisp when fried.

Chilled Salmon Terrine

Having a smart first course that can be made ahead and kept in the fridge until needed is really handy when entertaining. Top this terrine with a few pretty leaves and serve chilled with toast.

 Serves 8

 311 calories per serving

Special equipment
450g (1lb) loaf tin, 19 x 8.5cm (7½ x 3½in) and 5.5cm (2¼in) deep, with 750ml (1¼ pints) capacity

INGREDIENTS

- 200–250g (7–9oz) smoked salmon in long slices
- freshly ground black pepper
- 100g (3½oz) roasted salmon flakes
- 225g (8oz) full-fat cream cheese
- 115g (4oz) butter (room temperature)
- 1 tbsp lemon juice
- 1 tbsp hot horseradish sauce
- 4 tsp finely chopped fresh dill, plus small sprigs to garnish
- baby salad leaves, to garnish

1 Dampen the bottom and sides of the loaf tin using a pastry brush dipped in water. Line the tin with cling film so that it overhangs the sides. Cut 3 slices of salmon into long strips about 6cm (2½in) wide. Line the bottom and sides of the tin with the slices, allowing 3.5–5cm (1½–2in) overhang. (See below, Firm, well-shaped terrine, steps 1 and 2.) Sprinkle with pepper.

2 Make the pâté: put the salmon flakes, cream cheese, butter, lemon juice, and horseradish sauce in a food processor. Purée the mixture until smooth and season with pepper (you shouldn't need salt, as the salmon is salty).

3 Spoon one-third of the pâté into the salmon-lined tin and spread evenly to level the surface. Scatter over 2 teaspoons of the chopped dill. Continue with another third of the pâté, the remaining dill, and then the last of the pâté. Bring the smoked salmon overhang over it to cover (see below, Firm, well-shaped terrine, step 3), then the cling film overhang. Chill for at least 6 hours, preferably overnight, to firm up.

4 Serve the terrine straight from the fridge, as it will be easier to slice. Turn it out of its tin onto a serving plate. Peel off and discard the cling film and garnish the top with dill sprigs and baby leaves. Slice with a sharp knife.

KEYS TO PERFECTION

Firm, well-shaped terrine

1 Lining the tin with cling film makes the terrine easier to remove and helps to keep its shape. Dampen the tin first and smooth the cling film over the bottom and sides, plus allow some overhang. Don't worry about wrinkles.

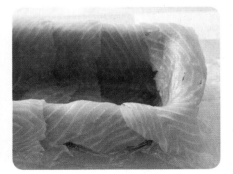

2 Line the tin with the salmon as neatly as you can. As the size of salmon slices can vary, you may need to trim or overlap them and patch up any gaps with leftovers. Lightly press the salmon strips so they stick together.

3 After adding the layers of pâté and dill, fold over the smoked salmon overhang, filling any gaps with leftover salmon and folding over the ends. Cover the terrine tightly with the cling film overhang before chilling.

Pan-fried Scallops with Warm Tomato Dressing

King scallops are always a treat, being particularly large and succulent. Here, dainty asparagus tips make the perfect base for them to sit on; like the scallops, they are cooked very briefly.

 Serves 4    260 calories per serving

INGREDIENTS

- 2–3 tbsp olive oil
- 100g (3½oz) asparagus tips, cut into long, thin, diagonal slices
- 12 king (large) shelled scallops, trimmed (see below, box)
- salt and freshly ground black pepper

FOR THE DRESSING

- 3 tomatoes
- 1 small shallot, finely chopped
- 1 garlic clove, finely chopped
- 4 tbsp extra virgin olive oil
- 1 tbsp lemon juice
- 1 tbsp finely chopped fresh parsley
- 1 tbsp finely snipped fresh chives

1 Make the dressing: skin the tomatoes and remove their seeds and juice (see below, Deseed the tomatoes). Cut the flesh into small dice. Put them in a small pan with the shallot, garlic, extra virgin olive oil, and lemon juice, and set aside.

2 Heat 2 tablespoons of the olive oil in a large, non-stick frying pan. Add the asparagus tips and stir-fry over a medium–high heat for 2–3 minutes or until just tender and starting to brown. Remove from the pan and keep warm.

3 If necessary, add a little more oil to the pan. When the oil is very hot, add the scallops. Season and cook briefly for 2–3 minutes (the cooking time depends on their size), turning once halfway through cooking (see below, Tender, golden scallops). When done, they should be opaque and browned on both sides. Remove from the pan and keep warm.

4 While the scallops are cooking, warm the dressing over a medium heat for 2 minutes, then take off the heat and stir in the parsley and chives. Season with salt and pepper. Divide the asparagus among 4 plates and top with the scallops. Serve with the warm dressing spooned around.

KEYS TO PERFECTION

Deseed the tomatoes

To ensure that the dressing is not too watery, remove the seeds and juice from the skinned tomatoes. Over a small bowl, scoop out the insides with a teaspoon, or gently squeeze with your hand, and discard.

Tender, golden scallops

The scallops must fry quickly, as they can soon become tough and rubbery. Get the oil very hot and press them down with a fish slice; the outsides should be golden brown, the centres slightly rare.

Buying and using scallops

Scallops must be very fresh, so check they smell sweet and their flesh is plump, soft, and creamy. Trim them using sharp kitchen scissors to cut off the crescent-shaped muscle found on the side of the body, as this can be slightly tough. If the scallops have their orange coral attached, you can leave it on, if you wish, as it is a delicacy.

Crispy Garlic Prawns with Lemon and Coriander Mayonnaise

This makes a lovely light, piquant first course. The tails are useful for dipping, so if you can't find peeled, tail-on prawns, buy shell-on prawns and peel them yourself, leaving the tail ends on.

 Serves 4    396 calories per serving

INGREDIENTS

- 16 raw peeled tiger prawns (with tails left on), deveined
- 3 tbsp olive oil
- 4 garlic cloves, finely chopped
- 1 tbsp chopped fresh coriander

FOR THE MAYONNAISE

- 2 large egg yolks
- 1 tsp Dijon mustard
- 1 garlic clove, crushed
- salt and freshly ground black pepper
- 150ml (5fl oz) olive oil
- 2–2½ tsp lemon juice
- ½ tsp finely grated lemon rind
- 1 tbsp chopped fresh coriander
- a generous splash of Tabasco
- pinch of caster sugar

1 Make the mayonnaise: place the egg yolks, mustard, garlic, and some salt and pepper in a bowl and combine using a hand-held blender. With the blender still on, add the oil very slowly, blending all the time, until it has all been mixed in and the mixture has thickened (see below, Creamy, smooth mayonnaise). Stir in 2 teaspoons of the lemon juice, the lemon rind, coriander, and Tabasco. Check the seasoning, adding a little sugar and more lemon juice if desired.

2 Season the prawns with salt and pepper. Just before serving, heat the oil in a large, non-stick frying pan over a high heat, add the garlic and prawns, and stir-fry for 1–2 minutes (see below, Tender prawns) until the prawns are just cooked and the garlic is golden and crisp. Do not let the garlic burn, or it will have a bitter taste.

3 Toss the coriander into the prawns, then pile the prawns onto 4 plates, spooning over the crispy garlic and any juices. Serve immediately with the lemon and coriander mayonnaise.

KEYS TO PERFECTION

Creamy, smooth mayonnaise

Pour in the oil, drop by drop at first, then in a slow, steady trickle, and blend continuously until the mixture thickens. If you add the oil too quickly at the beginning, the mayonnaise will start to separate.

Tender prawns

Fry the prawns over a high heat and keep them moving. If cooked too slowly or for too long, they can become tough and chewy. Take them off the heat as soon as they turn from opaque to pink all over.

My tips for curdled mayonnaise

If the mayonnaise separates, try beating in 1 tablespoon of hot water. If that doesn't work, you may need to start again by combining 1 fresh egg yolk and 75ml (2½fl oz) of oil as before. Once the eggs and oil have thickened, gradually stir in the curdled mayonnaise.

Twice-baked Mushroom and Camembert Soufflés

The beauty of this recipe is that the soufflés can be baked ahead and kept for several hours, then just before serving they can be re-baked and will come out of the oven all puffed up again.

 Serves 6   481 calories per serving

Special equipment
Six 150ml (5fl oz) ramekins, about 8cm (3¼in) diameter and 4.5cm (1¾in) deep

INGREDIENTS

- 60g (2oz) butter, plus extra for greasing
- 150g (5½oz) chestnut mushrooms, chopped into small, even-sized pieces
- salt and freshly ground black pepper
- 45g (1½oz) plain flour
- 300ml (10fl oz) full-fat hot milk
- 3 large eggs, separated
- 100g (3½oz) Camembert cheese, cut into small cubes
- rocket, to garnish

FOR THE SAUCE
- 300ml (10fl oz) double cream
- 4 tsp grainy mustard

KEYS TO PERFECTION (see overleaf)
Fast-fry the mushrooms; Make a thick, smooth soufflé base; Lighten the mixture; Bake light, fluffy soufflés; Re-bake the soufflés; Make a creamy sauce to finish

1 Generously butter the ramekins. Melt 15g (½oz) of the butter in a large, non-stick frying pan over a medium–high heat, add the mushrooms, and fry for 3–4 minutes or until they start to turn brown and all their juices are reduced (see p42, Fast-fry the mushrooms). Remove using a slotted spoon, drain on kitchen paper, season with salt and pepper, and set aside to cool. Preheat the oven to 220°C (fan 200°C/425°F/Gas 7).

2 Make the soufflé base: melt the remaining butter in a large pan over a medium heat. Stir in the flour and cook, whisking continuously, for 1 minute. Remove the pan from the heat and whisk in the hot milk very gradually. Return to the heat and bring to the boil, whisking all the time, until thickened. (See p42, Make a thick, smooth soufflé base.)

3 Cook for a few seconds, still stirring, then remove the pan from the heat. Beat in the egg yolks, one yolk at a time, then stir in the mushrooms and cheese and season with salt and pepper. Leave to cool a little.

4 Whisk the egg whites until they form soft peaks. Stir about 1 tablespoon of the egg whites into the egg-yolk mixture, then carefully fold in the rest of the whites. (See p42, Lighten the mixture.)

5 Divide the mixture evenly among the ramekins. Place them in a small roasting tin and pour enough boiling water into the tin to come halfway up the sides of the ramekins. Bake the soufflés for 15–18 minutes. (See p43, Bake light, fluffy soufflés.) Carefully remove the ramekins from the tin. Let the soufflés sit for 5–10 minutes.

6 Butter a large, shallow baking dish. Carefully unmould each soufflé and sit them in the dish (see p43, Re-bake the soufflés). (The soufflés can be made to this point several hours ahead and chilled in the dish covered with cling film.) Return the soufflés to the oven and bake for 10–12 minutes, or up to 15 minutes for chilled soufflés.

7 Meanwhile, make the sauce: heat the cream and mustard in a small pan over a medium heat and season with salt and pepper. When bubbles appear round the edge of the pan, lower the heat and simmer gently for 3–4 minutes (see p43, Make a creamy sauce to finish). To serve, spoon and drizzle a little sauce into the centre of each plate and sit a soufflé on top. Garnish with rocket and serve the rest of the sauce separately.

KEYS TO PERFECTION

Fast-fry the mushrooms

It's important to use quite a high heat when frying the mushrooms, so the juices are drawn out and reduce quickly. If the heat is too low, the mushrooms will steam rather than fry, which can create a lot of liquid and make the soufflés heavy.

Make a thick, smooth soufflé base

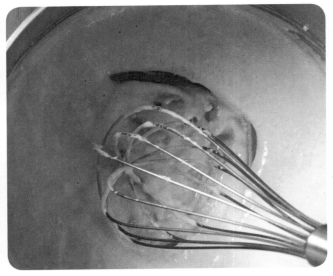

Add the milk to the flour and butter mixture ("roux") a little at a time, and whisk vigorously so it mixes in well and to prevent lumps from forming. When all the milk has been added and comes to the boil, the sauce should be quite thick, similar to the consistency of mayonnaise.

Lighten the mixture

1 Whisk the egg whites in a large bowl using an electric hand whisk on a high setting, or a hand-held balloon whisk, until they form soft peaks (but are not dry) and resemble fluffy clouds. Make sure the bowl and whisk are completely clean and free of grease, and don't under- or over-whisk the whites, otherwise they will lose their power to make your soufflés as light as air.

2 Stir just a little of the whisked whites into the cooled mixture before adding the rest. Fold in the rest of the egg whites using a large metal spoon or spatula rather than a wooden spoon, which can quickly deflate the egg whites. Gently stir the whites through the mixture in a figure-of-eight motion. This keeps the lightness of the whites and prevents the soufflés from sinking while cooking.

Bake light, fluffy soufflés

1 Fill the ramekins to the top with the mixture, so when the soufflés bake they will rise above the ramekins. To allow the soufflés to have the perfect "lift" and not catch on the ramekin sides, run your thumb nail around the inside of the rims to remove any excess mixture.

2 The soufflés are ready when they are risen and golden, and feel springy when touched. Never open the oven door while the soufflés are cooking or they are likely to sink. After the soufflés have rested they will shrink by about one-third, but don't worry. Once they have been re-baked they will become all puffed up again.

Re-bake the soufflés

To make it easier to turn out the baked soufflés, run a palette knife round the inside edge of each ramekin to loosen the sides. Then turn out the soufflé onto the palm of your hand and place it the right way up in a buttered baking dish. Make sure you butter the dish well, so the soufflés don't stick, and don't put the soufflés too close together, as they will expand. Re-bake the soufflés until puffy and golden.

Make a creamy sauce to finish

The simmering cream and mustard sauce will gradually thicken, so keep checking to see if the consistency is as you want it. When the sauce is thick enough to coat the back of a wooden spoon, take the pan off the heat. If you have the heat too high or cook for too long, the sauce will become very thick; if not cooked for long enough, it will be too thin.

Buy good equipment

Kitchen equipment is a long-term investment. Buy the best you can afford: good-quality pans, ovenware, knives, and other utensils all make preparation and cooking easier and more enjoyable, and will last longer.

Asparagus with Soft Poached Egg and Buttery Crumbs

Hollandaise sauce is traditionally served with asparagus, but there's no need for it here, as the poached eggs give a light texture to go with the rich, buttery crumbs. Serve with brown bread.

 Serves 4    230 calories per serving

INGREDIENTS

- 2–3 thick slices white bread (preferably 1 day old) or 50g (1¾oz) fresh white breadcrumbs
- 30g (1oz) butter, plus extra to serve
- ¼ tsp paprika
- salt and freshly ground black pepper
- 450g (1lb) asparagus spears
- 4 large eggs (see p49, box)

1 Make the breadcrumbs: cut the crusts off the bread. Tear the bread into large pieces, put them in a food processor, and process until they make fine crumbs. You will need 50g (1¾oz) of breadcrumbs. Heat the butter in a non-stick frying pan over a medium heat, add the breadcrumbs, and fry until evenly brown and crisp (see p48, Evenly crisp breadcrumbs). Add the paprika and a little salt and pepper. Remove from the pan and set aside.

2 Trim the asparagus spears and lay them in a wide-based sauté pan or frying pan. Pour enough boiling water over just to cover and bring to the boil, then reduce the heat slightly and simmer for about 3 minutes or until just tender. (See p48, Tender-crisp asparagus.) Drain and keep warm.

3 Poach the eggs gently in a pan of simmering salted water over a low heat for about 3 minutes. Remove using a slotted spoon and drain on kitchen paper. (See p49, Soft poached eggs.)

4 For each serving, lay some of the warm asparagus on a plate and dot with a small knob of butter. Carefully place a poached egg on top, season with a little salt and pepper, and scatter over the buttered breadcrumbs.

KEYS TO PERFECTION (*see overleaf*)
Evenly crisp breadcrumbs; Tender-crisp asparagus; Soft poached eggs

KEYS TO PERFECTION

Evenly crisp breadcrumbs

1 Use the pulse button of a food processor until the bread is reduced to same-sized crumbs. If the bread forms big lumps it will be more difficult to get the breadcrumbs evenly crisp.

2 When browning the breadcrumbs in the frying pan, you must keep stirring them with a wooden spoon or spatula, so they cook evenly and don't burn.

Tender-crisp asparagus

1 It's important to buy asparagus that is all the same width, so each spear cooks at the same rate. Before cooking the asparagus, trim the spears by removing the woody ends. Rather than using a knife to cut off the ends, snap them off with your fingers; the asparagus breaks off at the point where the stalk naturally starts to get tender.

2 A large, wide-based sauté pan or frying pan is good for cooking asparagus, as the spears can lay flat. Timing is key: if left to boil for too long, the asparagus will lose its colour and crisp texture. Test for doneness by inserting the tip of a sharp knife into a stalk. If it goes in easily and the asparagus feels tender but still firm, it is just right.

Soft poached eggs

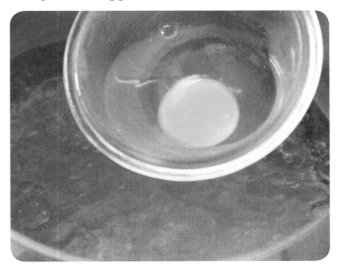

1 Use a slotted spoon to swirl the simmering water in the pan to make a vortex, then crack an egg into a small bowl or cup (this ensures the whites stay contained and won't spread in the water). Slide the egg into the water. Poach only 1 or 2 eggs at a time, so they have room to gently move around without touching each other.

2 As soon as the egg touches the water, turn the heat to low and set the timer for 3 minutes. Swirl the water around the edge of the egg white to gather it in and give the egg a neat shape. Keep the water at a gentle simmer to ensure the egg doesn't get too hard.

Buying, checking, and using eggs

When buying eggs, check them carefully to ensure they're fresh and that they don't have cracked shells. The "British Lion" mark indicates that the birds have been vaccinated against salmonella. Always use eggs before their "best before" date. This is vital from a safety point of view, but also because stale eggs have flat yolks and watery whites, which spoil both texture and taste.

3 When the egg is done, the egg white will look set and opaque and the yolk will look slightly cloudy with a bit of a wobble. Carefully lift the egg out using a slotted spoon and lay it on kitchen paper, so the excess water can drain away. Place the egg with the best side uppermost, in preparation for transferring it to the plate.

Caramelized Red Onion and Rocket Tartlets

These tartlets are easy to make with filo pastry – there's no rolling out, and its crisp texture makes a great contrast to the soft, creamy filling. You can prepare the tin and filling ahead.

 Serves 4    474 calories per serving    **Special equipment**
4-hole Yorkshire pudding tin

INGREDIENTS

- 1 large red onion
- 20g (¾oz) butter
- 2 tsp olive oil
- 1 large egg
- 150ml carton double cream
- salt and freshly ground black pepper
- 15g (½oz) rocket leaves
- 25g (scant 1oz) Parmesan cheese, coarsely grated
- 25g (scant 1oz) mature Cheddar cheese, coarsely grated

FOR THE FILO PASTRY CASES

- 25g (scant 1oz) butter, melted
- 2–3 large sheets shop-bought filo pastry (see p53, box)
- 4 tsp fresh thyme leaves

1 Finely slice the onion. Heat the butter and oil in a large, non-stick frying pan until the butter has melted. Add the onion slices and fry over a medium–low heat for about 15 minutes, stirring only occasionally, until soft and caramelized. Remove the onion, drain on kitchen paper, and set aside to cool. (See p52, Caramelize the onion.) Preheat the oven to 190°C (fan 170°C/375°F/Gas 5).

2 Prepare the filo pastry cases: brush a little of the melted butter in the hollows of the Yorkshire pudding tin. Using a sharp knife, cut 16 squares, measuring 11 x 11cm (4½ x 4½in), from the filo sheets (how many you get from each sheet depends on the brand of filo). Layer up 4 filo squares per hole, each at an angle to the previous squares, brushing melted butter and sprinkling thyme over each one. Scrunch up the pastry edges to add a bit of height. (See p53, Make crispy filo cases.)

3 In a small bowl, beat the egg, then stir in the cream and some salt and pepper. Roughly chop the rocket, setting aside just a few leaves for garnish. In a separate bowl, combine the two cheeses.

4 Carefully spoon the onion into the pastry cases. Scatter over half the cheese and the chopped rocket. Pour in the egg mixture, then top with the rest of the cheese.

5 Bake for 15–20 minutes or until the filling is just set and starting to turn golden brown at the edges. Remove from the tin and serve warm, garnished with the reserved rocket leaves.

KEYS TO PERFECTION (*see overleaf*)
Caramelize the onion; Make crispy filo cases

KEYS TO PERFECTION

Caramelize the onion

1 Peel the onion. Using a sharp chef's knife, quarter the onion lengthways. Cut the hard root from the base, then slice down each quarter lengthways into thin slices. This will give small, delicate pieces that are suited to the scale of the tartlet cases.

2 It's important to fry the onion in a mixture of butter and oil. The butter adds flavour and the oil helps to stop the butter from over-browning during the long cooking time needed to caramelize the onion. Fry the onion very slowly to bring out its sweetness. Stir occasionally to prevent it from burning, but not too often as you want it to start browning where it's in contact with the pan.

3 As the onion starts to turn brown and gets a bit sticky, stir so it doesn't burn and to bring the paler bits of onion to the bottom of the pan so they can also get brown. Scrape up the browned bits at the bottom of the pan using a spatula.

4 When the onion is done, it should be well reduced and evenly caramelized to a rich deep brown colour. Its flavour will become sweeter and more intense during the cooking process. Remove it using a slotted spoon and drain on kitchen paper.

Make crispy filo cases

1 Stack the filo pastry sheets on a board and cut out the 16 squares, each 11 x 11cm (4½ x 4½in), using a sharp knife in order to prevent the pastry from tearing as you cut. Filo pastry dries out extremely quickly and becomes very brittle, so keep the filo covered with a damp tea towel or cling film until you start lining the tins, which you should do as soon as possible.

2 For each case, brush one square of filo with butter and lay it in a hole in the buttered tin; the edges of the pastry square should extend over the rim. Sprinkle with thyme. Repeat for the three remaining squares of filo, laying each at an angle to the previous ones so they overlap, and buttering and sprinkling thyme over each layer. Layering the filo like this strengthens the pastry cases.

Buying and using filo pastry

This paper-thin pastry is not easy to make, but it's widely available in packets containing a number of ready-made sheets. Sizes of filo sheets can vary according to the manufacturer, so for this recipe you may need more than the number of sheets specified to be able to cut out enough squares. Careful handling is important. The sheets are extremely thin, so try not to split or tear them, as it may allow the filling to leak. If the pastry does tear, patch it up with another piece of buttered filo.

3 To add a bit of height and interest to the pastry cases, ruffle up the edges. Use your thumb and forefinger to bring up the sides so they're upright, then turn over the edges in small, soft folds, keeping the sides raised to maintain height. A bit of irregularity with the folds is fine and adds character to the cases.

Fish and Shellfish

Fish Pie with Crushed Potato Topping

The filling for this fish pie is a tasty blend of spinach, salmon, and hake. Instead of putting a classic mash on top, I've used quickly crushed potatoes, drizzled with olive oil to make them crunchy.

 Serves 6　　 525 calories per serving　　

Special equipment
1.7–2 litre (3–3½ pint) baking dish, about 25 x 18cm (10 x 7in) and 7.5cm (3in) deep

INGREDIENTS

- 75g (2½oz) butter, plus extra for greasing
- 1 large leek, trimmed and cut into 5mm (¼in) thick slices
- 50g (1¾oz) plain flour
- 600ml (1 pint) hot, full-fat milk
- 1½ tbsp chopped fresh dill
- finely grated rind of ½ lemon
- salt and freshly ground black pepper
- 400g (14oz) hake fillet, skinned and cut into 2.5cm (1in) cubes (see p59, box)
- 400g (14oz) salmon fillet, skinned and cut into 2.5cm (1in) cubes
- 200g (7oz) fresh spinach

FOR THE TOPPING

- 800g (1¾lb) new potatoes, such as Charlotte, scrubbed
- 2 tbsp olive oil, plus 2 tsp for drizzling

1 Grease the baking dish with butter. Melt 50g (1¾oz) of the butter in a large pan over a medium heat. Add the leek and fry for 3 minutes or until softened but not browned. Stir in the flour and cook, stirring, for 1–2 minutes. Remove from the heat and gradually pour in the hot milk. Return to a medium heat and stir until boiling, thickened, and smooth. Stir in the dill, lemon rind, and some salt and pepper. Add the hake and salmon to the sauce. Cook over a low heat for 2 minutes, stirring gently twice, just to start cooking the fish. (See p58, Make a smooth, creamy filling.)

2 Pour the fish mixture into the buttered baking dish and set aside to cool (see p58, Let the filling cool down). You can prepare up to this point 1 day ahead and refrigerate overnight.

3 Melt the remaining butter in a large, non-stick, deep-sided frying pan or sauté pan over a medium heat. Add the spinach and cook, stirring, for 1½–2 minutes or until it wilts. Drain thoroughly in a colander, pressing down with the back of a wooden spoon to extract excess moisture. Roughly chop and set aside. Preheat the oven to 200°C (fan 180°C/400°F/Gas 6).

4 Meanwhile, make the topping: put the potatoes in a large pan of cold salted water and bring to the boil. Cover and simmer for about 15 minutes or until tender. Drain well. Return the potatoes to the pan and, using a fork, break the potatoes down into rough, chunky pieces. (See p59, Make a crispy topping.) Stir in the olive oil and some salt and pepper.

5 Scatter the spinach on top of the cooled fish mixture, then spoon the potatoes over the spinach layer (see p59, Carefully add the topping). Drizzle over the remaining 2 teaspoons of oil and bake for 30–40 minutes or until the pie is bubbling at the edges and the topping is golden and crispy.

KEYS TO PERFECTION (*see overleaf*)
Make a smooth, creamy filling; Let the filling cool down; Make a crispy topping; Carefully add the topping

KEYS TO PERFECTION

Make a smooth, creamy filling

1 The leek should look wilted before you stir in the flour. However, you don't need to cook it completely, as it will finish cooking in the sauce. Stir the flour constantly for 1–2 minutes, making sure it is combined thoroughly with the butter. Don't let the butter or flour brown. You're aiming for a pale gold paste, or "roux".

2 I like to add hot milk when making a white sauce, as I find it blends into the roux more easily than cold milk and helps to prevent the sauce from turning lumpy. Bring the milk to a gentle simmer, then remove it from the heat. If you keep it simmering for too long, it will start to reduce in the pan. Add it gradually to the roux, stirring continuously.

Let the filling cool down

3 After adding the dill, lemon rind, and seasoning, add the fish to the sauce. Don't stir too much, or the fish may start to break up; you want to keep it in chunky pieces. Just give a couple of gentle turns using a wooden spoon so the fish is well coated with the white sauce.

Let the fish and sauce cool in the baking dish. This will provide a firmer base for when you spoon the potatoes over the top, so they won't sink in. Spoon the spinach over the sauce before adding the topping. The spinach must be well drained so the sauce doesn't get watery.

Make a crispy topping

1 Put the whole potatoes in a pan of cold water (if very large, cut them in half) and start the timing once the water comes to the boil. Reduce the heat slightly and let the water simmer gently. They will take about 15 minutes to cook. To test if the potatoes are done, insert the tip of a sharp knife; it should go in easily.

2 To crush the potatoes, use a fork to break each one into several chunky pieces. You don't want to break them down too much, and they don't need to be completely uniform in size. By crushing them the oil will be absorbed into the potato pieces, which will improve their flavour and make them golden when baked.

Carefully add the topping

Spoon the potatoes quite loosely over the top of the filling, rather than packing them down, so the broken edges can become crisp.

Buying and using hake

Hake is a member of the cod family and has a delicate flavour. Although it has a soft and flaky texture, if handled lightly it's still dense enough to work well and not break up in a fish pie. As when buying any fish, try to choose hake that has been responsibly sourced. Look out for the MSC (Marine Stewardship Council) ecolabel, which means the fish has come from a sustainable fishery.

Pan-fried Plaice with a Cream and Mushroom Sauce

This is a special occasion dish. The cooking is more or less last minute, so it's useful for times when you've invited guests but haven't time to cook ahead. Serve with mash and broccoli.

 Serves 4  509 calories per serving

INGREDIENTS

- 8 single plaice fillets, each about 75–90g (2½–3¼oz), or 4 double fillets, each about 150–180g (5½–6½oz) (see p84, Slice and skin the fillets, step 1)
- 45g (1½oz) plain flour
- salt and freshly ground black pepper
- 2 tbsp olive oil
- 15g (½oz) butter

FOR THE SAUCE

- 20g (¾oz) butter
- 200g (7oz) small white button mushrooms, thinly sliced
- 1 garlic clove, crushed
- 120ml (4fl oz) dry white wine
- 170ml carton double cream
- finely grated rind of 1 lemon
- juice of ½ lemon
- 2 tbsp chopped fresh dill
- fresh dill sprigs, to garnish

1 Prepare the plaice fillets as for sole: if they have their skin on, remove it; if you have bought double fillets, cut them in half lengthways first (see p84, Slice and skin the fillets). Rinse the fish, if necessary, and pat dry with kitchen paper. Sprinkle the flour onto a plate and season with salt and pepper. Coat both sides of the fillets in the seasoned flour.

2 Heat 1 tablespoon of the olive oil with the butter in a large, non-stick frying pan over a medium–high heat. Add 4 plaice fillets and fry for 1½–2 minutes or until golden (see below, Keep the fillets flat). Turn over and fry the other side for 1½–2 minutes. Do not let the butter brown. Transfer the fillets to a serving platter, cover with foil, and keep warm. Heat the remaining 1 tablespoon of oil and fry the remaining 4 fillets; transfer them to the platter.

3 Make the sauce: melt the butter in the frying pan. Add the mushrooms and fry over a medium–high heat for 2–3 minutes, then add the garlic and fry for 1–2 minutes. Pour in the wine, stir, and bring to the boil over a medium–high heat. Simmer for 1–2 minutes, then pour in the cream. Simmer, stirring, until the sauce thickens. (See below, Make a thick, creamy sauce.)

4 Stir in the lemon rind and juice, salt and pepper, and the chopped dill. Spoon the sauce over and around the fish and garnish with dill sprigs.

KEYS TO PERFECTION

Keep the fillets flat

Fry the unskinned side of the fillets first, as it will be the "presentation" side. Press down with a fish slice if needed to prevent curling.

Make a thick, creamy sauce

1 Fry the mushrooms until their juices run and they become tinged golden brown. Let the wine evaporate before adding the cream.

2 After the cream has been added, the sauce should simmer until it has thickened enough to coat the mushrooms (about 3 minutes).

Asian-style Fish Parcels

Cooking fish in parcels (or "en papillote") is such a delicate way to cook fish; it's healthy, too. All the flavours are trapped inside the bag, so as you open it you're treated to a tempting aroma.

 Serves 4    235 calories per serving    **Special equipment**
Parchment-lined foil (see p64, box)

INGREDIENTS

- 4 spring onions
- 1 small carrot
- 4 small pak choi, each 75–85g (2½–3oz)
- 4 pieces skinned cod loin or fillet, each about 200g (7oz)
- 2 tsp sesame oil, for brushing
- 4 tsp dark soy sauce
- salt and freshly ground black pepper
- 1 fresh, mild red chilli, deseeded and thinly sliced lengthways
- 1 tbsp rice wine
- 2 tsp finely grated fresh root ginger
- 2 garlic cloves, finely chopped
- ½ tsp caster sugar
- 1 tbsp sesame seeds

1 Preheat the oven to 230°C (fan 210°C/450°F/Gas 8). Trim and thinly slice the spring onions, slice the carrot into matchsticks, and cut the pak choi into quarters (see p64, Slice the vegetables uniformly). Pat the fish dry with kitchen paper. Set aside.

2 To make the parcels, cut four 30cm (12in) squares of parchment-lined foil. Lay them foil-side down and brush a little of the sesame oil in the middle of each square.

3 In the centre of each square, lay 4 pak choi quarters, scatter over one-quarter of the carrot sticks, pour ½ teaspoon of soy sauce over the vegetables, and place a fish fillet on top. Brush the fish with a little more of the sesame oil and season with salt and pepper. Scatter over the spring onions and chilli. (See p65, Make tightly sealed parcels, step 1.)

4 In a small bowl, mix the remaining 2 teaspoons of soy sauce with the rice wine, ginger, garlic, sugar, and 2 teaspoons of cold water. Spoon over the fish. Bring the parchment-lined foil up over each fish portion, fold over, and seal very tightly. (See p65, Make tightly sealed parcels, steps 2–4.)

5 Lay the parcels on a baking tray, with the folded ends uppermost, and bake for 12–15 minutes (depending on the thickness of the fish).

6 Meanwhile, toast the sesame seeds: heat a small, heavy-based frying pan over a medium heat. Tip in the sesame seeds and dry-fry for a few minutes, moving the seeds around in the pan so they don't burn, until they are toasted to a golden brown colour. Tip out of the pan and set aside.

7 Open up one of the parcels to test if the fish and vegetables are cooked. Do so carefully, as the contents will be very hot. When the fish is done it will look opaque and feel firm but tender. If you insert the tip of a small, sharp knife into one of the carrot sticks it will feel tender. When the fish and vegetables are cooked, remove all the parcels from the oven and leave to stand, unopened, for 5 minutes before serving.

8 Serve the fish, vegetables, and juices from the parcels on plates and sprinkle each portion with toasted sesame seeds. Alternatively, put the unopened parcels on plates and place the sesame seeds in a bowl so that diners can unwrap the parcels and help themselves.

KEYS TO PERFECTION (*see overleaf*)
Slice the vegetables uniformly; Make tightly sealed parcels

KEYS TO PERFECTION

Slice the vegetables uniformly

1 Using a sharp knife, trim the ends from the spring onions and slice the onions thinly on the diagonal. Sliced this way, they cook quickly and absorb other flavours easily.

2 Slice the carrot into uniform matchsticks. This will help them to cook evenly with the pak choi, spring onions, and fish. To make matchsticks, cut the carrot lengthways into 4 slices, then cut each slice in half widthways. Slice again, lengthways, into sticks no more than 5mm (¼in) wide.

About parchment-lined foil

This useful product is perfect for this recipe. Being double-sided, it combines the properties of both foil and baking parchment in one. The parchment protects the food and holds its shape better than foil alone, while the foil insulates the contents and promotes even cooking. It is strong enough not to tear and flexible too, so easy to fold over tightly and seal. If you can't find it, a layer of foil on a layer of ordinary baking parchment will work well – it's just a little more fiddly.

3 Select small pak choi and cut them uniformly to ensure even cooking. Using a sharp chef's knife, trim the root ends of the pak choi very slightly to neaten, but make sure you don't cut too far in or the leaves will start to separate. Cut each pak choi lengthways into quarters to give you 16 similar-sized pieces.

Make tightly sealed parcels

1 Wrapping and sealing the parcels tightly and securely will enclose all the flavours and aromas and keep the steam trapped inside, so it can cook the fish and vegetables efficiently. Lay the vegetables and fish in the middle of the parchment-lined foil square. There should be plenty of paper all round to bring up to create a parcel.

2 Carefully spoon the soy sauce and other flavourings over the fish and vegetables, distributing it evenly. This will create steam inside the parcel, which will gently cook the fish, making it very moist and tender. You don't need much liquid, as the fish and vegetables will release some of their own juices too.

3 For each parcel, bring up the 2 long sides of the parchment-lined foil to meet in the middle over the fish. Using both hands, hold the 2 edges firmly together, and fold them over tightly 2 or 3 times to secure. Press the central fold down onto the fish to seal.

4 To seal the ends of the parcel, fold in the corners of one end to almost meet in the middle and make 2 triangles, as if you were wrapping a present. Fold over the end 2 or 3 times to secure tightly. Repeat at the other end so that the parcel is completely sealed.

Grilled Trout with Chicory and Almonds

Chicory really complements grilled trout, especially when it's caramelized. Serve with new potatoes, so you can enjoy the buttery juices that gather in the grill pan and around the chicory.

 Serves 4    515 calories per serving

INGREDIENTS

- 85g (3oz) butter (room temperature)
- 1 tbsp chopped fresh dill, plus 4 large sprigs for stuffing and a few small sprigs to garnish
- salt and freshly ground black pepper
- 30g (1oz) flaked almonds
- 4 whole trout, each about 300g (10oz) with head and tail left on, gutted, cleaned, rinsed inside and out, dried, and small fins removed
- 2 small oranges: 1 cut into 8 thin slices and each slice halved; 1 cut into wedges, to garnish
- 3 small heads of green (sometimes called "white") chicory, damaged outside leaves removed and quartered lengthways
- ½ tsp caster sugar
- 2–3 tbsp fresh orange juice

1 In a bowl, mix 45g (1½oz) of the butter with the chopped dill. Season and set aside. Heat a small, non-stick frying pan until hot, tip in the almonds, and dry-fry over a medium heat until golden all over, turning often. Remove from the heat and drop a quarter of the dill butter into the pan. Set aside.

2 Preheat the grill on its highest setting. Remove the grid of the grill pan and line the grill pan with foil. Cut slashes across one side of each trout. Spread the remaining dill butter over the tops and undersides. Lay the trout in the grill pan, slashed-sides up, and stuff the cavities with the orange slices and large dill sprigs. Season. Reduce the heat to medium–high and grill the fish about 10cm (4in) from the heat. After 5–7 minutes, turn the fish over and grill for a further 4–5 minutes. (See below, Moist flesh, crispy skin.)

3 Meanwhile, melt the remaining butter in a large, non-stick frying pan over a medium–high heat. Add the chicory, cut-sides up, sprinkle with the sugar, turn, and fry until the undersides start to brown. Reduce the heat slightly, then turn again and add 2 tablespoons of the orange juice. Simmer until tender; add extra orange juice if needed. (See below, Sweet-tasting chicory.)

4 Gently reheat the almond and dill butter mixture. Serve the trout slashed-side uppermost, topped with the almonds, with the chicory alongside and the juices drizzled over. Garnish with the orange wedges and small dill sprigs.

KEYS TO PERFECTION

Moist flesh, crispy skin

1 Make 3 or 4 long, diagonal slits in the flesh, 1cm (½in) deep, using a sharp knife. Spread dill butter over the top, into the slashes, and underneath. This will keep the trout moist and give more flavour.

2 It's vital to preheat the grill for at least 5 minutes, so the fish starts cooking straight-away. Turn the trout carefully so it doesn't break, using a fish slice. When cooked, the flesh should be moist and the skin crisp.

Sweet-tasting chicory

Caramelizing chicory takes away its bitter taste. Just as the sugared leaves start to brown and caramelize (about 5 minutes), turn them over and add orange juice so the thicker undersides can finish cooking (2–3 minutes).

Salmon en Croûte with Watercress Sauce

This is an ideal dish for entertaining, as you can assemble the croûte ahead and chill it before baking. The combination of crisp pastry, succulent salmon, and watercress sauce is a real winner.

 Serves 8    618 calories per serving

INGREDIENTS

- 3 tbsp olive oil
- 3 shallots, finely chopped
- 200g (7oz) chestnut mushrooms, finely chopped
- 3 garlic cloves, finely chopped
- 1 tbsp lemon juice
- 125g (4½oz) watercress, chopped
- salt and freshly ground black pepper
- 2 tbsp full-fat crème fraîche
- 750g (1lb 10oz) shop-bought puff pastry (preferably all-butter)
- 2 pieces skinned salmon fillet, each 500g (1lb 2oz)
- 1 tbsp hot horseradish sauce
- 1 egg, beaten

FOR THE SAUCE

- 20g (¾oz) butter
- 1 shallot, finely chopped
- 15g (½oz) plain flour, plus extra for dusting
- 400ml (14fl oz) vegetable stock
- 100g (3½oz) frozen peas
- 100g (3½oz) watercress, chopped
- 5 tbsp full-fat crème fraîche
- 1 tbsp finely chopped fresh mint

KEYS TO PERFECTION (*see overleaf*)
Make a well-sealed parcel; Bake the croûte to perfection; Make a bright green sauce

1 Heat 2 tablespoons of the oil in a large, non-stick frying pan. Add the shallots and fry over a medium heat for 3–4 minutes or until softened, stirring occasionally. Increase the heat to high, stir in the mushrooms and garlic, and fry for 4–5 minutes or until the liquid has evaporated. Add the lemon juice. Take the pan off the heat and mix in the watercress until wilted. Season, transfer to a bowl, and set aside to cool, then stir in the crème fraîche. Preheat the oven to 220°C (fan 200°C/425°F/Gas 7).

2 Roll out half the pastry on a lightly floured surface. Trim to a rectangle 5cm (2in) larger all round than the salmon. Wrap the pastry trimmings in cling film and set aside. Place the rolled-out pastry on a large piece of baking parchment that will fit on a large baking sheet or in a shallow roasting tin. Lay one of the fillets in the middle of the pastry. Season and spread over the horseradish sauce, then the mushroom and watercress mixture. (See p70, Make a well-sealed parcel, steps 1 and 2.) Lay the other fillet on top. Season.

3 Roll out the remaining pastry to a rectangular shape that is about 7.5cm (3in) wider and 5cm (2in) longer than the bottom pastry layer. Brush the edge of the bottom layer with the beaten egg. Lay the pastry over the salmon and trim off the excess to give a 2cm (¾in) edge all round. Press, score, and crimp the edges. Re-roll the pastry trimmings thinly and cut them into strips. Brush the croûte all over with egg, lay the strips over in a decorative pattern, and brush these with egg. (See p70, Make a well-sealed parcel, steps 3 and 4.)

4 Carefully lift the croûte onto a large baking sheet, with the baking parchment still underneath. Bake for 30 minutes or until the pastry is golden brown. (See p71, Bake the croûte to perfection.)

5 Meanwhile, make the sauce: melt the butter in a medium pan. Stir in the shallot and fry for 2–3 minutes or until softened but not browned. Stir in the flour and cook for 1 minute. Take the pan off the heat and slowly stir in the stock. Return the pan to the heat and cook, stirring, over a medium–high heat, until the sauce has thickened slightly. Add the peas. Simmer for 2 minutes.

6 Remove the pan from the heat and stir in the watercress. Purée in a food processor until smooth. Pour the sauce back into the pan and set aside. When the croûte is done, remove it from the oven and leave to rest for 10 minutes. Meanwhile, stir the crème fraîche and mint into the sauce, season, and reheat. (See p71, Make a bright green sauce.) Transfer the croûte to a board or serving platter and serve in slices with the sauce.

KEYS TO PERFECTION

Make a well-sealed parcel

1 It's important to roll out the pastry so it's not too thick, as it needs to cook in the same time as the fish (the fish will become dry if overcooked). Roll it out so it's about the same thickness as a £1 coin – that way, it will bake to be light and crisp. The first piece of pastry (for the bottom of the croûte) should be 5cm (2in) larger all round than the size of a salmon fillet.

2 Spoon the mushroom and watercress filling carefully over the length of the bottom salmon fillet, then spread it over using a palette knife or round-bladed knife. Go almost up to the edge but not quite all the way, otherwise when you place the second fillet on top the weight of it may cause the filling to ooze out. Place the second fillet on top of the filling and season.

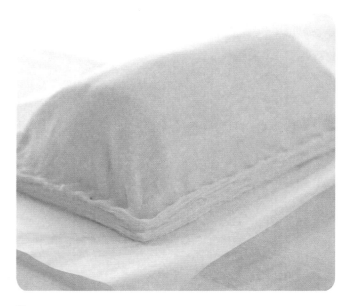

3 To make sure you don't stretch the pastry while covering the top of the salmon, lay it over a rolling pin to make it easier to lift and lower onto the fish. Press down the pastry edges well, or the filling may leak out when baking, then score the edges to secure the seal by gently tapping all around the cut sides using the back of a knife held horizontally.

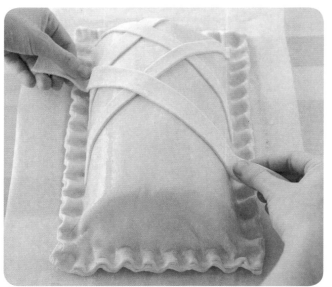

4 Crimp the edges using your fingers. Re-roll the pastry trimmings thinly and cut out 10–12 strips in 2 or 3 different sizes, varying from 1cm (½in) to 2.5cm (1in) wide and long enough to go over the domed part of the croûte. Trim to fit. Brush the croûte all over with beaten egg, then lay the strips over in a criss-cross pattern (you may not need all the pastry trimmings). Brush the strips with egg.

Bake the croûte to perfection

1 Transfer the pastry-wrapped salmon to a large baking sheet with the help of 2 fish slices to keep it stable. Retain the baking parchment underneath, as this will prevent the pastry from sticking to the sheet and make it easier to move once baked.

2 Baking the croûte at a high oven temperature will make the pastry light and crisp, especially on the base, and ensure that the salmon is cooked through. However, as the temperature is high, check after 20 minutes – if the pastry is already turning brown, lay a piece of foil loosely over the top to protect the pastry from becoming overdone while the salmon finishes cooking.

Make a bright green sauce

1 Watercress can quickly discolour if heated for too long, so to keep the sauce a good green colour, stir in the watercress off the heat: the heat of the sauce and pan will be sufficient to wilt the watercress while maintaining its colour. The peas will also help to boost the colour.

2 After puréeing the sauce, pour it back into the pan. Before serving, place it over a low heat and stir in the crème fraîche, mint, and salt and pepper. Heat through for as short a time as possible. As with the watercress, you want to retain the fresh green colour of the mint.

Mary's TOP TIPS

3

Use fresh herbs

Fresh herbs taste so much better than dried. They're widely available nowadays and are also easy to grow – you don't even need a garden. Simply sow or plant them in pots on the windowsill or outside the kitchen door.

Grilled Salmon with Thai Flavours

This is my take on the popular pairing of salmon and cucumber. Fish sauce ("nam pla") brings a special saltiness to the dish and complements the sweet and sour flavours. Serve with Thai rice.

 Serves 4  362 calories per serving

INGREDIENTS

- 4 pieces skinned salmon fillet, each about 175g (6oz)
- ground white pepper
- sunflower oil, for greasing
- ½ cucumber

FOR THE MARINADE

- 1 lemongrass stalk, tough outer layer removed
- 3 tbsp fish sauce (*nam pla*)
- 3 tbsp lime juice
- 1½ tsp finely chopped fresh root ginger
- 2 garlic cloves, finely chopped
- 1 fresh, Thai or mild red chilli, deseeded and finely chopped
- 2½ tsp caster sugar

1 Lay the salmon in a shallow, non-metallic dish in a single layer and season with pepper. Make the marinade: smash the lemongrass stalk with a rolling pin, slice it into thirds, and put the pieces in the dish with the salmon. Mix all the remaining marinade ingredients in a small bowl with 1 teaspoon of water. Set aside 2 tablespoons of the marinade and pour the rest over the salmon. Cover and chill for at least 2 hours (or overnight), turning the fish once.

2 Preheat the grill for 5 minutes on its highest setting. Meanwhile, line a baking tray or grill pan with foil and brush it with a little oil. Remove and discard the lemongrass from the marinade. Transfer the salmon from the marinade to the baking tray or grill pan, placing it skinned-side down. Spoon the marinade over the salmon and grill for about 10 minutes (see below, Succulent, flaky salmon). Do not turn the salmon, or it may break.

3 While the salmon is grilling, partially peel the cucumber (if the skin is tough, remove it all using a vegetable peeler). Cut the cucumber into wafer-thin slices, put the slices in a wide, shallow dish, and pour over the reserved marinade. (See below, Crunchy, decorative cucumber.)

4 Serve the salmon fillet with the cucumber slices alongside. Spoon the marinade from the cucumber over both the fish and the cucumber.

KEYS TO PERFECTION

Succulent, flaky salmon

To test if the salmon is done, pull back a small piece of flesh with a fork. It should flake easily and no longer look opaque inside. If it does, cook a minute or so longer, but be careful not to overcook the fish, as it will dry out.

Crunchy, decorative cucumber

1 Using a vegetable peeler or small, sharp knife, peel off 3 or 4 slices of skin down the cucumber, with a gap between each. This will give a pattern of dark and light stripes. If sliced very thinly, the cucumber will curl slightly.

2 Marinate the cucumber for about 10 minutes only. If it's left in the marinade for too long, it will lose its crunchy texture and bright colour. You want it to retain its vibrancy and bite.

Fish Curry with Coconut Milk

I've used a mixture of fish for this easy-to-cook, fragrant curry. Monkfish keeps its shape well and complements the slightly softer texture of cod loin. Serve with basmati rice and poppadums.

 Serves 4    385 calories per serving

INGREDIENTS

- 2 fresh, medium-hot green chillies
- 2 tbsp sunflower oil
- 1 onion, halved lengthways and thinly sliced
- 3 garlic cloves, finely chopped
- 2 tsp finely chopped fresh root ginger
- 1½ tsp garam masala
- 1 tsp ground coriander
- 1 tsp ground cumin
- ¼ tsp turmeric
- 1 tsp black mustard seeds
- 2 tsp plain flour
- 400ml can coconut milk
- 150ml (5fl oz) vegetable stock
- 2 tsp mango chutney
- 2 tbsp lime juice
- salt and freshly ground black pepper
- 400g (14oz) monkfish
- 300g (10oz) skinned cod loin
- 115g (4oz) fine green beans, stem ends trimmed
- 2 tbsp roughly chopped fresh coriander, to garnish

KEYS TO PERFECTION (*see overleaf*)
Make a spicy, smooth coconut sauce; Gently cook the fish

1 Deseed and finely shred the chillies (see p78, Make a spicy, smooth coconut sauce, step 1). Heat the oil in a large, deep-sided, non-stick frying pan or sauté pan. Add the onion and fry over a medium–high heat for 5–6 minutes or until it starts to brown, reducing the heat if it browns too quickly.

2 Add the garlic, ginger, and half the shredded chillies to the pan and fry for a further 2 minutes. Reduce the heat slightly and sprinkle in the garam masala, ground coriander, cumin, turmeric, and mustard seeds. Fry for 1 minute, then stir in the flour and cook for a further minute. (See p78, Make a spicy, smooth coconut sauce, steps 2 and 3.)

3 Pour in the coconut milk and then the stock. Increase the heat and bring to the boil, stirring. Let the liquid bubble for a couple of minutes while you continue to stir, to thicken the sauce slightly. Reduce the heat and stir in the mango chutney and lime juice. Season with salt and pepper. (See p78, Make a spicy, smooth coconut sauce, step 4.)

4 Remove the membrane from the monkfish and chop the monkfish and cod into chunky cubes, about 5cm (2in). (See p79, Gently cook the fish, steps 1 and 2.) Drop the beans into a pan of salted, boiling water and simmer for 4–5 minutes or until tender. Drain well, refresh in cold water for a few seconds, to keep the colour, and drain again.

5 Add the monkfish and cod to the curry sauce. Cover the pan and simmer gently for 4–5 minutes or until the fish is just cooked. Gently stir the beans into the curry and remove the pan from the heat. (See p79, Gently cook the fish, steps 3 and 4.) Before serving, scatter over the chopped coriander and remaining shredded chillies.

KEYS TO PERFECTION

Make a spicy, smooth coconut sauce

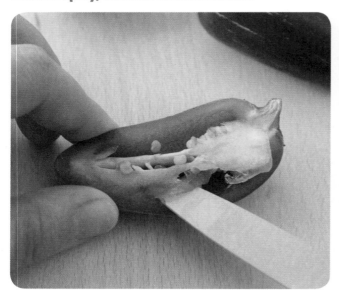

1 For the flavour of chilli without too much heat, remove the seeds. Slice the chilli in half lengthways with a small, sharp knife. Using the tip of the knife, scrape out the seeds and membrane and discard. To shred, flatten each chilli half and slice it lengthways into thin strips. When working with chillies, keep your hands away from your eyes, which the chilli will burn, and wash your hands well afterwards; you may like to wear latex or rubber gloves to be on the safe side.

2 Frying the spices briefly before adding the liquid prevents them from tasting raw and draws out their flavours, adding depth to the finished dish. However, you need to be careful not to let them burn. Reduce the heat to medium before adding the dry spices to the pan, and stir continuously as they fry.

3 I stir a little flour into the sauce before the coconut milk goes in. It's not traditional, but I find it helps to stabilize the sauce and stop it from separating. You don't want the sauce to be too thick, so only a little flour is required.

4 Slowly pour in the coconut milk and then the stock, stirring all the time to make a smooth sauce and prevent any lumps from forming. After the sauce has thickened slightly, add the mango chutney, lime juice, and salt and pepper.

Gently cook the fish

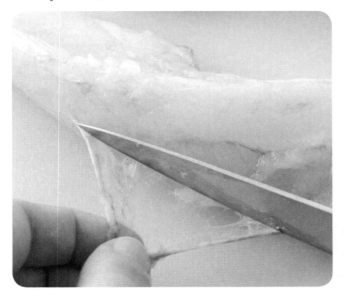

1 Before cooking the fish, remove the purple-grey membrane that covers the monkfish tail. If left on it will shrink around the fish during cooking and make it tough. Use the tip of a long, thin, sharp knife to nick the membrane so you can get the knife between it and the flesh, then very carefully pull the membrane away, being careful not to damage the flesh. You'll probably have to do this in several stages.

2 Pat the fish dry with kitchen paper, then cut it into cubes. It's best to have fairly large cubes, as they hold their shape better during cooking and stay more tender and succulent. If the fish (especially the cod) is cut too small, it can disintegrate and disappear into the sauce. Both cod and monkfish are firm white fish, and when cut into equal-sized cubes they take the same length of time to cook.

3 Lay the fish in the sauce so it's well covered. Don't stir, just let it sink into the sauce, then cover the pan. Time the cooking carefully so the fish will stay tender and in good-sized pieces.

4 After adding the green beans, remove the pan from the heat, so the fish doesn't overcook, and don't stir the curry any more than necessary, otherwise the cod may start to break up.

Pan-fried Tuna and Mixed Pea Stir-fry

Tuna steaks make an extra-special quick supper, and they can be marinating while you prepare the vegetables for the stir-fry. Make sure you buy sustainable tuna from a reputable supplier.

 Serves 4    370 calories per serving

INGREDIENTS

- 4 tbsp sunflower oil
- 2 tsp Chinese rice vinegar
- 1 garlic clove, crushed
- 4 tuna steaks, each about 150g (5½oz) and 2cm (¾in) thick
- salt and freshly ground black pepper
- 1 red pepper, halved, cored, and deseeded
- 8 spring onions, trimmed
- 200g (7oz) mangetout
- 150g (5½oz) sugarsnap peas
- 200g (7oz) beansprouts
- 2 tbsp dark soy sauce
- ¼ tsp five-spice powder

1 Mix 2 tablespoons of the oil with the rice vinegar and garlic in a shallow, non-metallic dish. Lay the tuna steaks in the marinade, season with pepper, and set aside for about 20 minutes while you prepare the vegetables. (See below, Tender, moist tuna, step 1.)

2 Slice the red pepper into long, thin strips. Cut the spring onions into long, thin, diagonal slices. Slice the mangetout and sugarsnap peas in half lengthways. Rinse the beansprouts in a colander and leave to drain.

3 Heat a large, non-stick, deep-sided frying pan, sauté pan, or wok. Remove the tuna steaks from the marinade, lay them in the hot, dry pan, and fry for 3 minutes over a high heat. Turn and fry the other side for 2–3 minutes (see below, Tender, moist tuna, step 2). Transfer to a warm plate, season with a little salt, cover with foil, and set aside while you fry the vegetables.

4 Heat another tablespoon of the oil in the pan, and with the heat on high, tip in the pepper and spring onions. Stir-fry for 1–2 minutes or until tinged brown. Pour in the remaining tablespoon of oil, add the mangetout and sugarsnap peas, and stir-fry for 2–3 minutes. They will turn a brighter green and be tender-crisp. Reduce the heat, then add the beansprouts, soy sauce, five-spice powder, and 2 tablespoons of water, and stir-fry for 1 minute. (See below, Super-quick vegetables.) Serve immediately with the tuna.

KEYS TO PERFECTION

Tender, moist tuna

1 Tuna is a lean, meaty fish, so it can dry out easily when cooked. Marinating will introduce moisture as well as add flavour. Lay the steaks in the dish in a single layer and turn them over so they're well coated in the marinade.

2 The pan must be really hot before putting in the steaks. As soon as they are browned underneath, turn and cook the other side. Do not overcook, or the steaks will be tough. You want the centres to be slightly pink.

Super-quick vegetables

Have all the vegetables sliced and close to hand, and set the pan over a high heat. When the oil is really hot, add the vegetables in the right sequence and fry quickly, stirring and tossing so they cook evenly.

Pan-fried Sole with Brown Shrimps

Serving little brown shrimps with lemon sole is my way of spoiling my supper guests. When the shrimps aren't available loose on their own, I buy the ones in cartons that are potted in butter.

 Serves 4   400 calories per serving

INGREDIENTS

- 100g (3½oz) frozen peas
- 8 single lemon sole fillets, each about 85–100g (3–3½oz), or 4 double fillets, each about 175–200g (6–7oz) (see p84, Slice and skin the fillets, step 1)
- 30g (1oz) plain flour
- salt and freshly ground black pepper
- 85g (3oz) butter
- 1 tbsp lemon juice
- 85g (3oz) cooked and peeled brown shrimps (see p85, box)
- 1 tbsp chopped fresh flat-leaf parsley
- lemon wedges, to serve

1 Tip the peas into a small pan of boiling salted water, bring back to the boil, and simmer for 2 minutes. Remove, drain, and set aside.

2 If the sole fillets have their skin on, remove it. If you have bought double fillets, cut them in half lengthways first. (See p84, Slice and skin the fillets.) Rinse the fillets if necessary and pat dry with kitchen paper.

3 Season the flour with salt and pepper. Dip the fillets into the seasoned flour to coat, and shake off any excess. Melt 30g (1oz) of the butter in a large, non-stick frying pan. Lay 4 fillets in the pan and fry gently over a medium–high heat for 2 minutes on each side. (See p84, Gently fry the fillets.) Remove the fish and keep warm. Fry the remaining 4 fillets.

4 Wipe the pan with kitchen paper, then add the remaining butter and melt over a medium–high heat until it starts to turn golden brown. Reduce the heat and stir in the lemon juice, shrimps, and reserved peas; warm through very briefly. (See p85, Make the shrimp sauce flavoursome.)

5 Season with pepper to taste and add more lemon juice if you wish, then mix in the parsley. Spoon the shrimps and peas over the sole and serve with a drizzle of the buttery juices and lemon wedges.

KEYS TO PERFECTION (*see overleaf*)
Slice and skin the fillets; Gently fry the fillets; Make the shrimp sauce flavoursome

KEYS TO PERFECTION

Slice and skin the fillets

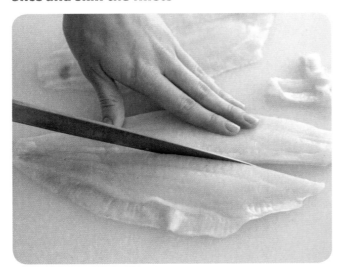

1 When buying sole or plaice, you may find what looks like one large fillet. This is the top or bottom half of the fish with the central bone removed, and consists of 2 smaller fillets, one on either side of where the bone would have been. It's best to divide these "double" fillets in half lengthways. Alternatively, you may find "single" fillets, which are already divided, so there is no need to cut them.

2 To skin the fish, lay each fillet skin-side down on a board. Put a little salt on your fingers so you can get a good grip on the skin (it can be slippery). Starting at the tail end, make an incision between the skin and flesh using a sharp, thin, long-bladed knife. Holding the knife at an angle, slide it along the skin, wiggling the skin as you go in order to separate it from the flesh.

Gently fry the fillets

1 Before frying the fish, sprinkle the flour onto a plate and season with salt and pepper. Place each fillet in the seasoned flour and drag it through the flour to coat. Gently shake off any excess flour to give a light coating that will protect the fish as it cooks.

2 When the butter starts to foam, and before it changes colour, lay 4 fillets in the pan with the unskinned-side down. Never overcrowd the pan by frying too many fish at once. Turn after 2 minutes and press down with a fish slice if the fillets start to curl. You want them to sizzle and brown slightly, but not overcook, so adjust heat as needed. When done, the fish will look opaque and flake easily.

Make the shrimp sauce flavoursome

1 Browning the butter for a quick sauce gives it a nutty flavour. Once the butter starts to change colour and release a nutty aroma (this will take about 2 minutes), swirl it around in the pan so that the butter can brown evenly.

2 As soon as the butter is a pale golden brown colour, reduce the heat, pour in the lemon juice, and stir in the shrimps and peas. The heat should be quite low, just enough to warm them through. Don't leave over the heat for any longer than 1 minute, or the peas will start to discolour and the shrimps become less juicy.

3 Season with pepper and taste the sauce to see if you need to add any more lemon juice. Mix in the parsley just before serving. If it is added too early, it will lose its colour.

Buying and using brown shrimps

Tiny, succulent, and packed with flavour, brown shrimps are traditionally the main ingredient of potted shrimps. They are translucent when raw, but turn amber-brown on cooking. Brown shrimps are fiddly to peel, but you can buy them in some supermarkets and fishmongers already cooked and peeled.

Spicy Crab Cakes

The ingredients in this recipe combine the fresh, spicy flavours of Thai crab cakes with the chunkier texture of American ones. Serve with stir-fried pak choi and long-grain rice or Chinese noodles.

 Serves 4   156 calories per serving

INGREDIENTS

- 2 x 170g cans white crab meat (preferably in large chunks)
- 2 spring onions, trimmed and finely chopped
- 1 small fresh red chilli, deseeded and finely chopped
- 30g (1oz) fresh white breadcrumbs
- 2 tbsp chopped fresh coriander
- finely grated rind of ½ lime
- 1 egg, beaten
- salt and freshly ground black pepper
- plain flour, for dusting
- 2–3 tbsp sunflower oil
- hot chilli sauce, to serve
- lime wedges, to serve

1 Drain the crab meat thoroughly, then pat it dry with kitchen paper to remove any excess liquid, so the mixture will not be too moist.

2 Put the spring onions, chilli, breadcrumbs, coriander, and lime rind in a medium bowl. Mix together and gently stir in the crab meat, without breaking up the chunks too much.

3 Stir in some of the egg, until the mixture is the right consistency, and season with salt and pepper. Divide the mixture into 8 equal-sized portions and shape into crab cakes. Chill for about 20 minutes. Lightly dust each crab cake with a little flour. (See below, Create a good texture.)

4 Heat 2 tablespoons of the oil in a frying pan. Fry the crab cakes on a medium–high heat for 2–3 minutes on each side or until they are golden brown and heated through, adding more oil if needed. Serve 2 crab cakes per person, with hot chilli sauce and lime wedges on the side.

KEYS TO PERFECTION

Create a good texture

1 Add the egg to the mixture a little at a time (you probably won't need it all). Use just enough to bind the mixture – it should hold together but not be too wet. Do not over-mix, or the crab will break up.

2 On a lightly floured surface, shape the mixture into flat cakes, 6cm (2½in) across, gently patting with your fingers; do not over-handle. Make all the cakes a similar size and shape for even cooking. Chill the cakes.

3 Sprinkle a little flour onto a plate, lay each crab cake in the flour, and turn to coat (the flour seals in moisture when frying and stops the cakes sticking to the pan). Gently shake off excess flour; it should be a light coating.

Quick Haddock with Tomato and Puy Lentils

When looking for ideas for simple midweek suppers, there's nothing better than a dish like this one, which is cooked in one pan. If you want something to go with it, a green salad is ideal.

 Serves 4   233 calories per serving

INGREDIENTS

- 2 tbsp olive oil
- 1 onion, coarsely chopped
- 2 garlic cloves, chopped
- 150ml (5fl oz) vegetable stock
- 400g can chopped plum tomatoes
- 1 tbsp sun-dried tomato paste
- ½ tsp hot smoked paprika (pimentón picante) (see below, box)
- 400g can green Puy lentils, rinsed and drained
- salt and freshly ground black pepper
- 4 pieces skinned haddock fillet, each about 125g (4½oz)
- chopped fresh flat-leaf parsley, to garnish

1 Heat the oil in a large, non-stick sauté pan or deep-sided frying pan with a lid. Add the onion and garlic and fry over a medium–high heat for 6–8 minutes or until browned, turning up the heat a little if necessary. Pour in the stock and stir to mix. (See below, Well-browned onions.)

2 Let the stock bubble briefly, then tip in the tomatoes. Stir in the sun-dried tomato paste, paprika, and lentils. Simmer for 8–10 minutes. Season to taste with salt and pepper.

3 Pat the fish dry with kitchen paper and season with salt and pepper. Lay the fillets on top of the tomatoes and lentils, pressing them lightly into the sauce but not submerging them fully, then cover the pan (see below, Moist, tender fish). Simmer over a low heat for 8–10 minutes or until the fish is just cooked and no longer opaque. The consistency of the sauce should be like a thick, spoonable soup. If you need to loosen it, simply pour in a little more hot water or stock at the end.

4 Transfer the fish and sauce to a warmed serving dish and serve immediately, garnished with chopped parsley.

KEYS TO PERFECTION

Well-browned onions

You want to create depth of flavour and colour, so make sure the onion is softened and well browned before you add the liquid. While adding the stock, stir in the sticky bits at the bottom of the pan for extra flavour.

Moist, tender fish

Lay the fish on the lentils and press lightly to partly submerge it. Keep the fillets whole, so they stay moist while cooking. Covering the pan ensures the fish steams. Simmer very gently, so the fish doesn't overcook.

Using smoked paprika

Smoked paprika brings a unique taste to the dish. There are 2 types: hot smoked paprika, as used for this recipe, and sweet smoked paprika. As a little can go a long way, add cautiously at first. The amount I have suggested gives a subtle background flavour to the fish that doesn't overpower, but if you like it smokier, check and adjust to your taste at the end of step 2.

Sea Bass with Creamy Lemon Sauce

The sauce has a silky-smooth texture that goes beautifully with the crispy-skinned sea bass. Fine green beans and new potatoes tossed with butter make the ideal accompaniments.

 Serves 4  292 calories per serving  **Special equipment**
Ridged cast-iron chargrill pan

INGREDIENTS

- 4 sea bass fillets, each about 100g (3½ oz)
- olive oil, for brushing
- salt and freshly ground black pepper

FOR THE SAUCE

- 50g (1¾oz) butter
- 150ml carton single cream
- juice and finely grated rind of ½ lemon
- 1 egg yolk
- 1 tsp plain flour
- ground white pepper
- 2 tsp finely snipped fresh chives

1 Make the sauce: melt the butter in a small pan. Remove it from the heat, then whisk in the cream, lemon juice, egg yolk, and flour until well mixed (see below, Smooth, creamy sauce). Stir in the lemon rind. Return the pan to a low heat and stir continuously until the mixture thickens enough to coat the back of a wooden spoon. Season with salt and white pepper. Set aside.

2 Preheat the chargrill pan over a high heat for about 5–10 minutes. Meanwhile, pat the fillets dry with kitchen paper and score the skin (see below, Crispy golden skin, step 1). Brush both sides of the fillets with olive oil and season with salt and black pepper.

3 Reduce the heat to medium–high and lay the fillets in the hot pan, skin-side down (see below, Crispy golden skin, step 2). Cook for 3–4 minutes until the skin is lightly charred and crisp. Carefully turn the fillets over using a fish slice, then chargrill for a further 1–2 minutes on the other side. You will probably need to cook the fish in batches.

4 Warm the sauce through briefly over a very low heat. Remove from the heat and stir in the chives. To serve, lay the fish on warmed plates, with the skin-side uppermost, and spoon over some of the sauce. Pour the rest of the sauce into a jug and hand it round separately.

KEYS TO PERFECTION

Smooth, creamy sauce

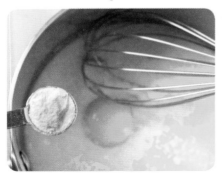

Sprinkle the flour into the sauce and whisk vigorously with a wire whisk as it goes in, so no lumps can form. Heat the sauce very gently, because the egg yolk and cream will curdle if they're overheated.

Crispy golden skin

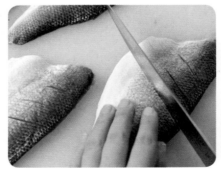

1 Using a sharp knife, score the fish skin by making 4 or 5 cuts to the point where you can see the flesh. Scoring the fillets helps to keep them flat in the pan, ensuring they don't curl up as they cook.

2 The pan must be very hot when you add the fillets, so that they can sear properly. Don't move the fish as it cooks, as it may break up and you'll lose the attractive charred pattern from the pan's ridges.

Poultry and Game

Country Chicken Casserole

Although this warming casserole is packed with vegetables, I like to serve it with mash to soak up the sauce. An added bonus is that it's cooked in one pan, keeping washing-up to a minimum!

 Serves 4    438 calories per serving

INGREDIENTS

- 8 bone-in chicken thighs
- salt and freshly ground black pepper
- 2 tbsp olive oil
- 15g (½oz) butter
- 1 onion, coarsely chopped
- 1 celery stick, thinly sliced
- 3 garlic cloves, finely chopped
- 2 medium carrots, halved lengthways and cut into chunks just under 1cm (½in) thick
- 2 medium parsnips, quartered and cut into chunks just under 1cm (½in) thick
- 1 large potato, about 300g (10oz), peeled and cut into 2.5–3cm (1–1¼in) cubes
- 200ml (7fl oz) white wine
- 1 tbsp Dijon mustard
- 2 tsp tomato purée
- 230g can chopped plum tomatoes
- 250ml (9fl oz) chicken stock
- 1 tbsp coarsely chopped fresh flat-leaf parsley

1 Remove the skin and fat from the chicken thighs and season the meat. Heat 1 tablespoon of the oil and the butter in a flameproof casserole until hot. Fry the chicken (skinned-side down first) in 2 batches over a medium–high heat until golden brown all over. Transfer to a large plate using a slotted spoon and set aside. (See p110, Succulent, golden brown chicken.)

2 Pour in the remaining tablespoon of oil. Tip in the onion and celery and fry for 2–3 minutes or until the onion starts to soften. Stir in the garlic followed by the carrots, parsnips, and potato. Reduce the heat to medium and fry for 4–5 minutes, stirring often, until the onion starts to brown. Preheat the oven to 160°C (fan 140°C/325°F/Gas 3).

3 Increase the heat and add the wine. Stir and let it bubble for about 2 minutes (see below, Enhance the flavour). Stir in the mustard and tomato purée, then the tomatoes and stock.

4 Return the chicken and its juices to the casserole (see below, Partially immerse the chicken). Bring to the boil, then reduce the heat, cover, and simmer for 10 minutes. Season with salt and pepper and transfer the casserole to the oven, covered. Cook for 50 minutes to 1 hour or until the chicken and vegetables are tender. Serve sprinkled with the parsley.

KEYS TO PERFECTION

Enhance the flavour

Let the wine bubble rapidly over a high heat, with the lid off, until it has reduced by about half. This drives off some of the alcohol and concentrates the flavour for the sauce. It will create a thick, syrupy liquid.

Partially immerse the chicken

Sit the chicken thighs on top of the vegetables and gently press them down so that they're about three-quarters immersed in the liquid; this will keep them tender and succulent, while retaining their golden brown colour.

Roast Chicken with Tarragon Butter and Roast Potatoes

I do like this way of roasting a chicken: spreading herb butter under the skin makes the meat extra moist and flavourful. While the roasted bird rests, turn up the oven for really crisp potatoes.

 Serves 4    676 calories per serving

INGREDIENTS

- 60g (2oz) butter (room temperature), plus extra for greasing and the legs
- 2 garlic cloves, crushed
- 1 tbsp chopped fresh tarragon, plus 3 extra sprigs
- salt and freshly ground black pepper
- 1.8kg (4lb) whole chicken
- 1 lemon, halved
- 1 small red onion, halved and sliced into about 20 small wedges

FOR THE ROAST POTATOES

- 1kg (2¼lb) fluffy potatoes, such as King Edward, peeled and cut into equal-sized pieces, about 5cm (2in)
- 3 fresh bay leaves, plus extra to garnish

FOR THE GRAVY

- 1 tbsp plain flour
- 300ml (10fl oz) chicken stock
- 3 tbsp red wine
- 1 tbsp redcurrant jelly

KEYS TO PERFECTION *(see overleaf)*
Prepare the chicken for roasting; Baste the chicken; Test for doneness; Make crispy roast potatoes; Make smooth, tasty gravy

1 Preheat the oven to 200°C (fan 180°C/400°F/Gas 6). Lightly grease a large roasting tin with butter. Make the tarragon butter: put the butter in a small bowl with the garlic and chopped tarragon and beat together with a small wooden spoon. Season with salt and pepper.

2 Sit the chicken, breast-side up, on a board and remove any string. Gently pull back the skin over the breasts and spread the tarragon butter under the skin over the flesh. Rub a little plain butter over the legs. Season the outside of the chicken with salt and pepper. Insert the lemon halves and tarragon sprigs in the cavity. Scatter the onion wedges in the centre of the roasting tin and sit the bird, breast-side up, on top. Roast for 50 minutes. (See p98, Prepare the chicken for roasting.)

3 While the chicken is in the oven, put the potatoes in a large pan. Cover with cold water and bring to the boil. Add salt and simmer for 5 minutes, then drain well. Return the potatoes to the pan and gently shake it over a very low heat. (See p99, Make crispy roast potatoes, step 1.) Set aside.

4 After 50 minutes' roasting, remove the tin, baste the chicken, and put the potatoes around the bird (see p98, Baste the chicken, and p99, Make crispy roast potatoes, step 2). Tuck the 3 bay leaves among the potatoes. Return the tin to the oven to roast for a further 50 minutes, turning the potatoes halfway through. When the chicken is done, transfer it to a large, warmed serving platter and cover with foil (see p98, Test for doneness).

5 Increase the oven temperature to 220°C (fan 200°C/425°F/Gas 7). Transfer the potatoes to a small roasting tin and pour over all but 1 tablespoon of the top layer of fat from the large roasting tin, leaving all the juices and the onion behind in the large tin. Baste the potatoes with the fat, so they are coated all over, then return them to the oven to roast for about 10 minutes to get really crisp. (See p99, Make crispy roast potatoes, step 3.)

6 Meanwhile, make the gravy: sit the large roasting tin on the hob. Sprinkle in the flour and whisk. Gradually blend in the stock with the whisk and bring to the boil. Simmer for 2 minutes, then stir in the wine and redcurrant jelly. Stir until thickened. Season and strain into a jug or gravy boat. (See p99, Make smooth, tasty gravy.) Remove the potatoes and sprinkle with salt. Garnish the chicken with bay leaves and serve with the potatoes and gravy.

KEYS TO PERFECTION

Prepare the chicken for roasting

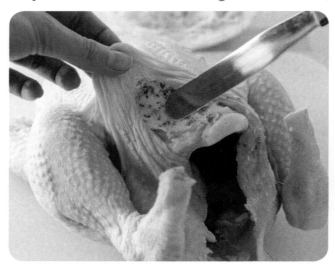

1 Spreading tarragon butter under the skin makes the chicken moist and flavoursome. Starting at the open-cavity end, loosen the skin over the breasts. Do each breast separately, and use your fingers to carefully free the skin from the flesh, easing your way as far down the "pockets" as possible without tearing the skin. Spread the butter evenly over the flesh. Bring the skin back over to cover the butter.

2 Rub plain butter over the legs, season the outside of the chicken, and put the lemon halves and tarragon sprigs in the cavity. Place the chicken on a little pile of onion wedges in the middle of the roasting tin. This will prevent the bird from sitting directly on the tin, so helps it to roast better and not stick, and also gives extra flavour to the chicken and later to the gravy.

Baste the chicken

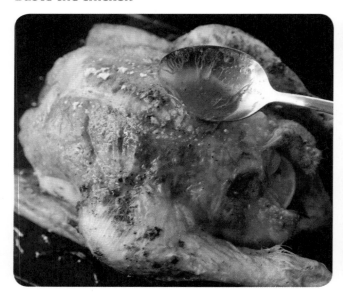

Halfway through cooking, baste the chicken all over with the buttery cooking juices to make it more succulent. If the breast skin is already golden brown at this point, cover the bird loosely with foil so that it doesn't burn later. After basting, add the par-boiled potatoes.

Test for doneness

Insert a small, sharp knife into the thickest part of the thigh; if the juices run clear, the chicken is cooked. If they are still pink, roast for a bit longer. Once done, let the bird rest for about 10 minutes, covered with foil to keep it warm, which will make the meat more succulent.

Make crispy roast potatoes

1 Roast potatoes will be crisper and fluff up more easily if they're par-boiled before roasting. Once the water comes to the boil, time them to simmer for just 5 minutes, or they will overcook and lose their shape. They should still be firm in the middle. Immediately tip the potatoes into a colander to drain, then return them to the pan and gently shake over a very low heat for about 1 minute. This will dry them off and create rough edges that will later go crispy.

2 After the chicken has roasted for 50 minutes and been basted, add the potatoes to the tin. Make sure they're in a single layer, so they cook on all sides, and turn them in the juices for maximum flavour and so they can turn crispy. If you're covering the chicken with foil, don't cover the potatoes, as they won't brown properly.

Make smooth, tasty gravy

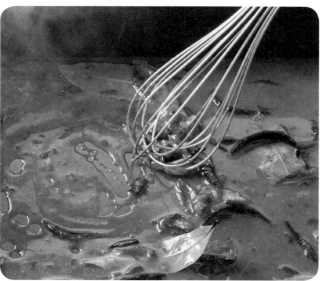

3 Once the chicken is cooked, transfer the potatoes to a smaller roasting tin using a slotted spoon, keeping them in a single layer so all sides can get crisp. Tip the large tin and pour off most of the top layer of fat (but not the juices) into the small tin. Baste with the fat. Increase the oven temperature so the high heat can finish off the crisping. If necessary, shake the tin after 5 minutes to stop sticking.

Making the gravy in the tin with the chicken juices gives the best flavour. Whisk in the flour to prevent lumps, and cook for 1–2 minutes to get rid of the raw taste. Add the stock a little at a time, whisking constantly for a smooth consistency. Simmer, then add the wine and redcurrant jelly. Stir to thicken. After the redcurrant jelly has dissolved, taste for seasoning. You may not need salt if the stock is salty. Strain.

Glazed Chicken with Cucumber Salsa

This is one of those very quick and easy suppers that is ideal for making when you get home from work. If you have any chicken left over, it's also good cold. Serve with long-grain rice or wild rice.

 Serves 4    325 calories per serving

INGREDIENTS

- 4 skinless, boneless chicken breasts
- olive oil, for greasing and drizzling
- 3 tbsp mango chutney
- 3 tbsp tomato ketchup
- 3 tbsp dark soy sauce
- 1 tbsp grainy mustard
- knob of butter
- lime wedges, to serve

FOR THE SALSA

- ½ cucumber, halved lengthways, deseeded, and chopped
- 4 spring onions, trimmed and finely chopped
- 1 fresh, mild green chilli, deseeded and finely chopped
- 15g (½oz) fresh coriander leaves with stalks, finely chopped
- 2 tsp capers (see below, box)
- 3 tbsp olive oil
- juice of 1 lime
- 1 tsp caster sugar
- freshly ground black pepper

1 Preheat the oven to 220°C (fan 200°C/425°F/Gas 7). Make deep cuts in the top of the chicken breasts (see below, Deeply flavoured, succulent chicken, step 1). Grease a small roasting tin, just large enough to accommodate the chicken breasts side by side, and put in the chicken.

2 Combine the chutney, ketchup, soy sauce, and mustard in a bowl and brush over the chicken (see below, Deeply flavoured, succulent chicken, step 2). Drizzle with oil and roast for 25 minutes, basting several times.

3 While the chicken is cooking, make the salsa: put all the ingredients into a bowl, add pepper to taste, and mix well (you shouldn't need salt, as the capers are salty).

4 When the chicken is cooked, remove it from the oven and pour the pan juices into a small pan. Set the chicken aside for 10 minutes. Keep warm.

5 Add the butter to the pan juices and simmer over a medium–high heat for a few minutes or until the juices reduce and just cover the bottom of the pan. Keep an eye on the glaze and stir frequently, so that it doesn't catch. Spoon the glaze over the chicken and serve hot, with the salsa and lime wedges on the side.

KEYS TO PERFECTION

Deeply flavoured, succulent chicken

1 Make 4 diagonal slashes across the top of each chicken breast, cutting about one-third of the way down. The cuts will allow the mango chutney mixture to flavour the flesh and the oven heat to penetrate.

2 Put the chicken in the tin, slashed-side up. Brush the chutney mixture liberally all over the chicken, working it deep into the cuts. During roasting, spoon the cooking juices over the chicken to help make the meat succulent.

Buying and using capers

Capers are sold in small jars, pickled in brine or packed in salt. The ones in brine tend to be the largest and are quite vinegary. For this recipe, I prefer the salted, tiny "nonpareille" capers, because their saltiness contrasts well with the sweetness of the chicken. You can rinse off the salt if you like, but I leave it on when I'm using a small quantity, as here.

Swiss Chicken, Spinach, and Mushroom Bake

For this quick-to-make, comforting supper dish, chicken breast fillets are baked with spinach and a creamy mushroom sauce and topped with Swiss Gruyère cheese.

 Serves 6　　 405 calories per serving

Special equipment
1.7–2 litre (3–3½ pint) baking dish, about 30 x 23cm (12 x 9in) and 5cm (2in) deep

INGREDIENTS

- 750g (1lb 10oz) fresh spinach
- ¼ tsp freshly grated nutmeg
- salt and freshly ground black pepper
- 725g (1lb 9oz) chicken breast fillets (mini chicken fillets)
- 2 tbsp olive oil
- 25g (scant 1oz) butter
- 200g (7oz) button mushrooms, halved or quartered according to size
- 1 garlic clove, crushed
- 200ml carton full-fat crème fraîche
- 75g (2½oz) Gruyère cheese, grated

1 Pick over the spinach leaves and trim off any thick, coarse stalks. Wash the spinach, place it in a large pan with some water still clinging to the leaves, cover, and cook for 5 minutes or until tender. Drain the spinach thoroughly in a colander, chop it coarsely, and return it to the pan. Add the nutmeg and plenty of salt and pepper, and toss the spinach briefly over a high heat, until dry. Transfer to the baking dish and spread the spinach over the bottom of the dish. (See pp104–105, Non-soggy spinach layer.)

2 Preheat the oven to 220°C (fan 200°C/425°F/Gas 7). Season the chicken fillets with salt and pepper. Heat the oil until hot in a large, non-stick frying pan, add half of the chicken fillets, and fry over a medium–high heat for 2 minutes, turning halfway. (See p105, Tender, golden chicken.) Transfer to the baking dish using a slotted spoon, arranging the fillets over the spinach in a single, even layer. Repeat with the remaining chicken.

3 Melt the butter in the frying pan, add the mushrooms, garlic, and some salt and pepper, and fry over a medium–high heat for 5 minutes, stirring frequently. Add the crème fraîche, a few spoonfuls at a time, and stir for 1–2 minutes over a medium heat to make a creamy sauce.

4 Pour the mushroom sauce over the chicken, then shake the dish and separate the fillets with a fork so that the sauce runs down between them. Sprinkle the cheese evenly over the top. Bake for 30 minutes. Remove from the oven and leave to settle for 5 minutes before serving.

KEYS TO PERFECTION (*see overleaf*)
Non-soggy spinach layer; Tender, golden chicken

KEYS TO PERFECTION

Non-soggy spinach layer

1 Wash the leaves in a large bowl or sink full of cold water to get rid of grit, then lift the leaves out a handful at a time, give them a good shake, and place them in a large pan. Push the leaves down with your hands until all of them are in. Don't worry if the pan seems rather full – the spinach will shrink as soon as it starts to cook.

2 Cover the pan with its lid and cook the spinach for 5 minutes over a high heat with only the water that is clinging to the leaves after rinsing and draining. Don't add any more water, as this will make the spinach soggy. Stir a few times during cooking, moving the uncooked leaves from the top to the bottom of the pan.

3 You may be surprised at the relatively small amount of spinach you're left with at the end of cooking, but the flavour is intense so you don't need a lot. Tip the contents of the pan into a colander held over the sink, and press and pound hard on the spinach using the edge of a wooden spatula to extract as much water as possible.

4 Tip half the spinach onto a board and chop coarsely with a large chef's knife, using a fork in your other hand to steady the leaves on the board. Return the chopped spinach to the pan, then chop the remaining half in the same way.

Non-soggy spinach layer (continued)

5 Add the nutmeg and plenty of seasoning to the spinach, then toss over a high heat for 1–2 minutes to drive off any surplus water. The spinach needs to be completely dry at this stage, or it will be too sloppy in the finished dish.

6 Tip the spinach out of the pan into the baking dish and spread it out as smoothly and evenly as possible using a spoon or spatula. The spinach should cover the entire bottom of the baking dish, right to the edges and into the corners.

Tender, golden chicken

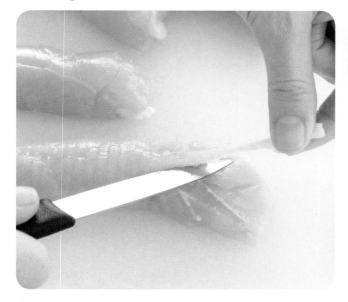

1 Chicken breast fillets are long, tender strips of meat available in most supermarkets, usually with 7 or 8 fillets per pack. Before cooking, remove the white tendon, which will be tough to eat. Use a small, sharp knife to tease one end of the tendon away from the flesh, then grip this end with your fingers and slide the blade along the length of the tendon to release it cleanly from the flesh.

2 Fry the chicken fillets for only 1 minute on each side. This is just long enough to give them a light golden colour on the outside, leaving them uncooked in the centre. It's important not to overcook the chicken at this stage, because it has yet to be baked with the spinach and sauce for 30 minutes, and you don't want the meat to become tough.

Mary's TOP TIPS 4

Get organized

Before you start to cook, clear any clutter from the worktop, gather the equipment you'll need, bring food to room temperature if required, and prepare the ingredients. You don't want any last-minute panics!

Chicken Tagine

Since this special dish tastes even better when cooked a day ahead and reheated, it's very handy to make when entertaining. Carry on the Moroccan theme and serve with couscous.

 Serves 4    350 calories per serving

INGREDIENTS

- 8 bone-in chicken thighs (see p111, box)
- salt and freshly ground black pepper
- 2 tbsp olive oil
- 1 large onion, coarsely chopped
- 20g (¾oz) fresh root ginger, finely chopped
- 2 tsp ground coriander
- 2 tsp ground cumin
- 1 tsp ground cinnamon
- 3 large ripe tomatoes, roughly chopped
- 2 large garlic cloves, crushed
- 1½ tsp harissa paste
- 1 tbsp runny honey
- 450ml (15fl oz) chicken stock
- 75g (2½oz) ready-to-eat dried apricots
- 75g (2½oz) ready-to-eat pitted prunes
- 1 preserved lemon (see p111, box)
- 4 tbsp coarsely chopped fresh coriander

KEYS TO PERFECTION (see overleaf)
Succulent, golden brown chicken; Soft, velvety fruit; Rich, mellow flavours

1 Skin, trim, and season the chicken. Heat the oil in a flameproof casserole over a medium–high heat until hot and fry the chicken in 2 batches until golden brown on all sides. (See p110, Succulent, golden brown chicken.) Remove using a slotted spoon, transfer to a large plate, and set aside.

2 Add the onion and ginger to the oil in the pan and soften over a low heat for 5 minutes, stirring frequently and scraping the bottom of the pan to release any sticky bits left from the chicken. Add the ground spices and fry for 2–3 minutes, stirring constantly.

3 Stir in the tomatoes and increase the heat to medium. Add the garlic, harissa paste, and honey, and stir well again. Pour in the stock and bring to the boil, stirring often. Return the reserved chicken to the pan, together with the juices that have collected on the plate.

4 Quarter the apricots, prunes, and preserved lemon, and remove the pips from the lemon (see p111, Soft, velvety fruit). Add the fruits to the pan. Press down the chicken and fruits to submerge them in the sauce.

5 Cover and simmer gently over a medium–low heat for 1 hour or until the chicken is tender and cooked through. Lift the lid and check occasionally during this time, turning the chicken over to ensure even cooking. Leave to cool, cover, and refrigerate overnight. (See p111, Rich, mellow flavours.)

6 The following day, slowly reheat the tagine for about 10 minutes or until the chicken is hot and the sauce gently bubbling. Stir in about half the chopped coriander and taste the sauce for seasoning. Serve hot, sprinkled with the remaining coriander.

KEYS TO PERFECTION

Succulent, golden brown chicken

1 If you're simmering chicken thighs in liquid, as in this recipe, it's best to remove the skin before cooking. This results in a less greasy sauce and helps keep the fat and calorie content down. To remove the skin, grip one end with your fingers and pull it away from the flesh – it should come off easily. Trim off any large pieces of white fat that may be clinging to the chicken flesh. Discard the fat.

2 Place the skinned chicken pieces on a large plate and season them well all over with salt and pepper. Do this just before cooking, or the salt will draw out the juices from the meat and make it dry.

3 Pick up each thigh, holding it firmly in shape, and add it to the hot oil with the smooth, skinned-side down. Fry 4 chicken thighs at a time. If you overcrowd the pan, the chicken will stew rather than fry and won't turn brown.

4 When the thighs are golden brown underneath, use tongs to turn them over. Don't use a fork, as this will pierce the meat and cause the juices to run out, making the chicken dry. Continue frying until the chicken is brown on all sides. Don't rush the browning stage – it can take as long as 12 minutes or so. Remove the chicken using a slotted spoon and set aside on a plate while you fry the second batch.

Soft, velvety fruit

Buying and using preserved lemons

Preserved lemons can be found in jars at most supermarkets. They come whole, packed in brine, and look tiny compared with fresh lemons, but their tangy, sour-salty flavour packs a very big punch. Preserved lemons are traditional in Moroccan tagines and can be left in or out before serving, as you prefer. I find it's a nice surprise to come across the occasional piece of lemon in the sauce.

Using a pair of sharp kitchen scissors, snip the apricots and prunes into quarters, so that during the cooking time they will soften and almost melt into the sauce to give it a velvety consistency. Cut the lemon into quarters lengthways and flick out the tiny pips with the tip of a small, sharp knife. Discard the pips.

Rich, mellow flavours

The benefits of chicken thighs

Chicken thighs are richer in flavour and less expensive than chicken breasts. They also remain moist for longer, which is why they're the best choice for a slow-cooked dish such as this tagine. They are available bone-in or boneless, but I prefer to cook them on the bone, as it gives a better flavour and helps to keep the meat in shape. You can either leave the skin on, or remove it – which is best for this recipe.

As with most spicy dishes, the resting and chilling time allows the flavours to mellow and mature. When the chicken is cooked, remove the casserole from the heat. Leave the tagine to go completely cold, then cover it with a lid and refrigerate overnight. The following day, bring the dish to room temperature and then reheat it slowly.

Chicken Korma

This is a light, fragrant, creamy curry, ideal for those who like their curries mild, and it doesn't take long to make. Basmati rice goes well with it, as does some warm naan bread on the side.

 Serves 4    445 calories per serving

INGREDIENTS

- 4 tbsp sunflower oil
- 2 skinless, boneless chicken breasts, about 280g (9½oz) in total, cut into 3.5cm (1½in) chunks
- 500–550g (1lb 2oz–1¼lb) skinless, boneless chicken thighs, cut into 3.5cm (1½in) chunks
- 1 onion, halved and thinly sliced
- 6 cardamom pods, slit down one side
- ½ cinnamon stick, about 6cm (2½in) long
- 3 garlic cloves, crushed
- 2 tsp finely grated fresh root ginger
- 1 tsp ground coriander
- 1½ tsp garam masala
- ¼ tsp turmeric
- ½ tsp mild chilli powder
- 150g (5½oz) plain, full-fat yogurt (room temperature)
- 1 tbsp ground almonds
- 4–5 tbsp double cream
- ¼ tsp freshly ground black pepper
- salt
- chopped fresh coriander, to garnish

1 Heat 2 tablespoons of the oil in a large, non-stick sauté pan. Add the chopped chicken breasts and thighs and fry over a medium–high heat for 6–8 minutes until starting to colour, stirring occasionally. Transfer to a large plate using a slotted spoon and set aside.

2 Pour the remaining 2 tablespoons of oil in the pan and add the onion, cardamom pods, cinnamon, garlic, and ginger. Fry for about 5 minutes or until the onion starts to brown.

3 Stir in the ground coriander, garam masala, turmeric, and chilli powder, and fry for 1 minute. Return the chicken to the pan together with any juices and cook, stirring, for 2 more minutes.

4 Reduce the heat to medium–low and add the yogurt gradually. Pour in 200ml (7fl oz) of water, cover, and simmer over a low heat for 15–20 minutes or until the chicken is tender. (See below, Smooth, creamy sauce.)

5 Stir in the ground almonds and 3 tablespoons of the cream. Season with the pepper and some salt and remove the cinnamon stick. Spoon over a drizzle of the remaining cream and scatter a little coriander over each serving.

KEYS TO PERFECTION
Smooth, creamy sauce

1 To prevent the yogurt from curdling, bring it to room temperature before using and stir it in just a tablespoonful at a time over a gentle heat, rather than tipping it in all at once. Stir well between each spoonful.

2 As the chicken simmers, check the sauce's consistency. Add a drop more water if needed, but not too much as the sauce should coat the chicken. When added, the almonds will thicken the sauce slightly and the cream will enrich it.

Spanish-style Chicken Paprika

I like this dish for casual entertaining: you can make it ahead and finish it in the oven before serving. If it's been in the fridge, allow a bit longer to heat up. Serve with a mix of long-grain and wild rice.

 Serves 4

 443 calories per serving

Special equipment
 1.7–2 litre (3–3½ pint) baking dish, about 25 x 18cm (10 x 7in) and 7.5cm (3in) deep

INGREDIENTS

- 115g (4oz) chorizo, cut into 1cm (½in) thick slices and then small cubes
- 3 tbsp olive oil
- 1 onion, halved lengthways and thinly sliced
- 2 garlic cloves, finely chopped
- 4 skinless, boneless chicken breasts, about 140g (5oz) each
- salt and freshly ground black pepper
- 250g (9oz) chestnut mushrooms, cut into 1cm (½in) thick slices
- 2 tsp paprika
- 1 tsp cornflour
- 150ml (5fl oz) chicken stock
- 170ml carton full-fat soured cream
- 12 pitted plump green olives
- 1 tbsp chopped fresh flat-leaf parsley, to garnish

1 Heat a large, non-stick frying pan or sauté pan. Add the chorizo and fry until crispy. Remove using a slotted spoon, drain on kitchen paper, and set aside. Keep 1 tablespoon of the chorizo oil in the pan and drain off any excess. Add 1 tablespoon of the olive oil. (See below, Use the chorizo oil for frying.) When hot, add the onion and garlic and fry for 6–8 minutes over a medium heat, stirring occasionally, until the onion starts to brown. Spread the onion over the bottom of the baking dish.

2 Preheat the oven to 200°C (fan 180°C/400°F/Gas 6). Pour another tablespoon of the oil into the pan. Season the chicken and brown over a medium heat for 10 minutes, turning once. Place on top of the onion.

3 Add the final tablespoon of oil to the pan, tip in the mushrooms, and season with pepper. Fry for about 3 minutes over a medium–high heat, stirring occasionally, until starting to brown. Stir in the paprika and cornflour. Pour in the stock, stirring to deglaze the bottom of the pan, and simmer for 1 minute. Stir in the soured cream and heat until just starting to bubble.

4 Pour the mushroom sauce over the chicken in the dish. Scatter over the chorizo and olives. Cover with foil and bake for 15–20 minutes or until bubbling around the edges. Serve sprinkled with the parsley.

KEYS TO PERFECTION
Use the chorizo oil for frying

1 Fry the chorizo in a hot, dry pan over a medium heat for about 1 minute until the fat starts to run, then increase the heat for 2 minutes until crispy. Stir frequently so it doesn't burn. Remove using a slotted spoon.

2 Use 1 tablespoon of the spicy red oil released by the chorizo for frying the onion and garlic: its smoky paprika flavour adds depth to the dish. Don't use any more, as it can overpower; instead, top up with olive oil.

Stir-fried Duck

Stir-frying is all about speed, movement, high heat, and using little oil, making this recipe fresh, quick, and healthy. Serve with cooked egg noodles, plain boiled or tossed into the wok at the end.

Serves 2   524 calories per serving

INGREDIENTS

- 2 oranges
- 3 tbsp dark soy sauce
- 2 duck breasts, each about 175g (6oz)
- ¾ tsp five-spice powder
- freshly ground black pepper
- 1 red pepper, deseeded
- 5cm (2in) piece of fresh root ginger, peeled
- 6 spring onions, trimmed
- 1 fresh red chilli, deseeded
- 225g (8oz) Tenderstem broccoli (see p118, box)
- 225g can water chestnuts, drained
- 2 tbsp sunflower oil
- 1 tbsp runny honey
- sesame oil, for sprinkling

KEYS TO PERFECTION (*see overleaf*)
Prepare the ingredients for stir-frying; Stir-fry to finish

1 Squeeze the juice from 1 of the oranges, pour it into a bowl, and add the soy sauce. Peel and segment the other orange, holding it over the bowl to catch the juice (see p118, Prepare the ingredients for stir-frying, step 1). Set the juice mixture and segments aside, keeping them separate.

2 Remove the skin and fat layer from the duck and discard. Slice the meat into strips, about 5cm (2in) long and no more than 5mm (¼in) thick, then cut each strip lengthways in half (see p118, Prepare the ingredients for stir-frying, step 2). Put the strips into a bowl, sprinkle with the five-spice powder and a good grinding of pepper, and mix well. Set aside.

3 Slice the red pepper, ginger, spring onions, and chilli into strips about the same size as the duck. Cut the florets off the broccoli stems and set the florets aside. Cut the broccoli stems into thin strips. (See p118, Prepare the ingredients for stir-frying, step 3.) Finely slice the water chestnuts.

4 Heat a wok or large, deep-sided, non-stick frying pan or sauté pan over a high heat until very hot. Pour in the sunflower oil and heat until it just begins to smoke. Add the duck and honey and stir-fry for a few minutes or until brown, then remove to a plate and set aside. Add the ginger, spring onions, and chilli to the hot oil and stir-fry for a few minutes until softened, then add the red pepper and broccoli stems and stir-fry for a few minutes more until softened. (See p119, Stir-fry to finish.)

5 Pour the reserved orange juice mixture into the wok, then add the broccoli florets and water chestnuts. Stir-fry for a few minutes more before tossing in the reserved cooked duck and orange segments to heat through. Sprinkle with sesame oil, to taste, and more soy sauce if you like. Serve immediately.

KEYS TO PERFECTION

Prepare the ingredients for stir-frying

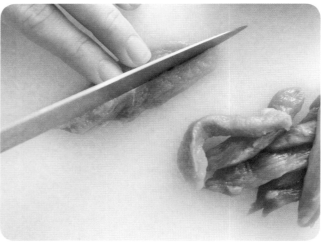

1 After removing the peel and pith from the orange using a sharp knife, cut down both sides of each membrane to free the segments from the core. Use a small, sharp knife and hold the orange over the bowl containing the orange juice and soy sauce, so the juice from the fruit falls into the bowl.

2 For fast, even cooking, all the ingredients need to be a similar size. Start with the duck, slicing it across the grain into thin strips about 5cm (2in) long and maximum 5mm (¼in) thick, then cut each strip lengthways in half. Slicing it this way means that long fibres are cut through, giving tender meat; it also exposes a greater cut surface to the heat, so the duck cooks more quickly while retaining its shape.

Using broccoli for stir-fries

Tenderstem broccoli is thin and delicate and therefore good for stir-fries, because both the stems and florets cook in super-quick time. You can also use ordinary broccoli for this recipe, provided you discard the thick, woody stalks and cut off the stems just below the florets, slicing them very finely. Separate the florets into tiny sprigs, otherwise they won't cook quickly enough.

3 Now slice the red pepper, peeled ginger, trimmed spring onions, deseeded chilli, and broccoli stems into strips approximately the same length and thickness as the duck. Slicing the vegetables finely like this means that they can cook quickly yet remain al dente, and enables them to absorb the flavours of the oil and spices while frying.

Stir-fry to finish

1 The great thing about a stir-fry is that it cooks in next to no time, but you need to get everything ready beforehand because once you start cooking you shouldn't stop. Put all the prepared ingredients into bowls, grouping them according to their cooking time, and line them up, ready to toss into the pan one after the other.

2 When you're ready to cook, get the wok as hot as possible over a high heat. Hold your hand over the pan – you should feel the heat rising. Add a drop of oil to test; it will sizzle when the wok is ready. Add the remaining oil and swirl it around the wok until it just begins to smoke very slightly.

Stir-frying with and without a wok

A wok isn't essential for stir-frying, but it does have several benefits – the main one being that the rounded shape and large size allow the food to be tossed around easily. If you don't have a wok, it's fine to use a large, deep-sided, non-stick sauté pan or frying pan instead. When stir-frying, you want to ensure you don't have the pan more than one-third full, so there's plenty of space for moving the ingredients around quickly and easily.

3 Throughout the cooking process, keep the heat under the wok as high as possible. Tip the ingredients into the hot oil, in the correct sequence, and then keep them constantly on the move around the bottom and sides of the wok by shaking the pan and tossing the contents together with a wok shovel, spatula, or two wooden spoons.

Pheasant Breasts with Apple and Cider

Supper always feels special when I cook pheasant. Here, I've teamed it with apples and cider, as they go so well with the richness of the meat. Serve with curly kale.

Serves 4   581 calories per serving

INGREDIENTS

- 4 boneless pheasant breasts, skinned
- 2 tbsp plain flour
- salt and freshly ground black pepper
- 1 tbsp olive oil
- 25g (scant 1oz) butter
- 150g (5½oz) smoked streaky bacon, cut into 1cm (½in) pieces
- 1 crisp dessert apple, such as Braeburn or Cox, peeled, cored, and cut into 1cm (½in) cubes
- 4 shallots, thinly sliced
- 300ml (10fl oz) dry cider
- 150ml (5fl oz) pheasant or chicken stock
- 1 tbsp redcurrant jelly
- 120ml (4fl oz) full-fat crème fraîche
- 1½ tsp finely chopped fresh sage
- 1½ tsp finely chopped fresh thyme

1 Place the pheasant breasts on a board and cover with cling film. Pound with the base of a saucepan to flatten very slightly. Put the flour on a plate, season, and coat the pheasant in the flour. Heat the oil and butter in a large, deep-sided, non-stick frying pan or sauté pan over a medium–high heat. As soon as the butter is foaming, add the meat, skinned-side down. Fry for 2 minutes on each side until golden brown, pressing it flat with a fish slice. Transfer the meat to a dish and set aside.

2 Put the bacon in the pan and cook for 5 minutes over a medium–low heat, stirring often. Add the apple and shallots and fry for 5 minutes over a medium heat, stirring frequently or until softened and lightly coloured. Add the cider, stock, redcurrant jelly, and some salt and pepper. Bring to the boil, stirring constantly until the jelly has melted. Reduce the heat and return the pheasant and its juices to the pan. Simmer gently for 2 minutes, turning the breasts halfway and basting frequently. Remove the pheasant to a board, cover loosely with foil, and leave to rest for 10 minutes.

3 Meanwhile, increase the heat to high and stir the crème fraîche into the sauce. Add 1 teaspoon each of sage and thyme and simmer gently until thickened. Season. Slice the pheasant and arrange on warmed plates (see below, Tender, thinly sliced pheasant). Spoon the sauce over and around the meat. Serve immediately, sprinkled with the remaining sage and thyme.

KEYS TO PERFECTION

Tender, thinly sliced pheasant

1 After the pheasant has rested, slice the breasts thinly on the diagonal with a sharp chef's knife or carving knife. Ideally, slice no more than 5mm (¼in) thick.

2 If you keep the slices close together as you carve the pheasant breasts, you can easily transfer each breast to a dinner plate with a fish slice.

Venison Cottage Pie

Roughly mashed carrots and potatoes make the perfect rustic topping for this wintry pie, as the taste and texture hold their own against the robust flavour of the venison.

 Serves 6

 606 calories per serving

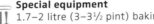 **Special equipment**
1.7–2 litre (3–3½ pint) baking dish, about 30 x 23cm (12 x 9in) and 5cm (2in) deep

INGREDIENTS

- 900g (2lb) stewing venison (see p125, box), cut into bite-sized cubes
- 600ml (1 pint) red wine
- finely grated rind and juice of 1 orange
- finely grated rind of 1 lemon
- 1 heaped tsp allspice berries, crushed
- salt and freshly ground black pepper
- 30g (1oz) plain flour
- 2–3 tbsp sunflower oil
- 1 piece smoked streaky bacon, about 200g (7oz), cut into 1cm (½in) cubes
- 1 large onion, coarsely chopped
- 250g (9oz) chestnut mushrooms, quartered
- 2 bay leaves
- 2 tbsp redcurrant jelly

FOR THE TOPPING

- 800g (1¾lb) carrots, cut into 1cm (½in) thick slices
- 800g (1¾lb) smooth potatoes, such as Desirée, peeled and quartered
- 50g (1¾oz) butter (room temperature)

KEYS TO PERFECTION *(see overleaf)*
Marinate and dry the meat; Make a stable mash topping; Assemble the pie carefully

1 Put the venison into a large, non-metallic bowl. Pour in the wine and add the orange rind and juice, lemon rind, allspice, and black pepper. Stir well, submerging the meat. Cover with cling film and marinate in the fridge for a minimum of 12 hours, preferably up to 2 days. Remove the meat using a slotted spoon, drain, and pat dry with kitchen paper, then transfer it to another large bowl. (See p124, Marinate and dry the meat.) Reserve the marinade.

2 Preheat the oven to 160°C (fan 140°C/325°F/Gas 3). Spread out the flour on a large plate or tray and season. Coat one-third of the meat in the flour. Heat 2 tablespoons of the oil in a large, non-stick frying pan until hot. Fry the floured meat over a medium–high heat until browned all over; this should take about 6 minutes. Remove the meat from the pan using a slotted spoon and transfer to a bowl or large plate. Set aside. Divide the remaining meat into 2 batches and repeat the flouring and browning, adding more oil if needed.

3 Tip the oil and juices from the frying pan into a flameproof casserole. Add the bacon to the casserole and fry over a medium heat until the fat begins to run, then add the onion and fry for about 5 minutes, stirring occasionally, until the bacon and onion are lightly coloured. Stir in the mushrooms and fry for a few minutes until the juices run.

4 Tip in the venison and its juices and pour over the reserved marinade. Stir, then add up to 150ml (5fl oz) cold water, just enough so the liquid barely covers the meat. Stir again, increase the heat, and bring to a simmer. Add the bay leaves, redcurrant jelly, and season with salt. Cover, transfer to the oven, and cook for 2 hours or until the venison is tender.

5 Meanwhile, make the topping: cook the carrots and potatoes together in a large pan of salted boiling water for 15–20 minutes or until tender. Drain in a colander, return to the pan with half the butter, and mash roughly with a potato masher. (See p124, Make a stable mash topping.) Season.

6 Remove the casserole from the oven and increase the oven temperature to 200°C (fan 180°C/400°F/Gas 6). Transfer just the meat and vegetables to the baking dish and spread them out in an even layer. Discard the bay leaves. Measure 200ml (7fl oz) of the gravy and pour this over the meat and vegetables. Spread over the mash and mark it in a criss-cross pattern with a fork. Grind over black pepper and dot with the remaining butter. (See p125, Assemble the pie carefully.) Bake for 30–40 minutes until golden. Reheat the remaining gravy in a pan, pour it into a jug, and hand it round separately.

KEYS TO PERFECTION

Marinate and dry the meat

1 Stir the marinating venison every now and then, pressing the chunks of meat under the liquid with the back of a spoon. You can marinate the meat for as little as 12 hours, but 2 days is ideal (stirring about 3 times during this period). Keep the bowl covered between stirrings, to prevent evaporation.

2 After marinating, make sure the meat is as dry as possible before coating it in flour, otherwise it won't brown. Drain the pieces well when you lift them out of the liquid using a slotted spoon, then tip each spoonful onto a double sheet of kitchen paper and pat the meat thoroughly dry with more paper. Reserve the marinade.

Make a stable mash topping

1 The mash should be quite stiff, so that it holds its own above the meat and gravy. Carrots are more watery than potatoes, so take care to drain them well with the potatoes. Shake the colander to get rid of as much water as possible, then return the vegetables to the pan and toss them over a low heat for a few minutes until they're quite dry.

2 Remove the pan from the heat and mash the carrots and potatoes with half the butter, simply breaking them up roughly with a potato masher, just enough to mix them together. When combining carrots in a mash like this, it's best not to over-mash and make the mixture too smooth or it will go sloppy.

Assemble the pie carefully

1 For a perfect cottage pie, it's all about ratio and consistency – juicy meat and gravy at the bottom and a good, thick layer of mash on top. Transfer the meat and vegetables from the casserole to the dish using a slotted spoon, leaving behind as much of the gravy as possible. This is the way to control the amount of liquid that goes in the dish.

2 Now you should add just enough gravy to moisten the meat without making the pie too runny. If there's too much gravy, it will bubble up into the mash during baking and make it sloppy. Pour the measured gravy slowly over the venison, shaking the dish so that the liquid flows between the pieces of meat.

Using stewing venison

Butchers often sell ready-cubed "stewing venison" without identifying the cut. Generally, it's either shoulder or shin, both of which are suitable for this pie. Venison is a lean, low-fat meat that benefits from marinating before cooking to help make it juicy and tender. Steeping the cubes of meat in a marinade softens the tough fibres of the meat and gives it more flavour.

3 Spoon the mash on top of the meat mixture, then spread it out using a palette knife to make as even a layer as possible. Take care to go right to the edge of the dish, to seal in the gravy and prevent it from seeping up the sides. Finally, make criss-cross markings with a fork, grind over pepper liberally, and dot the top with knobs of butter.

Meat

Peppered Fillet of Beef

This is an easy roast, with guaranteed "wow factor" and no waste at all. Mustard and peppercorns protect the meat from the intense heat of the oven, while giving a zingy crust around each slice.

🍽 Serves 6   🕐 388 calories per serving

INGREDIENTS

- 1 centre-cut piece of beef fillet, 1.25kg (2¾lb) (room temperature)
- 1 tbsp olive oil
- 2 tbsp Dijon mustard
- 6 tbsp black peppercorns, coarsely crushed

FOR THE GRAVY

- 30g (1oz) butter
- 1 tbsp plain flour
- 150ml (5fl oz) red wine
- 250ml (9fl oz) beef stock
- 2 tsp redcurrant jelly
- 1 tsp Dijon mustard
- salt

1 Rub the beef all over with the oil. Heat a large, non-stick frying pan (or roasting tin if the fillet is too large) and brown the beef on all sides, except the ends (see below, Sear the beef). Remove the beef from the pan and leave until cold. Preheat the oven to 220°C (fan 200°C/425°F/Gas 7).

2 Spread the mustard over the seared beef, except the ends, then roll the mustard-covered sides in the crushed peppercorns (see below, Make a peppery crust). You can sear and coat the fillet up to 12 hours ahead (if you do so, keep the fillet in the fridge and bring to room temperature 1–2 hours before roasting). Place the beef on a rack in a roasting tin and roast for 25 minutes. Transfer the beef to a carving board and let it rest for 10 minutes.

3 Meanwhile, make the gravy: put the butter in the roasting tin and place the tin on the hob over a medium–low heat. Stir until the butter has melted, scraping up bits on the bottom of the tin, then sprinkle in the flour and cook for 1–2 minutes, whisking constantly with a wire whisk.

4 Slowly whisk in the wine and stock and bring to the boil, then add the redcurrant jelly and mustard. Simmer for a few minutes, whisking all the time, until the jelly has melted and the gravy thickens. Add salt to taste. Carve the beef into thick slices and serve with the gravy in a jug or gravy boat.

KEYS TO PERFECTION

Buying and cooking fillet of beef

The thickest part of the fillet – called the centre or middle cut – is essential for even cooking, as it will be the same thickness along its length. Don't doubt the roasting time in this recipe – 25 minutes in the oven guarantees perfect rare beef every time. If you prefer beef medium rare, roast it for 30 minutes.

Sear the beef

Once the frying pan is very hot, sear the fillet for 1 minute on all sides (except the ends) until the outside is brown. This releases juices that caramelize and give depth of flavour.

Make a peppery crust

After spreading mustard over the sides of the cooled beef, put the crushed peppercorns on a sheet of greaseproof paper and roll the beef in them until evenly coated.

Steak and Guinness Pie

This is a classic, hearty pie. To make it ahead, cook the meat to the end of step 3, then leave it in the fridge overnight before finishing off the pie. Serve with mash and seasonal green vegetables.

 Serves 6

 650 calories per serving

Special equipment
1.2 litre (2 pint) pie dish, about 27 x 20cm (10½ x 8in) and 5cm (2in) deep

INGREDIENTS

- 900g (2lb) braising steak, cut into bite-sized cubes
- 30g (1oz) plain flour
- 1 tsp mustard powder
- salt and freshly ground black pepper
- 2–3 tbsp sunflower oil
- 1 large onion, coarsely chopped
- 3 celery sticks, cut diagonally into slices 2.5cm (1in) thick
- 2 large carrots, cut into rings 1cm (½in) thick, then quartered
- 500ml (16fl oz) Guinness
- 200ml (7fl oz) beef stock
- 2 tbsp redcurrant jelly
- 2 bay leaves
- 500g (1lb 2oz) shop-bought puff pastry (preferably all-butter)
- 2 tbsp chopped fresh parsley
- 2 tsp chopped fresh thyme
- 1 egg, beaten

KEYS TO PERFECTION (*see overleaf*)
Brown the meat well; Make a well-fitting, decorative pie lid

1 Preheat the oven to 160°C (fan 140°C/325°F/Gas 3). Pat the meat dry with kitchen paper. Put the flour on a large plate or tray and season with the mustard, ½ teaspoon of salt, and a few grindings of pepper. Coat one-third of the meat in the flour. Heat 2 tablespoons of the oil in a large, non-stick frying pan until hot and fry the floured meat over a medium–high heat. (See p132, Brown the meat well.) Remove the meat from the pan using a slotted spoon and transfer to a flameproof casserole. Divide the remaining meat into 2 batches and repeat the flouring and browning, adding more oil if needed.

2 Add the onion to the frying pan, with a little more oil if necessary, and fry for 3 minutes or until golden brown, stirring frequently. Add the celery and carrots and stir to mix, then fry for 2 minutes before tipping the vegetables on top of the meat in the casserole.

3 Pour the Guinness and stock into the casserole and add the redcurrant jelly. Mix well and bring to the boil, stirring. Add the bay leaves and season with salt and pepper. Cover the casserole, transfer it to the oven, and cook for 2½ hours or until the meat is tender. Remove the casserole from the oven, taste the gravy for seasoning, and leave until cold.

4 Make the pastry lid: preheat the oven to 220°C (fan 200°C/425°F/Gas 7). Roll out the pastry and cut out a lid and a strip for the lip of the pie dish. Remove the bay leaves from the casserole and stir in the parsley and thyme, then transfer the meat and vegetables to the pie dish using a large spoon, together with enough of the gravy to come just below the lip of the dish. Reserve any remaining gravy. Brush water around the lip of the dish; cut the pastry strip into smaller pieces and place the strips on the moistened lip. Moisten the strips, cover with the lid, and press to seal. (See pp132–33, Make a well-fitting, decorative pie lid, steps 1–3.)

5 Trim, "knock up", and scallop the edge, then brush the pastry lid with beaten egg to glaze. Use the trimmings to make decorations and re-glaze with as much of the remaining egg as needed. Cut a small slit in the centre of the lid. (See p133, Make a well-fitting, decorative pie lid, steps 4–6.)

6 Bake the pie for 30–35 minutes or until the pastry is risen and golden brown. If you have any gravy left over, reheat until bubbling, pour it into a jug, and serve alongside the pie.

KEYS TO PERFECTION

Brown the meat well

1 Flour will thicken the gravy during the long time in the oven, but it needs to be cooked at the initial frying stage, otherwise it will taste raw in the finished dish. Before frying the batches of meat, toss the chunks in the seasoned flour until lightly coated on all sides.

2 Make sure the oil is really hot before browning. This is vital to sear the meat and give it a good colour and flavour. Place the floured beef chunks in the oil, spacing the pieces well apart, and fry over a medium–high heat until browned on all sides (this takes 6 minutes or so). Remove the meat using a slotted spoon, so that the fat and juices remain in the pan.

Make a well-fitting, decorative pie lid

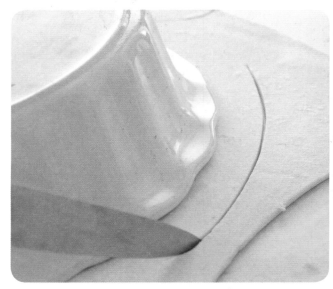

1 Roll out the pastry on a lightly floured, cool surface until it is about 5mm (¼in) thick. Place your pie dish upside down in the centre of the pastry and press it down quite firmly. With a small, sharp knife, cut out a lid that is about 2cm (¾in) larger all round than the outside edge of the dish.

2 Lift off the dish and set aside the excess pastry. Using the pie dish indentation as a guide, cut off the strip from around the outside of the pastry lid. Spoon the cold pie filling into the dish, mounding it up slightly in the centre and adding enough gravy to come just below the lip of the dish. Brush the lip with water and attach the pastry strip to it, cutting it into smaller pieces and joining them together as needed.

Make a well-fitting, decorative pie lid (continued)

3 Check the size of the pastry lid over the pie dish and roll it out a little larger if necessary. You don't want to have to stretch the pastry to fit it over the dish, as this would cause shrinkage when baking. Brush the pastry strip with water, then roll the pastry lid loosely around the rolling pin, lift it over the dish, and gently unroll it. Press all around the edge to seal the lid to the strip.

4 Trim off any surplus pastry with the knife if necessary, cutting downwards against the edge of the dish. "Knock up" the edge of the pastry by holding the back of the knife horizontally against the edge and tapping all the way round. This will help the pastry rise evenly.

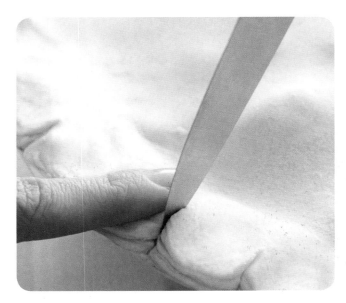

5 For an attractive finish, scallop all round the edge of the pie by making indentations with the back of the knife and your forefinger, alternating the knife marks and finger indentations. Brush all over the pastry with beaten egg, using a pastry brush. Coat the surface lightly; too much egg will prevent the pastry from puffing up.

6 Roll out some pastry trimmings and cut out leaf shapes. Make patterns using the back of the knife. Place the pastry leaves on top of the pie and brush all over the lid again with more egg. Cut a small slit, about 2cm (¾in) long, in the middle of the lid, to allow steam to escape during baking. This prevents the pastry from becoming soggy.

Ribeye Steak with Caramelized Shallots

For the most tender steaks that are full of flavour, ask your butcher to cut them from the sirloin end of the rib. Spinach and rösti (see pp216–17) make the perfect accompaniments.

 Serves 2

 615 calories per serving

 **Special equipment**
Ridged cast-iron chargrill pan

INGREDIENTS

- 30g (1oz) butter
- 3 echalion (banana) shallots (see below, box), halved lengthways
- 30g (1oz) caster sugar
- 200ml (7fl oz) hot beef stock
- 2 ribeye steaks, about 200g (7oz) each (room temperature)
- 2 tbsp sunflower oil
- salt and freshly ground black pepper
- 90ml (3fl oz) red wine
- 1 fresh red chilli, deseeded and finely chopped
- 1 garlic clove, finely chopped
- ½ tsp Dijon mustard
- 2 tbsp chopped fresh flat-leaf parsley
- 1 tbsp full-fat crème fraîche

1 Melt the butter in a non-stick frying pan over a medium heat. When the butter bubbles, add the shallots and fry for 3–4 minutes until golden brown on each side, turning once. Sprinkle in the sugar, stir, and allow to colour and caramelize for a few minutes, then stir in half the stock. Bring to the boil, cover the pan, and reduce the heat to low. Simmer for 10 minutes, turning and basting once (see below, Soft, caramelized shallots).

2 Preheat the chargrill pan over a high heat for 5–10 minutes or until piping hot. Meanwhile, wipe the steaks dry with kitchen paper, brush them on both sides with oil, and season with pepper. Place the steaks in the pan and grill for 2–3 minutes on each side for rare to medium rare (see below, Juicy, chargrilled steaks). Lift the steaks out of the pan, season with salt and more pepper if required, and let them rest.

3 Pour the wine and remaining stock into the chargrill pan and scrape to release the sticky bits. Add the chilli and garlic. Simmer until reduced by about half. Take off the heat and stir in the mustard and parsley.

4 To serve, reheat the shallots and stir in the crème fraîche. Arrange 3 shallot halves on each plate and spoon over their sauce. Place the steaks alongside or on top, and drizzle with the wine and stock mixture.

KEYS TO PERFECTION

Echalion (banana) shallots

Echalions, also known as banana shallots, are best for this recipe. Not only is their long oval shape appealing, but being a cross between an onion and a shallot they are easier to peel than ordinary shallots and stay in shape when cut in half. If you can't find echalions in the shops, ordinary shallots will do.

Soft, caramelized shallots

To ensure even cooking, turn and baste the shallots with the stock halfway through. At the end, they should feel soft when pierced with a fork yet still retain their shape.

Juicy, chargrilled steaks

As the steaks grill, press them with a fish slice but don't move them around. This way they will look good with charred lines and will cook perfectly in the time given.

Mary's TOP TIPS 5

Stock up on staples

Keep a well-stocked storecupboard and have back-up in the freezer of bread, milk, and stock. It's always reassuring to know you have the basics to hand so you can rustle up an impromptu meal.

Spicy Schnitzels with Lemon and Garlic Mayonnaise

This is a classic Wiener schnitzel, except I've used pork instead of veal, as it's less expensive and more available, but just as tender. I like to serve it with a simply dressed tomato and red onion salad.

 Serves 4   452 calories per serving

INGREDIENTS

- 150g (5½oz) stale white bread slices, at least 1 day old
- 1 tsp black peppercorns, coarsely crushed
- ½ tsp smoked paprika
- ½ tsp salt
- ¼ tsp crushed dried chillies
- 4 thinly cut pork escalopes, about 450g (1lb) in total, trimmed of fat
- 2 tbsp plain flour
- 1 egg, beaten
- 3–5 tbsp sunflower oil
- lemon wedges, to serve

FOR THE LEMON AND GARLIC MAYONNAISE

- 4 heaped tbsp mayonnaise
- 4 tbsp finely chopped fresh flat-leaf parsley
- 1 garlic clove, crushed
- finely grated rind of 1 lemon
- squeeze of lemon juice

1 Preheat the oven to 160°C (fan 140°C/325°F/Gas 3). Spread the bread on a baking sheet and bake for 20 minutes or until crisp and dry, turning halfway through cooking. Remove from the oven and leave to cool a little, then break the slices (with their crusts) into pieces and drop them into a food processor fitted with a metal blade. Add the peppercorns, paprika, salt, and chillies and blitz to fine crumbs.

2 Beat out the escalopes and coat first in the flour, then in the egg, and finally in the breadcrumbs (see below, Prepare the escalopes for frying). In a small bowl, combine all the ingredients for the lemon and garlic mayonnaise. Cover and chill the mayonnaise in the fridge until serving time.

3 Heat 3 tablespoons of the oil in a large, non-stick frying pan over a medium heat. Add 2 of the crumbed escalopes (schnitzels) and fry for 1–2 minutes on each side or until golden brown and crisp. As they fry, press down hard with a fish slice to ensure they make contact with the pan. Drain and keep warm while frying the rest. If you need more oil, ensure it is hot before adding the meat. Serve immediately, with the mayonnaise and lemon wedges.

KEYS TO PERFECTION

Prepare the escalopes for frying

1 Cover an escalope with cling film and pound to flatten using a heavy-based pan (a pan is better than a rolling pin as it's flat, so doesn't leave ridge marks). Beat the meat as thinly as possible without tearing it.

2 Coat the escalopes in the spicy breadcrumb mixture. You want an even coating of flour (shake off the excess), then egg (let excess drain back into the dish), then breadcrumbs (pat them firmly into the egg so they stick).

Prepare the dish a day ahead

You can prepare the garlic and lemon mayonnaise and get the schnitzels ready for frying up to 24 hours ahead. If not frying the schnitzels straightaway, arrange them in a single layer on a large plate and put them in the fridge uncovered, or the coating will go soggy.

Roast Loin of Pork

Crispy crackling is hard to resist, but it's not always easy to get right if you keep the skin on the pork. If you cook the skin separately, as shown here, you'll have success every time.

 Serves 6 generously

 565 calories per serving

Special equipment
Stanley knife (or ask your butcher to make the incisions)

INGREDIENTS

- 1 boned loin of pork, 1.65kg (3lb 10oz)
- 4 tsp olive oil
- 2 tsp coarse sea salt
- salt and freshly ground black pepper
- 20g (¾oz) fresh rosemary sprigs

FOR THE STUFFING

- 30g (1oz) butter
- 1 onion, finely chopped
- 125g (4½oz) fresh white breadcrumbs
- 1 large egg, beaten
- 3 tbsp coarsely chopped fresh sage
- 1 tbsp finely chopped fresh rosemary
- 1 heaped tbsp capers, chopped
- 2 tsp anchovy paste
- finely grated rind of 1 orange

FOR THE GRAVY

- 20g (¾oz) butter
- 20g (¾oz) plain flour
- 100ml (3½fl oz) dry white wine
- 300ml (10fl oz) chicken stock
- juice of 1 orange (5–6 tbsp)
- 2 tsp redcurrant jelly
- 2 tsp Dijon or grainy mustard
- 1 tsp very finely chopped fresh sage

KEYS TO PERFECTION (see overleaf)
Make crispy crackling; Stuff, roll, and tie the loin

1 Make the stuffing: melt the butter in a small, non-stick frying pan, add the onion, and fry for 8–10 minutes over a medium–low heat until softened but not browned, stirring occasionally. Put the remaining stuffing ingredients into a bowl. Add the softened onion and the butter and mix well.

2 Remove the skin from the pork and make small incisions all over the skin using the Stanley knife (see p142, Make crispy crackling). Alternatively, ask the butcher to do this. Rub the skin with 2 teaspoons of the oil, then the coarse sea salt. Place the skin, salted-side up, on a rack in a roasting tin.

3 Preheat the oven to 220°C (fan 200°C/425°F/Gas 7). Place the pork joint, skinned-side down, on a board and open out the meat to make room for the stuffing. Place the stuffing on the pork, then fold over and roll the meat to enclose it. Turn the meat over so that the join is underneath. Tie the joint with string. Brush with the remaining 2 teaspoons of oil, sprinkle with salt and pepper, and tuck rosemary sprigs under the string. Put the pork in a roasting tin. (See pp142–43, Stuff, roll, and tie the loin.)

4 Place the pork on a low rack in the oven, with the tin of crackling on the shelf above. Roast for 30 minutes, then reduce the oven temperature to 180°C (fan 160°C/350°F/Gas 4) and roast for a further 1½ hours. (If you have a meat thermometer, the internal temperature should reach 75°C/165°F.) Check after 30–45 minutes to see if the crackling is crisp enough. If it is, remove it from the oven and keep it warm. Transfer the pork to a board, cover loosely with a tent of foil, and set aside to rest for 20 minutes.

5 Make the gravy: put the butter in the roasting tin and place the tin on the hob over a medium–low heat. Stir until the butter has melted, scraping up any sediment from the bottom of the tin, then sprinkle in the flour and cook for 1–2 minutes, whisking constantly.

6 Pour in the wine and whisk vigorously to combine, then slowly whisk in the stock and orange juice and bring to the boil. Add the redcurrant jelly, mustard, and sage. Simmer over a medium–high heat for about 5 minutes, whisking all the time, until the jelly has melted and the gravy thickens. Season with salt and pepper. Keep on a very gentle simmer until serving time, whisking occasionally.

7 Cut the crackling into strips with scissors or a sharp knife, or snap it with your fingers. Remove the string from the pork, carve, and serve with the crackling and piping-hot gravy in a jug or gravy boat.

KEYS TO PERFECTION

Make crispy crackling

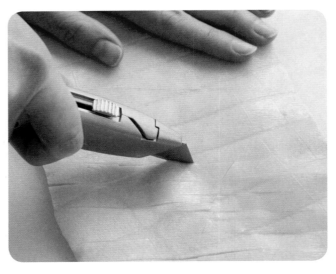

1 Remove the skin from the joint. Using a very sharp chef's knife in a sawing action, cut horizontally between the meat and the skin, taking most of the fat away with the skin.

2 Using a Stanley knife, make parallel cuts in the skin, about 1cm (½in) apart, working from the centre out, then from the centre out to the opposite side. Cut right through the skin into the fat beneath. Massage olive oil into the skin, then rub coarse sea salt all over the surface, working it into the cuts with your fingers. Place the skin on a rack in a roasting tin with the salted-side facing up.

Stuff, roll, and tie the loin

1 To open out, or "butterfly" the joint, place the loin flat on a board, skinned-side down. Using a very sharp chef's knife and starting at the fattier side of the joint, make a horizontal cut through the centre of the thick, meaty part of the loin, stopping short of the opposite edge. Work slowly, using a sawing action with the knife.

2 Lift up the flap of meat and fold it back like the page of a book, so that the joint lies flat on the board.

Stuff, roll, and tie the loin (continued)

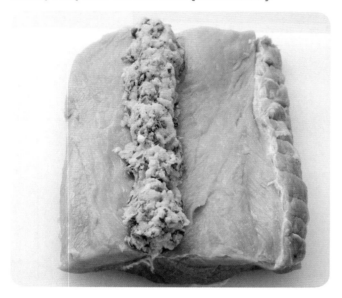

3 Place the caper and herb stuffing along the central groove created by opening out the loin, and squash it into a long sausage shape using your hands.

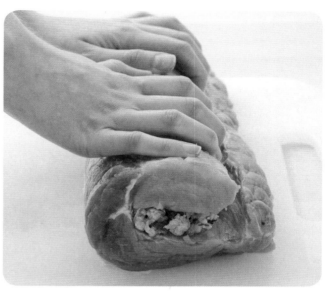

4 Cover the stuffing with the flap of meat, folding it over and tucking it in. Now roll the pork over and keep rolling firmly. The join should end up underneath.

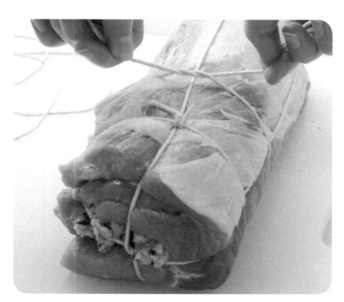

5 Take a length of string that is 6 times longer than the length of the joint and run it lengthways around the bottom and top of the joint. Cross the string at one end of the joint and run it lengthways again, this time around the sides of the joint. Tie at one end. Cut 4 pieces of string about 20cm (8in) longer than the circumference of the joint and tie them at regular intervals around the meat.

6 Oil and season the joint all over, and tuck sprigs of rosemary under the string on top of the joint. Put the pork in a roasting tin.

Pork Chops Arrabbiata

Arrabbiata is a tomato sauce made spicy with crushed chillies, and it really livens up grilled pork chops for a no-fuss supper. Serve with spaghetti tossed in olive oil and shredded basil.

 Serves 4    340 calories per serving

INGREDIENTS

- 2 red peppers, halved, cored, and deseeded
- olive oil, for brushing
- 4 boneless, lean pork chops, about 175g (6oz) each and ideally 2.5cm (1in) thick
- salt and freshly ground black pepper

FOR THE SAUCE

- 2 tbsp olive oil
- 1 onion, finely chopped
- 2 garlic cloves, finely chopped
- 400g can chopped tomatoes
- 1 tsp sugar
- ¼ tsp dried crushed chillies

1 Preheat the grill to its highest setting for 5 minutes. Place the pepper halves, cut-side down, on a lightly oiled baking sheet and grill about 10cm (4in) from the heat for 15–20 minutes or until well blistered and charred. Transfer the peppers to a plastic food bag, seal, and leave to cool.

2 While the peppers are grilling, make the sauce: heat the oil in a medium pan, add the onion and garlic, and fry over a medium–high heat for 5–6 minutes or until softened and starting to brown. Stir in the tomatoes, sugar, and chillies. Simmer for 12–15 minutes, stirring occasionally. When the peppers are cool, remove them from the bag and peel off the skins. Chop two of the pepper halves into small pieces and stir into the sauce. (See below, Thick, piquant sauce.) Season. Set aside with the remaining pepper halves.

3 Lightly trim the chops, brush both sides with oil, and season with pepper. Grill the chops about 10cm (4in) from the heat for about 8 minutes on each side or until the juices run clear. Remove to a warmed serving dish, season with salt, and keep warm. (See below, Moist, tender pork.)

4 Grill the remaining pepper halves for about 1 minute to heat through, then cut into long, thin strips. Reheat the sauce and serve with the grilled chops and sliced peppers.

KEYS TO PERFECTION

Thick, piquant sauce

Simmer the sauce until it's fairly thick but still moist, then add the chopped red pepper. It should be chopped fairly small so it blends in well. As well as enlivening the flavour, the peppers will add good texture.

Moist, tender pork

1 Remove and discard a little of the fat, but not too much, as a thin layer of fat keeps the meat moist as it grills and also improves the flavour. Oil and season with pepper but not salt at this stage, as salt draws out the juices.

2 Time the grilling carefully, because if the pork is overcooked it will be dry. It's important to have the grill very hot, and watch the chops as they cook, turning only once with tongs. Add salt after cooking.

Glazed Ham with Spiced Cranberry Relish

I like to decorate this glazed ham the traditional way – in a diamond pattern, studded with cloves. The subtly spiced, fruity flavourings and cranberry relish make it that little bit special.

Serves 10   560 calories per serving

INGREDIENTS

- 1 unsmoked, dry-cured boneless gammon joint (from the hock or middle), about 2.4kg (5¼lb), tied with string (see p148, box)
- 1 litre (1¾ pints) dry farmhouse cider
- 500ml (16fl oz) orange juice from a carton
- 15cm (6in) cinnamon stick, snapped in half
- 5 star anise

FOR THE RELISH
- 2 oranges
- 8 heaped tbsp mango chutney
- 5 heaped tbsp cranberry sauce
- ½ tsp five-spice powder
- salt and freshly ground black pepper

FOR THE DECORATION
- 4 tbsp mango chutney
- about 30 whole cloves

KEYS TO PERFECTION *(see overleaf)*
Cook the gammon in liquid; Decorate and glaze the ham before roasting

1 Make the relish: finely grate the rind of the oranges into a small bowl. Peel and segment the oranges, holding them over the bowl to catch the juice. Roughly chop the segments and place in a medium pan with the orange rind and juice, mango chutney, cranberry sauce, and five-spice powder.

2 Bring to the boil and simmer over a medium–high heat for about 5 minutes or until thickened, stirring often. Remove from the heat, add a good pinch of salt and a few grindings of pepper, and pour into a small heatproof bowl. Leave to cool, cover, and chill in the fridge until serving time.

3 Preheat the oven to 160°C (fan 140°C/325°F/Gas 3). Place the gammon, skin-side up, in a large, lidded, ovenproof pan or flameproof casserole. Pour in the cider and orange juice and top up with cold water so that the liquid covers the gammon (you will need about 750ml/1¼ pints water). Add the cinnamon and star anise, cover the pan, and bring the liquid to the boil on the hob, then allow it to simmer for a few minutes. Transfer to the oven and cook for 2 hours. Remove the pan from the oven and turn the joint over in the liquid. Set aside until lukewarm, turning over once or twice during this time, then lift the meat out of the liquid and place it on a large board. Discard the liquid. (See p148, Cook the gammon in liquid.)

4 To decorate, remove the string from the ham and strip off the skin, leaving a thin layer of fat behind on the meat. Discard the skin. Score the fat in a diamond pattern. Brush the mango chutney all over the fat, then stud with cloves. (See p149, Decorate and glaze the ham before roasting.)

5 Preheat the oven to 220°C (fan 200°C/425°F/Gas 7). Stand the ham on a rack in a roasting tin and roast for 25–30 minutes or until bubbling and glazed to a light golden colour.

6 Transfer the ham to a carving board, cover loosely with foil, and leave to stand for 15–20 minutes before carving into thick or thin slices, as you wish. This resting time lets the juices be distributed more evenly through the meat so that the fibres relax, making the meat easy to carve into neat slices. Serve hot, with the chilled relish on the side.

KEYS TO PERFECTION

Cook the gammon in liquid

1 It's important that the gammon fits snugly in the pan, skin-side up, and is totally covered by liquid. For this size of joint, use a 25cm (10in) lidded ovenproof pan or a flameproof casserole with a capacity of 5 litres (8¾ pints).

2 With the lid on the pan, bring the liquid to the boil over a high heat. This may take longer than you think, about 10 minutes, but it's essential for the cooking time in the oven to be accurate. Once the liquid is bubbling, let it simmer for a few minutes to get the cooking started before transferring the pan to the oven.

Buying and cooking gammon

Gammon is the name given to the cured hind leg of a pig. Confusingly, gammon changes its name to ham when it's cooked. Unsmoked gammon does not need soaking before cooking. If you prefer the stronger, saltier taste of smoked ham, check if it needs soaking or not (with supermarket gammon the instructions will be on the label). If you buy a different-sized joint, the formula for the cooking time in the liquid is 20 minutes per 500g (1lb 2oz), plus 20 minutes. Whatever the size of joint, the roasting time remains the same.

3 At the end of cooking, you can check the internal temperature of the ham if you have a meat thermometer – it should be around 80°C (175°F). Let the ham cool down in the liquid for at least 2–3 hours. During this time, the meat will continue cooking in the residual heat, which will help redistribute the juices evenly through the meat and make it easier to slice.

Decorate and glaze the ham before roasting

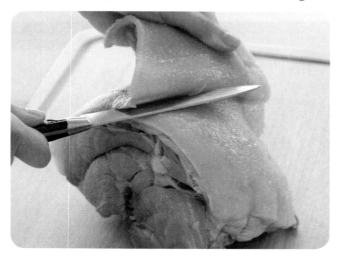

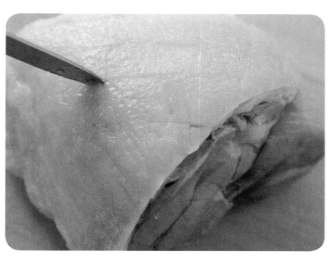

1 Cut the string off the ham, then using a sharp knife, strip the skin away from the fat. Start at one end of the joint and cut slowly using a horizontal sawing action, holding the skin in one hand while you cut with the knife in the other.

2 With the tip of the same knife, score parallel diagonal lines in the fat to make a diamond pattern. For this size of gammon joint, cutting 8 lines in one direction and 9 lines in the other will make an attractive pattern, but you could do more or fewer, as you prefer and according to the size of your joint.

Preparing the ham and relish ahead

The gammon can be prepared up to the end of step 3 of the method several hours in advance. Once roasted, you can keep the ham in the fridge for up to 5 days and slice it as and when you need it. When the ham is sliced straight from the fridge, you'll be able to get thinner slices and up to double the number of servings. The cranberry relish can be made several days ahead and kept in a rigid container in the fridge. It's best served chilled.

3 Brush the mango chutney evenly all over the top of the ham, working it into the cuts in the fat, then press cloves into the intersections of the diamond shapes. The chutney glaze gives the fat a deliciously sweet finish and the cloves give a decorative effect.

Lamb Kofta Kebabs with Tzatziki

Porridge oats may seem an unlikely ingredient for these hot, spicy kebabs, but I got the idea from an Indian friend, who said there's nothing better for binding the mixture and giving a good texture.

 Serves 4   386 calories per serving    **Special equipment**
12 wooden skewers, about 20cm (8in) long

INGREDIENTS

- 500g (1lb 2oz) minced lamb
- 1 small onion, very finely chopped
- 20g (¾oz) piece of fresh root ginger, peeled and very finely chopped
- 1 garlic clove, very finely chopped
- 1 tsp harissa paste
- 1 heaped tbsp porridge oats
- 1 large egg, beaten
- 15g (½oz) fresh coriander leaves and stalks, very finely chopped, plus 1–2 tbsp chopped leaves, to garnish
- salt and freshly ground black pepper

FOR THE TZATZIKI

- 2 tbsp chopped fresh mint
- 1 garlic clove, crushed
- 2 tsp mint sauce
- ½ tsp caster sugar
- 200g carton Greek-style yogurt
- ¼ cucumber, about 75g (2½oz), peeled and diced
- extra virgin olive oil, to drizzle

1 Put the lamb into a large bowl with the onion, ginger, garlic, harissa paste, oats, and egg. Add the coriander leaves and stalks and season well. Mix everything together with your hands until well combined (see below, Mould well for firm kebabs, step 1). Cover and chill in the fridge for 1–48 hours.

2 Make the tzatziki: put the mint, garlic, mint sauce, sugar, and some salt into a bowl. Stir with a fork, then whisk in the yogurt. Add the cucumber. Cover and chill until serving time. Soak the skewers (see below, box).

3 Drain the skewers and preheat the grill to its highest setting. Divide the lamb mixture into 12 equal-sized portions, roll each into a ball, and mould to shape around the skewers (see below, Mould well for firm kebabs, step 2).

4 Arrange the skewers on the grill rack over a grill pan. Grill for 8–10 minutes or until the kebabs are sizzling and turning brown. Turn them once and do not overcook – they should be juicy.

5 Transfer the tzatziki to a serving bowl and drizzle with the oil. Serve the kebabs, on or off the skewers, drizzled with the pan juices and sprinkled with the coriander leaves. Hand round the bowl of tzatziki separately.

KEYS TO PERFECTION
Mould well for firm kebabs

1 Use your hands to combine all the kebab ingredients, pressing and squeezing the meat for several minutes until it looks almost like a paste. Chill the mixture.

2 Form the chilled mixture into 12 balls and push a skewer through the centre of each. With wet hands, squish the meat around the skewer into a long torpedo shape.

Soak the skewers before use

Wooden skewers are best for these kebabs, because the meat sticks to them better than it does to metal skewers. To prevent the wood from burning under the grill, soak the skewers in a dish of cold water for 6 hours before using.

Slow-roast Lamb Lyonnaise

Cooking the lamb slowly, on a bed of potatoes and parsnips, ensures everything becomes very tender with lots of flavour. It's a meal in itself, but I like to serve a green vegetable, too.

 Serves 6    774 calories per serving

INGREDIENTS

- 1 whole shoulder of lamb, about 2.25kg (5lb), blade bone removed and tied, and excess fat removed
- 1 tbsp olive oil, plus extra for greasing
- 4 tsp chopped fresh rosemary
- 4 tsp chopped fresh thyme
- 2 garlic cloves, crushed
- salt and freshly ground black pepper
- 1 tbsp redcurrant jelly

FOR THE VEGETABLE LAYER

- 1kg (2¼lb) fluffy potatoes, such as King Edward
- 750g (1lb 10oz) parsnips
- 1 large onion
- 6 garlic cloves
- a few fresh thyme sprigs
- a few fresh rosemary sprigs
- 425ml (14½fl oz) dry white wine
- 425ml (14½fl oz) chicken stock

KEYS TO PERFECTION *(see overleaf)*
Add flavour to the meat; Prepare the vegetables for even cooking; Make a flavoursome redcurrant gravy

1 Make incisions in the top of the lamb with a small, sharp knife. Put the oil into a small bowl with 2 teaspoons each of the chopped rosemary and thyme, the garlic, ½ teaspoon of salt, and a good grinding of pepper. Mix to a paste and rub all over the skin of the lamb, working it into the incisions with your fingers. (See p154, Add flavour to the meat.)

2 Preheat the oven to 220°C (fan 200°C/425°F/Gas 7). Prepare the vegetable layer: peel all the vegetables (including the garlic), then cut the potatoes into slices about 5mm (¼in) thick, the parsnips into slices about 1cm (½in) thick, and the onion into thin rings. Brush the inside of a large roasting tin with oil. Put the vegetables into the tin with some salt and pepper and add the garlic cloves and sprigs of thyme and rosemary. Combine the wine and stock together and pour over the vegetables. (See p154, Prepare the vegetables for even cooking.)

3 Place the lamb on top of the vegetables, put the roasting tin in the oven, and roast for 40 minutes until the lamb is golden brown. Reduce the oven temperature to 160°C (fan 140°C/325°F/Gas 3) and roast for a further 4 hours.

4 Transfer the lamb to a carving board, cover loosely with foil, and leave to rest for 15–20 minutes. Meanwhile, lift the vegetables out of the cooking liquid with a slotted spoon and transfer them to a baking dish. Place the dish in the oven while you make the gravy.

5 Pour the cooking liquid into a jug and leave it to stand for about 5 minutes or until the fat has risen to the top. Scoop off the fat with a spoon, then pour the remaining juices into a pan and add the redcurrant jelly. Bring to the boil, whisking all the time, then reduce the heat. Add the remaining 2 teaspoons each of chopped rosemary and thyme, and taste for seasoning. Leave to simmer gently on the hob while the lamb rests, whisking occasionally, until you are ready to serve. (See p155, Make a flavoursome redcurrant gravy.)

6 To serve, remove the string from the lamb and carve the meat into thick slices. Serve with the dish of potatoes, parsnips, and onion, and the gravy in a jug or gravy boat.

KEYS TO PERFECTION

Add flavour to the meat

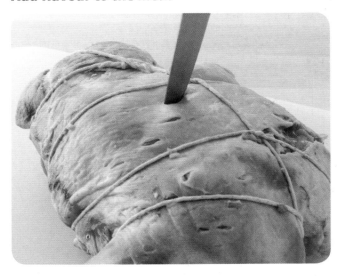

1 To inject flavour into the meat and ensure crispy skin, make about 12 deep slits in the lamb with a sharp knife. Space these incisions at regular intervals all over the top part of the lamb (the side with the skin), cutting through the skin deep into the meat to make little "pockets" about 2cm (¾in) long.

2 Use a teaspoon to mix the oil, herbs, garlic, and seasoning to a paste in a small bowl, then tip the paste on top of the lamb and spread it out with your fingers. Rub the paste all over the skin, pressing it into the incisions in the meat.

Prepare the vegetables for even cooking

1 The vegetables are all sliced into different thicknesses according to how long they take to cook. Cut the parsnips on the diagonal, and don't worry if the cores seem a little tough. The parsnips are cooked for so long that any toughness will disappear. Don't be tempted to slice the potatoes ahead of time and keep them in water, as this will wash away some of the starch that's needed to hold them together.

2 When the potato, parsnip, and onion slices are in the roasting tin with the seasoning, jumble the vegetables up with your hands to mix everything together, then spread them out in an even layer so that they all take the same time to cook. Push the whole garlic cloves and sprigs of thyme and rosemary in among the vegetables and drench them with the white wine and chicken stock.

Make a flavoursome redcurrant gravy

1 Shoulder of lamb is fairly fatty compared with the leg and loin. During long, slow roasting, the fat melts into the meat and vegetables to make them very tender and flavoursome, but the gravy is better without it. After removing the vegetables from the liquid using a slotted spoon, pour the juices from the roasting tin into a jug and set aside. The fat will rise to the top and float on the surface.

2 Using a metal spoon, skim the fat off the surface and discard. Do this slowly and carefully, a spoonful at a time, trying not to disturb the juices underneath. You won't manage to remove all of the fat, but it doesn't matter at this stage.

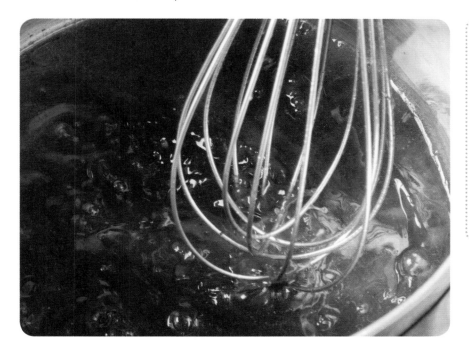

Buying and carving shoulder of lamb

Shoulder of lamb is one of the best joints to slow-roast for succulent and juicy meat, but it has an odd shape that can be difficult to carve. For ease of carving, ask your butcher to remove the blade bone and then tie the meat with string to hold it together. Remove the string before carving.

3 Bring the gravy to the boil over a high heat, whisking continuously, then reduce the heat and let it simmer, whisking occasionally. Any remaining fat will disperse throughout the gravy and the redcurrant jelly will absorb any greasiness.

Greek Lamb Pilaf with Orzo

This one-pot meal needs only a green salad to accompany it. You can make it a day ahead up to the end of step 3. To serve, heat it until bubbling, add the orzo, and continue with the recipe.

 Serves 6   535 calories per serving

INGREDIENTS

- 6 lamb neck fillets, about 800–900g (1¾–2lb) in total
- 2–3 tbsp olive oil
- 1 large onion, finely chopped
- 2 garlic cloves, crushed
- ½ tsp ground cinnamon
- ½ tsp ground allspice
- 400g can chopped tomatoes
- 2 tbsp tomato purée
- 300ml (10fl oz) dry white wine
- 2 tbsp lemon juice
- 2 tsp sugar
- 1 chicken stock cube
- 1 tbsp chopped fresh thyme
- salt and freshly ground black pepper
- 250g (9oz) orzo (see below, box)

TO SERVE

- 85g (3oz) feta cheese
- 1 tbsp chopped fresh thyme
- 1 tbsp chopped fresh mint
- finely grated rind of 1 lemon (optional)

1 Preheat the oven to 160°C (fan 140°C/325°F/Gas 3). Cut each neck fillet in half lengthways, without trimming away any fat, then cut each halved fillet crossways into 6–8 bite-sized pieces (see below, Use the right lamb). Heat 2 tablespoons of the oil in a large, non-stick frying pan until hot, and sear the lamb in 4 batches over a medium–high heat until browned on all sides. You may need to add another tablespoon of oil. As each batch is seared, transfer the lamb to a large flameproof casserole using a slotted spoon.

2 Reduce the heat and add the onion to the frying pan. Fry, stirring often, for 3 minutes until golden brown. Add the garlic, cinnamon, and allspice and fry for 1–2 minutes, then add the onion mix to the casserole.

3 Pour the canned tomatoes over the meat and onion. Fill the tomato can twice with water and add to the casserole. Stir, then add the tomato purée, wine, lemon juice, and sugar. Crumble in the stock cube and add the thyme, ½ teaspoon of salt, and pepper to taste. Bring to the boil, stirring, then cover the pan and transfer to the oven. Cook for 2 hours, stirring halfway.

4 Stir in the orzo, cover the pan again, and return to the oven. Cook for a further 20 minutes or until the orzo is plump and tender, stirring halfway (see below, Time the orzo). To serve, gently stir the meat and orzo, crumble the feta over the top, and sprinkle with the herbs and lemon rind, if using.

KEYS TO PERFECTION

Use the right lamb

Neck fillets are ideal for this dish: marbled with fat, the meat becomes juicy and tender when slow-cooked. Don't confuse them with the leaner loin fillets, which would become dry.

Time the orzo

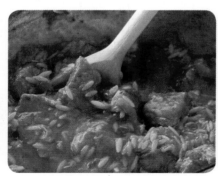

Orzo swells quickly to several times its size, so don't use too much and be careful not to overcook it. Stir after 10 minutes' cooking, or it can clump together and stick to the pan.

Buying and using orzo

Orzo looks like large grains of rice, but it is in fact a small pasta shape made from durum wheat. Mostly used in soups and stews, it is readily available in the pasta section at supermarkets and Italian delicatessens. I like it in this Greek stew, because it swells to just the right size if cooked properly and complements the lamb.

Pasta and Rice

Creamy Seafood Linguine

This creamy pasta dish reminds me of summer's warmth and relaxing holidays. However, it's delicious at any time of the year, bringing you a taste of the sea wherever you are.

 Serves 4    581 calories per serving

INGREDIENTS

- 500g (1lb 2oz) baby squid, either whole or pre-prepared baby squid pouches (see p162, box)
- 300ml (10fl oz) dry white wine
- 2 garlic cloves, crushed
- salt and freshly ground black pepper
- 300ml (10fl oz) double cream
- finely grated rind of 1 lemon
- juice of ½ lemon
- 400g (14oz) linguine
- knob of butter
- ½ tsp anchovy paste
- 150g (5½oz) cooked, peeled king prawns
- 25g (scant 1oz) fresh flat-leaf parsley, chopped

1 If using whole squid, prepare it as follows: pull the tentacles from the body pouch (the head and guts will be attached), then cut off the tentacles just below the eyes. Retain the tentacles and discard the head and guts. At the top of the tentacles you may find a small, hard black "beak"; squeeze it out and discard it. Feel inside the pouch and remove and discard the "quill" (a clear sliver of cartilage that feels like a plastic shard). Wash the inside of the pouch thoroughly and peel off the spotty purplish outer skin. Rinse the tentacles in cold water.

2 Slice the pouches into rings, about 5mm (¼in) wide. Put the rings and prepared tentacles (if using whole squid) into a flameproof casserole with the wine and garlic. Grind in plenty of black pepper. Bring to a simmer over a medium heat, cover the pan, and simmer gently for 10 minutes. Transfer the squid to a bowl and set aside. (See p162, Well-prepared, tender squid.)

3 Add the cream, lemon rind and juice to the liquid in the pan. Let it bubble over a high heat for 5–7 minutes, occasionally stirring it in from the edge of the pan with a wooden spoon. Simmer the sauce until thickened and reduced by about half.

4 Cook the linguine in a large pan of salted boiling water for 10–15 minutes, or according to packet instructions. Drain, reserving a cupful of the pasta cooking water. (See p163, Cook pasta the foolproof way.)

5 Add the butter and anchovy paste to the cream sauce, stirring until they are melted. Taste for seasoning, adding salt if needed. Stir in the reserved squid, the prawns, and half the parsley. Leave the sauce over a low heat to gently warm through the squid and prawns. Don't let them overcook, or they will become rubbery.

6 Add the cooked linguine to the sauce and toss to mix, adding a splash or two of the reserved pasta cooking water to get the consistency you like (you may not need it all). Tip into a serving bowl, sprinkle with the remaining parsley, and serve immediately.

KEYS TO PERFECTION (see overleaf)
Well-prepared, tender squid; Cook pasta the foolproof way

KEYS TO PERFECTION

Well-prepared, tender squid

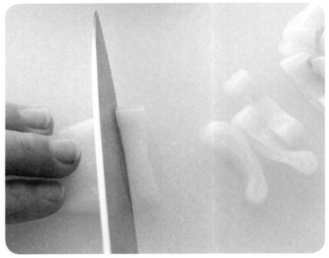

1 Lay the squid on a board. If using whole squid, hold the body pouch with one hand and pull the tentacles with the other. The tentacles should come away easily, together with the head and guts. Using a sharp knife, cut off the tentacles just below the eyes and discard the head and guts. Remove the "beak" from the tentacles, if necessary, and discard. Take out the "quill" from inside the pouch and discard. Repeat for all the squid.

2 Thoroughly rinse the inside of the pouch and peel away the dark outer skin, so you're left with white meat. Rinse the tentacles under cold running water. Whether you're using whole squid or pre-prepared pouches, slice the pouches across into equal-sized rings.

Buying and using squid

You can buy squid rings, but sometimes these can be quite large and chewy. I prefer to buy whole baby squid, as shown here, then prepare and slice it into rings myself. Alternatively, pre-prepared baby squid pouches are available, which reduce the preparation time, but they won't have the decorative tentacles attached.

3 Cook the squid rings and tentacles, if using, in a covered casserole with the wine and garlic until tender. The squid will turn opaque and will shrink in size. Using a slotted spoon, lift the cooked squid out of the wine a few pieces at a time and transfer to a bowl. Hold the spoon against the side of the pan and let the liquid drain through. The wine in the pan, now flavoured by the squid, will be used as the base for a delicious creamy sauce.

Cook pasta the foolproof way

1 Three-quarters fill a 5 litre (8¾ pint) pan with cold water. With the lid on the pan, bring the water to the boil over a high heat. Add 1 tablespoon of salt (the water will bubble furiously), then add the linguine. Lower the strands into the water and bend and coil them around as they soften until they're submerged.

2 Bring the water back to a rolling boil and cook the linguine over a high heat with the pan uncovered. Stir from time to time to keep the strands separate and prevent them from sticking together.

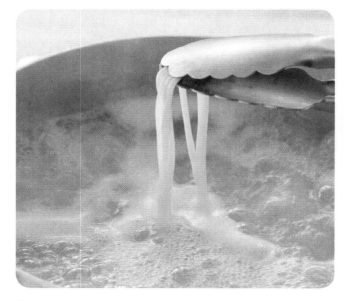

3 After 10 minutes, lift out a strand or two with tongs and bite into the pasta. The usual cooking time is 10 minutes for al dente (tender but firm to the bite) or 12–15 minutes if you like your pasta a little softer. Scoop out a cupful of the cooking water and reserve. This will be used when you coat the linguine in the sauce – the starch in the water helps the sauce cling to the pasta.

4 Tip the contents of the pan into a large colander placed over the sink and shake the colander to let the water drain through. This prevents the pasta from becoming waterlogged and soggy.

Penne with Cherry Tomato Sauce

There is so much flavour in this simple, colourful pasta dish, it doesn't need any meat or fish added. It's the perfect vegetarian supper, topped with pecorino cheese to finish it off.

 Serves 4    555 calories per serving

INGREDIENTS

- 30g (1oz) pine nuts
- 4 tbsp olive oil
- 1 onion, finely chopped
- 3 garlic cloves, crushed
- 400g (14oz) cherry vine tomatoes, halved
- ½ tsp caster sugar
- salt and freshly ground black pepper
- 350g (12oz) penne
- 250g (9oz) Tenderstem broccoli tips, ends trimmed and halved lengthways
- 1 tbsp chopped fresh flat-leaf parsley
- 3 tbsp shredded fresh basil
- 50g (1¾oz) pecorino cheese, grated or shaved into strips

1 Heat a large, non-stick frying pan until hot. Add the pine nuts and dry-fry over a medium–low heat for a few minutes, tossing them in the pan, until golden brown. Tip them into a small bowl and set aside.

2 Heat 2 tablespoons of the oil in the same frying pan. Add the onion and garlic and fry for 6–8 minutes or until softened and just starting to brown. Add another tablespoon of oil and heat, then stir in the tomatoes and sugar. Fry for 2–3 minutes or until the tomatoes have softened and released their juices but have not lost their shape. Season and set aside.

3 Plunge the penne into a large pan of salted boiling water and cook for 10–12 minutes. About 3 minutes before the end of the cooking time, add the broccoli. Reserve some of the cooking water (see below, Use the pasta cooking water, step 1). Drain the pasta and broccoli.

4 Heat the tomatoes through and stir in about 4 tablespoons of the pasta cooking water (see below, Use the pasta cooking water, step 2). Tip the pasta and broccoli into the tomatoes and toss gently with a couple more tablespoons of the cooking water, if needed. Stir in the parsley and basil. To serve, scatter over the pine nuts, drizzle over the remaining tablespoon of oil, sprinkle over the pecorino, and add an extra grinding of pepper.

KEYS TO PERFECTION

Use the pasta cooking water

1 After the pasta is cooked, scoop out and reserve a couple of ladlefuls of the cooking water for the sauce. The starch in the water helps the sauce cling to the pasta, and it also extends the sauce.

2 Spoon some of the reserved pasta water into the tomato juices – about 4 tablespoons to start with. You're aiming for a light sauce, just enough to coat the pasta. You don't want to drown it and can add more if you need to.

Cannelloni with Double Cheese Sauce

I've used both a tomato and a béchamel sauce for this luxurious version of the classic cannelloni. Using a combination of beef and pork is traditional in northern Italy and gives great flavour.

 Serves 6

 630 calories per serving

Special equipment
2.2–2.5 litre (4–4½ pint) baking dish, about 35 x 25cm (14 x 10in) and 5cm (2in) deep

INGREDIENTS

- 3 tbsp olive oil
- 1 onion, very finely chopped, plus ¼ onion
- 1 carrot, very finely chopped
- 2 celery sticks, very finely chopped
- 300g (10oz) minced beef
- 300g (10oz) minced pork
- 1 large garlic clove, crushed
- 3 tbsp tomato purée
- 75ml (2½fl oz) red wine
- 1½ tbsp chopped fresh thyme
- salt and freshly ground black pepper
- 600ml (1 pint) full-fat or semi-skimmed milk
- 1 bay leaf
- a few black peppercorns
- 40g (1¼oz) butter
- 40g (1¼oz) plain flour
- a few gratings of nutmeg
- 680g jar passata
- 18 cannelloni tubes
- 75g (2½oz) mature Cheddar cheese, coarsely grated
- 40g (1¼oz) Parmesan cheese, coarsely grated

KEYS TO PERFECTION *(see overleaf)*
Make a classic, smooth béchamel sauce; Fill and arrange the tubes with care

1 Make the filling: heat the oil in a large, deep, non-stick frying pan over a medium heat. Add the chopped onion, carrot, and celery and fry gently for about 10 minutes or until softened but not browned, stirring often. Add the beef, pork, and garlic and fry for about 5 minutes or until the meat loses its redness, stirring frequently and breaking up lumps with a wooden spoon.

2 Stir in the tomato purée, wine, 1 tablespoon of the thyme, and some salt and pepper. Cook for about 10 minutes, stirring often, until the mixture is quite dry. Remove from the heat and set aside.

3 Make the béchamel sauce: pour the milk into a small pan, add the bay leaf, peppercorns, and onion quarter and bring just to the boil. Cover the pan, remove from the heat, and leave to infuse for 30 minutes, then strain into a jug. Melt the butter in a pan over a medium heat, add the flour, and cook for 1–2 minutes. Remove the pan from the heat and gradually add the strained milk, whisking all the time. Return to the heat and whisk until the sauce thickens. Season with the nutmeg and salt and pepper. Set aside. (See p168, Make a classic, smooth béchamel sauce.)

4 Heat the passata in a pan with 200ml (7fl oz) of water, the remaining ½ tablespoon of thyme, and some salt and pepper. Cover the bottom of the baking dish with about half the passata mixture.

5 Stir 6 tablespoons of the béchamel sauce into the meat, pressing with a fork to mash the mixture together. Fill the cannelloni tubes with the meat mixture and arrange side by side in the dish. (See p169, Fill and arrange the tubes with care.) If you have any leftover meat mixture, tuck it in between the tubes. Cover with the remaining passata mixture, and wiggle the tubes apart so that the passata runs between them.

6 Pour the remaining béchamel sauce over the cannelloni and shake the dish so that it settles evenly around the tubes. Sprinkle over the Cheddar and Parmesan, then leave to stand for at least 2 hours (see p169, box).

7 When you are ready to bake, preheat the oven to 190°C (fan 170°C/375°F/Gas 5). Bake the cannelloni for 45 minutes or until bubbling and golden brown. Check that the tubes are soft by piercing them with a skewer, and cook a little longer if necessary.

KEYS TO PERFECTION

Make a classic, smooth béchamel sauce

1 First, infuse the milk with the flavourings: "scald" the milk in a pan over a medium–high heat (that is, bring it to just below boiling point). Watch carefully, and turn off the heat as soon as you see tiny bubbles appear around the edge, as the milk can quickly boil over or scorch on the bottom of the pan. Cover the pan and remove from the heat. Leave to infuse for about 30 minutes, then strain the milk into a jug to remove the flavourings.

2 Melt the butter over a medium heat until it foams, then sprinkle in the flour and mix it immediately with the butter using a small balloon whisk. Keep whisking for 1–2 minutes. The butter and flour mixture ("roux") must cook properly, or you'll taste raw flour in the sauce. When the mixture changes colour from white to pale golden, remove the pan from the heat. Don't let this "blond roux" turn brown, as the colour and flavour of the sauce will be impaired.

3 With the pan off the heat, pour in the strained milk a little at a time, whisking constantly and vigorously to work it into the roux and keep the sauce smooth. Not all recipes for béchamel sauce use hot or warm milk, but I find the roux absorbs it better than cold milk, and it also helps to prevent lumps from forming.

4 Once you've added all the milk, return the pan to a medium heat and cook for a few minutes more until the sauce thickens, still whisking continuously. The finished sauce should have a medium–thick consistency. If it coats the back of a wooden spoon without running off, it is ready to use.

Fill and arrange the tubes with care

1 Filling the tubes can be a messy job, but it's not difficult once you get the hang of it. First, make the meat mixture as smooth and dry as possible; a lumpy, sloppy mixture will be harder to work with. As you cook the meat, break up any lumps with a wooden spoon, then once the sauce is cooked, mash the béchamel into the meat mixture with a fork to make the filling even smoother. The béchamel will help to bind the meat together.

2 Hold a cannelloni tube upright in the palm of your hand so that the bottom end is sealed off. Take a teaspoonful of the meat mixture and push it into the tube right down to the bottom, using the handle of the spoon if you find this helps. Repeat with more filling until the tube is full along its entire length.

Prepare ahead for best results

I like to prepare and assemble cannelloni (and lasagne) several hours before baking, and leave it covered at room temperature, as it allows the sauces to get absorbed into the pasta, making it softer and more flavoursome. You can do this the day before, which is ideal if you're entertaining and want to get ahead. If keeping it overnight, cover the dish and place it in the fridge. Allow the cannelloni to come to room temperature for about an hour before baking, or it won't cook through in the time.

3 Lay the tubes in a single layer in the baking dish, which should measure about 35 x 25cm (14 x 10in) and 5cm (2in) deep. The size doesn't have to be exact, because it depends on the cannelloni you're using, but you should be able to leave a small gap between each tube. This allows room for the sauces to run between the tubes and lets the oven heat penetrate.

My New Spaghetti Carbonara

By adding chestnut mushrooms and some streaky bacon, I've made this a more special pasta dish. It's perfect for when you want to have supper made and ready to eat in under half an hour.

 Serves 4    694 calories per serving

INGREDIENTS

- 350g (12oz) spaghetti
- salt and freshly ground black pepper
- 150g (5½oz) unsmoked streaky bacon, cut across into thin strips
- 3 tbsp olive oil
- 150g (5½oz) small chestnut mushrooms, quartered
- 2 garlic cloves, crushed
- 2 large eggs, beaten
- 85g (3oz) Parmesan cheese, grated
- 4 tbsp double cream
- 1 tbsp chopped fresh flat-leaf parsley

1 Cook the spaghetti in a large pan of salted, boiling water for about 10 minutes (or according to packet instructions) until just tender. Meanwhile, heat a large, deep, non-stick frying pan or sauté pan, add the bacon, and fry over a low heat until the fat starts to run. Pour in 1 tablespoon of the oil, increase the heat, and fry for 3–5 minutes or until the bacon is crisp, stirring. Remove using a slotted spoon and transfer to kitchen paper to drain.

2 Pour the remaining 2 tablespoons of oil into the frying pan, add the mushrooms and garlic, and fry over a medium–high heat for 3–4 minutes or until the mushrooms are golden. Set aside.

3 In a small bowl, combine the eggs and most of the Parmesan (reserve 2 tablespoons for sprinkling). Season with salt and pepper. When the pasta is almost done, return the frying pan to a low heat. Scoop out a cupful of the pasta cooking water and reserve. Drain the pasta in a colander or large sieve.

4 Tip the spaghetti into the pan with the bacon and mushrooms. Remove the pan from the heat and mix in the eggs and cheese. Stir in the cream and 120ml (4fl oz) of the reserved pasta cooking water. (See below, Creamy, smooth eggs and sauce.) Place the spaghetti on 4 plates or bowls (see box, left) and scatter over the parsley, reserved Parmesan, and a grinding of pepper.

KEYS TO PERFECTION

Creamy, smooth eggs and sauce

1 Mix in the eggs and cheese quickly off the heat, so the warmth of the pan and the other ingredients cook the eggs enough to lightly set them and keep them smooth, without scrambling them. Use tongs to lift the pasta.

2 Pour in the double cream and enough pasta cooking water to make a sauce that will coat the spaghetti strands. The consistency should be creamy. The high fat content in the double cream will enhance this.

How to serve spaghetti

You can, of course, simply pile spaghetti onto plates or into bowls in an informal way. However, for a neater, more stylish presentation, twirl the pasta around a long-pronged fork and place the twirl in a pile in the centre of a plate, helping it off with a small fork; then, using the same technique, lay another, smaller pasta twirl on top of the first.

Mary's TOP TIPS
6

Attractive presentation

Try to present your meals beautifully, on serving dishes that set off the food well. Even the simplest garnish, such as shavings of Parmesan cheese or a scattering of fresh herbs, can make a dish look so much more appetizing.

Smoked Salmon and Haddock Kedgeree

Gently spiced and slightly creamy, this is one of my supper-time favourites. The crispy onion topping isn't traditional, but it provides a wonderful contrast of colour, flavour, and texture.

 Serves 4    567 calories per serving

INGREDIENTS

- 2 tbsp sunflower oil
- 3 onions (2 halved and thinly sliced, 1 finely chopped)
- salt and freshly ground black pepper
- 350g (12oz) smoked undyed haddock fillets
- 100g (3½oz) smoked salmon
- 250g (9oz) basmati rice
- 3 cardamom pods, split
- ½ cinnamon stick, about 3cm (1¼in) long
- ½ tsp turmeric
- 2 large eggs
- 30g (1oz) butter
- 100ml (3½fl oz) single cream
- 2 tbsp finely chopped fresh coriander
- cayenne pepper, to taste
- juice of ½ lemon

1 Heat 1 tablespoon of the oil and fry the sliced onions (see below, Make the topping crispy). Season with salt and pepper, drain on kitchen paper, and set aside in a warm place. Put the haddock, skin-side down, in a large frying pan and pour over enough water to just cover. Simmer, covered, over a low heat for 5–8 minutes until opaque and cooked through. Remove from the heat. Lay the smoked salmon in the liquid, cover, and let stand for 2 minutes. Drain the fish and discard any skin and bones. Set aside.

2 Prepare the rice (see below, Rinse the rice). Heat the remaining tablespoon of oil in a large, non-stick, deep-sided frying pan or sauté pan. Add the chopped onion, cardamom pods, and cinnamon and fry over a medium–high heat until the onion is golden, about 5 minutes. Stir the drained rice into the onion in the pan. Pour in 450ml (15fl oz) cold water and stir in the turmeric. Bring to the boil. Reduce the heat to low, stir, cover, and cook for 12–15 minutes or until the water is absorbed. Take the rice off the heat and let it stand, covered, for 5 minutes before fluffing up the grains with a fork. Boil, peel, and quarter the eggs (see below, Lightly hard-boil the eggs).

3 Flake the fish into large pieces. Remove the cinnamon stick from the rice and carefully stir in the butter, cream, coriander, fish, and eggs. Season with salt and cayenne pepper, and add the lemon juice. Heat through over a low heat, stirring gently once or twice only so you don't break up the fish. Serve the kedgeree with the warm crispy onion on top.

KEYS TO PERFECTION

Make the topping crispy

Fry the onions slowly in a large, non-stick frying pan over a medium heat for 20–25 minutes, stirring occasionally. You're aiming for a crispy texture and deep golden colour.

Rinse the rice

Put the rice in a sieve and hold under cold running water until the water runs clear. This removes the starch and prevents clumping, making the rice lighter and fluffier. Drain well.

Lightly hard-boil the eggs

Place the eggs in a small pan, cover with cold water, and bring to the boil. Simmer for 6 minutes, at which point the white should be set and firm but the yolks slightly soft.

Lemon Chicken Risotto

Enjoy the relaxing process of stirring a risotto as it cooks – it's a very satisfying thing to make. Use a good stock, as the quality of the stock is very important for the overall flavour of any risotto.

 Serves 4    686 calories per serving

INGREDIENTS

- 2 skinless, boneless chicken breasts, cut into bite-sized pieces
- salt and freshly ground black pepper
- 2 tbsp olive oil
- 150g (5½oz) pancetta, finely diced
- 1 onion, finely chopped
- 1 garlic clove, crushed
- 300g (10oz) risotto rice (see p179, box)
- 150ml (5fl oz) dry white wine
- 1.2 litres (2 pints) hot chicken stock
- 175g (6oz) frozen peas, thawed
- large knob of butter
- finely grated rind and juice of 1 lemon
- 1 tbsp chopped fresh flat-leaf parsley
- 1 tbsp chopped fresh mint
- a few fresh basil leaves, finely shredded

1 Season the chicken. Heat the oil in a large, deep, non-stick frying pan or wide-based, non-stick pan over a medium heat until hot. Add the chicken and cook, stirring often, for 3–5 minutes or until golden on all sides and just tender. Remove with a slotted spoon, transfer to a plate, and set aside.

2 Put half the pancetta in the pan and fry, stirring, for 3–5 minutes or until crisp. Scoop out using a slotted spoon and leave to drain on kitchen paper.

3 Add the onion and garlic to the pan with the remaining pancetta. Reduce the heat to low and fry for 8–10 minutes or until the onion is softened but not browned, stirring occasionally. Increase the heat to medium and add the rice. Cook for a few minutes until the grains are coated and shiny, stirring almost all the time. (See p178, Heat the stock and rice.)

4 Pour in the wine and simmer, stirring, until it has been absorbed. Now add the hot stock gradually, a ladleful at a time. Stir constantly and wait until each ladleful has been absorbed before adding more. After 10 minutes, just after adding a ladleful of stock, stir in the peas, then continue with the stirring and adding stock for a further 8–10 minutes or until the stock is almost all used up. (See pp178–79, Add the liquids gradually.)

5 Add the chicken and the remaining stock, and stir gently until the chicken is heated through and the stock absorbed. At this stage, the rice should be plump, slightly sticky, and al dente.

6 Remove the pan from the heat and gently stir in the butter, lemon rind, parsley, and mint. Taste for seasoning, then sprinkle the lemon juice over the top and cover the pan. Leave for 5 minutes (see p179, Let the risotto rest). Gently fork through the risotto and serve immediately, topped with the reserved crispy pancetta and the shredded basil.

KEYS TO PERFECTION (*see overleaf*)
Heat the stock and rice; Add the liquids gradually; Let the risotto rest

KEYS TO PERFECTION

Heat the stock and rice

1 Both the stock and the rice must be hot before they're combined, so the rice can absorb the stock and release its starch slowly during cooking, to give a creamy texture. Bring the stock just to the boil and keep it simmering all the time while you're making the risotto.

2 Stir the rice into the onion, garlic, and pancetta and fry for several minutes so it reaches the required temperature before adding the liquid. The rice will become shiny and change colour, but it shouldn't turn brown. Watch carefully, stir often, and listen – you'll know the rice is ready for the liquid when you hear a quiet "popping" sound.

Add the liquids gradually

1 For a silky-smooth consistency, it's vital that the liquids are added to the rice gradually. First, pour in the wine – it will splutter, hiss, and steam. Stir to combine with the rice mixture and then keep stirring until you can see it no more.

2 Add the first ladleful of hot stock and stir until it disappears. This is the beginning of the gentle nurturing phase, when you need to stand by the hob and add the stock a ladleful at a time, waiting for it to be absorbed before adding more. The total cooking time should be about 20 minutes, but this can vary slightly depending on the type of rice and the exact degree of heat.

Add the liquids gradually (continued)

3 Keep patiently adding the stock and stirring until it's absorbed. The rice and liquid should be gently simmering throughout, so if needed adjust the heat under the pan. Add the peas about halfway through the cooking time, just after adding a ladleful of stock.

4 Towards the finish, when the stock is coming to an end and before you add the chicken, check the consistency of the risotto by drawing a line through the middle with a spatula or spoon – the two sides should stay apart. If it's too wet and soupy, cook a little longer without adding the last of the stock. If it seems too dry, add more stock. The rice should have a slightly "nutty" bite to each grain.

Let the risotto rest

The different types of risotto rice

You may find three types of risotto rice in the shops – Arborio, Carnaroli, and Vialone Nano. Often, the packet will be labelled simply "risotto rice", which is invariably Arborio. You can experiment with different types to see which one you like best. My favourite is Arborio. I find it has just the right amount of starchiness to get the creamy consistency I like.

The all-important final stage of this recipe is the resting. Once removed from the hob, the rice will continue to cook in the residual heat of the risotto. Leave it covered and undisturbed to let the butter and lemon juice do their work.

My Special Egg-fried Rice

Fresh herbs and five-spice powder bring a new fragrance to this rice dish. Instead of stir-frying the egg with the rice, as is usual, I've made a very thin omelette to give the egg more structure.

 Serves 6    305 calories per serving   **Special equipment**
23–24cm (9–9½in) non-stick frying pan

INGREDIENTS

- 250g (9oz) long-grain rice, rinsed and drained (see below, box)
- salt and freshly ground black pepper
- 50g (1¾oz) frozen peas
- 2 large eggs
- 2 tbsp sunflower oil
- 1 red pepper, deseeded and diced
- 8 spring onions, trimmed and thinly sliced
- 2 garlic cloves, finely chopped
- 1 tsp five-spice powder
- 2 tsp sesame oil
- 2 tsp dark soy sauce mixed with 1 tsp water, plus extra soy sauce to serve (optional)
- 140g (5oz) beansprouts
- 1 tbsp snipped fresh chives, plus extra to garnish
- 50g (1¾oz) roasted cashew nuts, to serve

1 Put the rice in a medium pan, pour over 450ml (15fl oz) of cold water, and add 1 teaspoon of salt. Bring the water to the boil. Stir, reduce the heat to low, and cover with a tight-fitting lid. Simmer gently for 12–15 minutes or until all the water has been absorbed. Take the pan off the heat and let it stand, covered, for 5 minutes. Fluff up the grains, separating them with a fork.

2 While the rice is cooking, cook the peas in a pan of salted boiling water for 2 minutes. Drain and set aside. Make the omelette: beat the eggs in a bowl and season. Heat 1 tablespoon of the sunflower oil in the frying pan over a medium heat. Pour in the egg and cook for 2 minutes. Slice the omelette finely. (See below, Make a thin omelette.)

3 Heat the remaining tablespoon of sunflower oil in a wok or a large, deep-sided, non-stick frying pan or sauté pan. Tip in the red pepper and fry over a high heat, stirring, for 2–3 minutes. Add the spring onions, garlic, and five-spice powder, and stir-fry for 1 minute.

4 Reduce the heat to medium and stir in the sesame oil, the soy sauce mixed with water, the rice and peas, the omelette, and the beansprouts. Gently stir-fry for 1–2 minutes or until heated through. Stir in the chives and serve sprinkled with extra chives, the cashews, and a splash of soy sauce, if you like.

KEYS TO PERFECTION
Make a thin omelette

Prepare the rice for cooking

To make really light, tender rice and to ensure it isn't mushy, it's essential to measure the grains and water accurately. Before cooking the rice, put it in a large sieve and rinse under cold running water until the water runs clear, then drain well.

1 As you pour the egg into the pan for the omelette, tilt the pan so the egg completely covers the bottom to an even thickness. It will look set and no longer runny when done. Do not turn the omelette.

2 When the omelette is cooked, slide it onto a board and let it cool slightly, so that it will be easier to handle. Roll it up tightly like a cigar, then use a sharp knife to slice it across into very thin ribbons.

Classic Pad Thai

Thai cooks wouldn't make more than one or two portions of this dish at a time, as the ingredients would overcrowd the pan and not cook as well. To guarantee perfection, I follow the same rules.

 Serves 2　　 641 calories per serving

INGREDIENTS

- 115g (4oz) dried Thai rice noodles (*gueyteow*)
- 1 tbsp palm sugar (*namtarn peep*) or light muscovado sugar
- 1 tsp tamarind paste (*makham piek*)
- 1 tsp shrimp paste (*kapi*)
- juice of 1 lime
- 2 tbsp fish sauce (*nam pla*)
- 2 tbsp sunflower oil
- 1 small red onion, sliced into thin half-moons
- 1 small red chilli, deseeded and thinly shredded lengthways
- 1 tbsp finely chopped fresh root ginger
- 1 garlic clove, finely chopped
- 200g (7oz) raw, peeled king prawns, deveined and halved crossways
- 2 large eggs
- 2 tbsp chopped fresh coriander

TO SERVE

- 30g (1oz) peanuts, very finely chopped
- 30g (1oz) beansprouts
- 2 spring onions, trimmed and finely shredded lengthways
- 2 lime wedges

1 Lay the noodles flat in a wide, shallow pan and pour in 1 litre (1¾ pints) of cold water. Bring to the boil, then simmer over a medium heat for 10 minutes. Drain the noodles and rinse under cold running water until cold. Set aside. (See below, Keep the noodles separate.) Put the palm sugar into a small bowl with the tamarind and shrimp pastes. With a small spoon, mix in the lime juice and fish sauce until evenly blended.

2 Heat a wok or large, deep-sided, non-stick frying pan or sauté pan over a high heat until hot. Spoon in the oil and heat until hot, then add the onion, chilli, ginger, and garlic. Let the ingredients sizzle over a medium–high heat for 30–60 seconds or until just starting to brown, then add the prawns and stir vigorously for 30–60 seconds or until they begin to turn pink at the edges.

3 Pour in the lime juice mixture and stir-fry for about 1 minute or until the prawns are pink all over. Now tip in the noodles and stir constantly for 1½ minutes. Scoop the stir-fry to one side and crack the eggs into the empty part of the wok. Allow them to set around the edges for about 1 minute before stirring for a further minute until softly scrambled.

4 Mix the eggs into the noodles with the coriander and keep stirring for a minute or so until the mixture is dry. Serve immediately, topped with the peanuts, beansprouts, and spring onions, and a lime wedge on each plate.

KEYS TO PERFECTION

Keep the noodles separate

1 Rice noodles stick together if not prepared properly. Use lots of water for boiling, and swish around with a spatula between the strands as they cook to keep them separate.

2 As you rinse and drain the noodles, shake the colander and lift and separate the strands with your hands. If they start to feel sticky before you stir-fry, rinse and drain again.

Vegetables

At-a-glance Guide to Cooking Vegetables

Most vegetables can be cooked in a number of different ways, as indicated in the chart below. The cooking times given here are guidelines only, as timings vary according to the size and quantities of vegetables and the temperature of the hob or oven. More detailed information on each cooking method is given later in this chapter.

VEGETABLE	BOILING *see pp194–95*	BRAISING *see pp194–95*	STEAMING *see pp194–95*
 Cabbages	Remove tough outer leaves and thick stalks; shred leaves. Cook 4 mins.	Remove tough outer leaves and thick stalks; shred leaves. Cook 40 mins.	Remove tough outer leaves and thick stalks; shred leaves. Cook 6 mins.
 Brussels sprouts	Remove tough or discoloured outer leaves; trim stalks; halve lengthways. Cook 3 mins.	Not suitable	Remove tough or discoloured outer leaves; trim stalks; halve lengthways. Cook 6 mins.
 Broccoli	Trim stalk; cut into equal-sized florets. Cook 3 mins.	Not suitable	Trim stalk; cut into equal-sized florets. Cook 6 mins.
 Cauliflower	Remove tough central core; cut into equal-sized florets. Cook 5 mins.	Not suitable	Remove tough central core; cut into equal-sized florets. Cook 7 mins.
 Spinach & Chard	Trim thick stalks; shred large leaves. Cook with just water that clings to the leaves for 3–5 mins.	Trim thick stalks. Cook 6 mins.	Trim thick stalks; shred large leaves. Cook 3–5 mins.
 Pak choi	Cut lengthways into quarters. Cook 2 mins.	Cut lengthways in half or quarters. Cook 12 mins.	Cut lengthways into quarters. Cook 3 mins.
 Tomatoes	Not suitable	Remove stalk; halve crossways. Cook cut-side down 5 mins.	Not suitable
 Courgettes	Trim ends; thickly slice. Cook 2 mins.	Not suitable	Trim ends; thickly slice. Cook 5 mins.
 Squash & Pumpkin	Peel; halve lengthways; deseed; cut into 3cm (1in) chunks. Cook 5 mins.	Not suitable	Peel; halve lengthways; deseed; cut into 3cm (1in) chunks. Cook 8 mins.
 Aubergines	Trim ends; cut into 3cm (1in) chunks or 1cm (½in) thick slices. Cook 3 mins.	Trim ends; cut into 3cm (1in) chunks. Cook 15 mins.	Not suitable
 Peppers	Not suitable	Not suitable	Not suitable
 Sweetcorn/ Baby corn	Cobs: remove leaves and threads; cut stalk. Cook cobs 10 mins, loose kernels 2 mins, baby corn 4 mins.	Not suitable	Cobs: remove leaves and threads; cut stalk. Cook cobs 12 mins, loose kernels 5 mins, baby corn 6 mins.
 Globe artichokes	Trim stalk; discard dry outer leaves. Add 1 tsp lemon juice to the water. Cook 10–20 mins.	Not suitable	Trim stalk; discard dry outer leaves; sprinkle with lemon juice. Cook 20–30 mins.
 Broad beans	Pod the beans. Cook 3 mins. Rinse in cold water; slip off skins, if liked.	Not suitable	Pod the beans. Cook 5 mins. Rinse in cold water; slip off skins, if liked.
 Green beans	Trim stem end. Cook 4 mins.	Not suitable	Trim stem end. Cook 6 mins.

ROASTING *see pp200–201*	CHARGRILLING & GRILLING *see pp206–207*	SAUTÉING *see pp212–13*	STIR-FRYING *see pp218–19*
Not suitable	Not suitable	Remove tough outer leaves and thick stalks; shred leaves. Cook 5 mins.	Remove tough outer leaves and thick stalks; shred leaves. Cook 4 mins.
Not suitable	Not suitable	Remove tough or discoloured outer leaves; trim stalks; halve lengthways. Par-boil 2 mins, then sauté 4 mins.	Remove tough or discoloured outer leaves; trim stalks; halve lengthways. Par-boil 2 mins, then stir-fry 2 mins.
Trim stalk; cut into equal-sized florets. Cook 20 mins.	Not suitable	Trim stalk; cut into equal-sized florets. Blanch 2 mins, then sauté 4 mins.	Trim stalk; cut into equal-sized florets. Blanch 2 mins, then stir-fry 2 mins.
Remove tough central core; cut into equal-sized florets. Cook 25 mins.	Not suitable	Remove central core; cut into equal-sized florets. Par-boil 2 mins, then sauté 5 mins.	Remove central core; cut into equal-sized florets. Par-boil 2 mins, then stir-fry 4 mins.
Not suitable	Not suitable	Trim thick stalks; shred large leaves. Cook 5–6 mins.	Trim thick stalks; shred large leaves. Cook 5–6 mins.
Not suitable	Chargrill only: cut lengthways in half or quarters. Cook 2 mins each side.	Not suitable	Cut stems into wide strips; shred leaves. Cook stems 2 mins, leaves 30 seconds.
Remove stalk; halve crossways. Cook cut-side up 15 mins.	Remove stalk; halve crossways. Cook cut-side down 4 mins.	Not suitable	Not suitable
Trim ends; cut into 3cm (1in) chunks. Cook 20 mins.	Trim ends; cut into 1cm (½in) slices. Cook 2 mins each side.	Trim ends; thinly slice. Cook 4 mins.	Trim ends; thinly slice or dice. Cook 2–3 mins.
Peel; halve lengthways; deseed; cut into 5cm (2in) chunks. Cook 25 mins.	Chargrill squash only: peel; halve lengthways; deseed; cut into 2cm (¾in) thick slices. Cook 5 mins each side.	Squash only: peel; halve lengthways; deseed; cut into 3cm (1in) chunks. Cook 10 mins.	Not suitable
Trim ends; cut into 4cm (1½in) chunks. Cook 25 mins.	Trim ends; cut into 1cm (½in) thick slices. Cook 5 mins each side.	Trim ends; cut into 3cm (1in) chunks. Cook 10 mins.	Trim ends; cut into 3cm (1in) chunks. Cook 10 mins.
Halve lengthways; core; deseed. Cut into 4cm (1½in) chunks, if liked. Cook 25–30 mins.	Halve lengthways; core; deseed. Cook 8 mins each side.	Halve lengthways; core; deseed. Cut into 1cm (½in) thick slices. Cook 6 mins.	Halve lengthways; core; deseed. Cut into 1cm (½in) thick slices. Cook 4 mins.
Cobs: remove leaves and threads; cut stalk. Par-boil cobs 8 mins, roast 10 mins.	Baby corn: thread on skewers with other suitable vegetables. Cook 4 mins each side.	Not suitable	Baby corn: cut into 2cm (¾in) pieces or in half lengthways. Cook 3 mins.
Not suitable	Not suitable	Not suitable	Not suitable
Not suitable	Not suitable	Not suitable	Not suitable
Not suitable	Not suitable	Not suitable	Trim stem end; cut in half crossways. Cook 4 mins.

At-a-glance Guide to Cooking Vegetables (continued)

VEGETABLE	BOILING *see pp194–95*	BRAISING *see pp194–95*	STEAMING *see pp194–95*
Peas	Pod the peas. Cook 3 mins.	Pod the peas. Cook 7 mins.	Not suitable
Mangetout & Sugarsnaps	Trim stem end. Cook 2 mins.	Not suitable	Trim stem end. Cook 4 mins.
Onions	Trim ends; peel. Cook whole 25 mins.	Trim ends; peel; halve lengthways. Cook cut-side down 35 mins.	Not suitable
Shallots	Trim ends; peel. Cook whole 12 mins.	Trim ends; peel; halve lengthways. Cook 20 mins.	Not suitable
Leeks	Discard outer leaves; trim base; cut into 3cm (1in) slices. Cook 4 mins.	Discard outer leaves; trim base; cut into 3cm (1in) slices. Cook 15 mins.	Discard outer leaves; trim base; cut into 3cm (1in) slices. Cook 8 mins.
Fennel	Trim roots and stem tips; quarter. Cook 8 mins.	Trim roots and stem tips; quarter. Cook 30 mins.	Trim roots and stem tips; quarter. Cook 15 mins.
Celeriac	Peel; cut into 5cm (2in) chunks. Cook 15 mins.	Peel; cut into 2.5–5cm (1–2in) chunks. Cook 40 mins.	Peel; cut into 5cm (2in) chunks. Cook 25 mins.
Celery	Trim; cut into 7cm (2¾in) long sticks. Cook 5 mins.	Trim; cut into 7cm (2¾in) long sticks. Cook 40 mins.	Not suitable
Asparagus	Snap off woody ends; leave whole. Cook 3–4 mins.	Snap off woody ends; halve lengthways. Cook 12 mins.	Snap off woody ends; leave whole. Cook 8 mins.
Carrots	Peel; trim; slice into sticks or rounds. Cook 3–4 mins.	Peel; trim; slice into sticks or rounds. Cook 15 mins.	Peel; trim; slice into sticks or rounds. Cook 10 mins.
Parsnips	Peel; trim; cut into 2cm (¾in) slices. Cook 8 mins.	Peel; trim; slice into sticks or rounds. Cook 15 mins.	Peel; trim; cut into 2cm (¾in) slices. Cook 12 mins.
Beetroot	Leave whole, do not trim. Cook 30 mins. Slip off skins when cooked.	Peel; trim; cut into quarters. Cook 40 mins.	Leave whole, do not trim. Cook 40 mins. Slip off skins when cooked.
Swedes & Turnips	Peel; trim; cut into 4cm (1½in) chunks. Cook 15 mins.	Peel; trim; cut into 3cm (1in) chunks. Cook 30 mins.	Peel; trim; cut into 3cm (1in) chunks. Cook 25 mins.
Potatoes	Maincrop potatoes: peel; cut into 6cm (2½in) chunks. Cook 20 mins. New potatoes: scrub skins. Cook 12 mins.	Maincrop potatoes: peel; cut into 6cm (2½in) chunks. Cook 35 mins. New potatoes: scrub skins; halve crossways. Cook 20 mins.	Maincrop potatoes: peel; cut into 5cm (2in) chunks. Cook 30 mins. New potatoes: scrub skins; halve crossways. Cook 30 mins.
Sweet potatoes	Peel; trim; cut into 6cm (2½in) chunks. Cook 20 mins.	Peel; trim; slice into sticks or rounds. Cook 15 mins.	Peel; trim; cut into 3cm (1in) chunks. Cook 30 mins.
Jerusalem artichokes	Cook 20 mins. Peel, if liked.	Not suitable	Cook 30 mins. Peel, if liked.
Mushrooms	Not suitable	Not suitable	Not suitable

ROASTING *see pp200–201*	CHARGRILLING & GRILLING *see pp206–207*	SAUTÉING *see pp212–13*	STIR-FRYING *see pp218–19*
Not suitable	Not suitable	Not suitable	Not suitable
Not suitable	Not suitable	Trim stem end. Blanch 2 mins, then sauté 2 mins.	Trim stem end; halve lengthways, if liked. Blanch 2 mins, then stir-fry 2 mins.
Trim ends; peel; cut into wedges. Cook 30 mins.	Not suitable	Trim ends; peel; slice or chop. Cook 4–6 mins.	Trim ends; peel; slice or chop. Cook 4 mins.
Trim ends; peel; halve lengthways, if liked. Cook 20 mins.	Not suitable	Trim ends; peel; quarter or slice. Cook 6 mins.	Trim ends; peel; quarter or slice. Cook 5 mins.
Discard outer leaves; trim base; cut into 5cm (2in) lengths. Cook 20 mins.	Chargrill only: discard outer leaves; trim base; halve lengthways; cut into 10cm (4in) lengths. Cook cut-side down 4 mins, turn and cook 2 mins.	Discard outer leaves; trim base; cut into 3cm (1in) slices. Cook 4 mins.	Discard outer leaves; trim base; cut into 2cm (¾in) slices. Cook 4 mins.
Trim roots and stem tips; quarter. Cook 30 mins.	Trim roots and stem tips; slice lengthways into 1cm (½in) slices. Cook 5 mins each side (if grilling, par-boil 3 mins first).	Trim roots and stem tips; quarter. Cook 10 mins.	Trim roots and stem tips; slice finely. Cook 3 mins.
Peel; cut into 2.5–5cm (1–2in) chunks. Cook 25 mins.	Not suitable	Not suitable	Not suitable
Trim; cut into 7cm (2¾in) long sticks. Cook 25 mins.	Not suitable	Trim; cut into 1cm (½in) slices. Cook 4 mins.	Trim; cut into 1cm (½in) slices. Cook 3 mins.
Snap off woody ends; leave whole. Cook 25 mins.	Snap off woody ends; leave whole. Cook 10 mins, turning occasionally.	Snap off woody ends; cut each stalk into thirds. Cook 8 mins.	Snap off woody ends; slice thinly. Cook 4 mins.
Peel; trim; slice into sticks. Cook 25 mins.	Not suitable	Peel; trim; slice into sticks or quartered rounds. Cook 10 mins.	Peel; trim; slice into matchsticks. Cook 5 mins.
Peel; trim; quarter lengthways. Cook 35–40 mins.	Not suitable	Not suitable	Not suitable
Peel; trim; quarter; add 3 tbsp water; cover with foil. Cook 30 mins.	Not suitable	Peel; trim; quarter. Cook 25 mins.	Not suitable
Peel; trim; cut into 5cm (2in) chunks. Cook 40 mins.	Not suitable	Peel; trim; cut into 3cm (1in) chunks. Cook 20 mins.	Not suitable
Maincrop potatoes: peel; cut into 5cm (2in) chunks. Par-boil 5 mins; roast 60 mins. New potatoes: scrub skins; cut into 3mm (⅛in) slices. Cook 40 mins.	Not suitable	Maincrop potatoes: Peel; cut into 3cm (1in) chunks. New potatoes: scrub skins; cut into 2cm (¾in) slices. Cook 25 mins.	Not suitable
Peel; trim; cut into 6cm (2½in) chunks. Cook 30 mins.	Not suitable	Peel; trim; cut into 2cm (¾in) slices. Cook 15 mins.	Not suitable
Not suitable	Not suitable	Not suitable	Not suitable
Wipe with damp kitchen paper. Cook whole 10–15 mins.	Wipe with damp kitchen paper. Cook whole 5 mins, turning once.	Wipe with damp kitchen paper; cut into 5mm (¼in) slices. Cook 5 mins.	Wipe with damp kitchen paper; cut into 5mm (¼in) slices. Cook 3 mins.

Stir-fried Spinach with Raisins and Pine Nuts

Raisins bring a touch of sweetness to the spinach, which can be bitter, while butter introduces a mellow flavour, giving a perfect balance. The pine nuts add crunch. Serve with grilled meats.

 Serves 4  256 calories per serving

INGREDIENTS

- 300g (10oz) fresh spinach
- 3 tbsp olive oil
- 1 red onion, halved and thinly sliced
- 30g (1oz) butter
- 2 garlic cloves, crushed
- 45g (1½oz) pine nuts, toasted
- 30g (1oz) raisins (preferably crimson raisins)
- salt and freshly ground black pepper

1 Wash and drain the spinach; trim off the tough stalks and coarsely shred the leaves (see below, Prepare the spinach for stir-frying).

2 Heat a large, deep-sided, non-stick frying pan or wok over a high heat until very hot. Pour in the oil and heat until very hot. Add the onion, reduce the heat to medium, and stir-fry for a few minutes until softened and tinged a light golden brown.

3 Add the butter and garlic and stir to mix with the onion. When the butter has melted, throw a large handful of the spinach into the pan. Toss until the spinach leaves wilt, then add the remaining spinach in handfuls and keep stir-frying until all the spinach is in the pan. This whole process should take about 5 minutes in total.

4 Reduce the heat and toss in the pine nuts and raisins, plus salt and pepper to taste. Stir-fry for another minute or so, just to heat through the nuts and raisins, then tip the contents of the pan into a warmed serving dish and serve at once.

KEYS TO PERFECTION

Prepare the spinach for stir-frying

1 Plunge the spinach into cold water in a large bowl or sink and swish the water about to get rid of grit. Drain in a colander, but not too thoroughly, as the leaves should still have a little water clinging to them for stir-frying.

2 Pick over the leaves and discard any that are discoloured. If the leaves are young, the stalks should be thin enough to stir-fry, but thick stalks should be removed as they will not soften down in the short cooking time.

3 Working a batch at a time, put a mound of spinach on a board. Using a chef's knife, slice across the leaves to coarsely shred them. The shreds should be 1–2cm (½–¾in) wide. Repeat for the remaining batches.

Vegetable Gratin

A gratin is great for preparing ahead – especially for a Sunday lunch, when everything needs to come together at once. Squash is irresistible combined with leeks, cabbage, and a cheese sauce.

 Serves 6   ● 393 calories per serving    **Special equipment**
1.7–2 litre (3–3½ pint) baking dish, about 30 x 23cm (12 x 9in) and 5cm (2in) deep

INGREDIENTS

- 1 butternut squash, about 750g (1lb 10oz)
- 2 tbsp olive oil
- salt and freshly ground black pepper
- 250g (9oz) leeks, trimmed and thickly sliced
- 200g (7oz) savoy cabbage, shredded
- 60g (2oz) butter
- 60g (2oz) plain flour
- 600ml (1 pint) hot milk
- 90g (3¼oz) Red Leicester cheese, coarsely grated
- 90g (3¼oz) mature Cheddar cheese, coarsely grated
- 1 tsp Dijon mustard

1 Preheat the oven to 220°C (fan 200°C/425°F/Gas 7). Peel and deseed the squash and cut it into chunks (see below, Prepare the squash for roasting). Put the chunks into the baking dish. Pour over the olive oil, season, and stir to coat the squash in the oil. Roast for 20–25 minutes or until just tender.

2 While the squash is roasting, plunge the leeks into a large pan of salted boiling water over a high heat and bring back to the boil. Reduce the heat slightly and simmer for 3 minutes. Add the cabbage and simmer for a further 1 minute. Drain the leeks and cabbage in a colander.

3 Melt the butter in a pan over a medium heat, sprinkle in the flour, and whisk using a small balloon whisk for 1–2 minutes until pale golden. Remove from the heat and gradually add the milk, whisking constantly.

4 Return the pan to a medium heat and continue whisking until the sauce bubbles and thickens. Remove from the heat. Combine both the cheeses; add half to the sauce with the mustard and whisk until smooth.

5 Remove the squash from the oven and reduce the temperature to 200°C (fan 180°C/400°F/Gas 6). Add the leeks and cabbage and stir to mix. Pour the sauce over the vegetables, cover with the remaining grated cheese and a grinding of pepper, and bake for 30–35 minutes or until golden brown.

KEYS TO PERFECTION

Prepare the squash for roasting

1 Roasting the squash keeps it chunky and improves the flavour (boiling would make it soggy). First, use a sharp chef's knife to slice off both ends and discard, then divide the squash in half by cutting across its "waist".

2 Stand each piece on its trimmed end and shave off the peel from top to bottom, holding the squash firmly and sawing with the knife. It can be difficult, as some skins can be very tough. Cut each piece in half lengthways.

3 With a teaspoon, scrape out the seeds and stringy fibres and discard. Cut each piece of squash lengthways into quarters, then slice across into 5cm (2in) chunks. When roasted, the edges will become slightly caramelized.

How to Boil, Steam, and Braise Vegetables

There are several ways of cooking vegetables using water or stock. Boiling is quick and versatile, steaming preserves maximum nutrients, while braising enhances the flavour of vegetables.

How to boil vegetables

Most vegetables (greens and roots) can be boiled. Drop them into a large pan of boiling salted water and bring back to the boil as quickly as possible. Reduce the heat and simmer until the vegetables are just tender, then drain. Don't boil them for too long, or their flavour and texture will be impaired, and they will lose colour and nutrients.

Blanch green vegetables

When stir-frying or sautéing green vegetables you may like to blanch them first, to speed up the cooking time. Put them into a pan of boiling salted water, leave for a few minutes so they start to cook, rinse under cold running water until cold, then drain. This will stop further cooking and set the green colour.

How to steam vegetables

Steaming is a healthy way of cooking delicate vegetables, such as broccoli or asparagus. Put them in a single layer in a steamer placed above a pan of rapidly boiling water. Sprinkle with a little salt. Cover the steamer with a tight-fitting lid and steam until

Beetroot is great boiled or steamed and used in salads.

just tender. If you don't have a steamer, use a large saucepan with a steamer basket, or a wok with a lid and a bamboo steamer.

Enlivening plain vegetables

Plain boiled or steamed vegetables are made more interesting if they're dressed, however simply. Toss them with butter or some good-quality olive oil, and add some fresh herbs just before serving.

How to braise vegetables

Cabbage, celery, carrots, and other root vegetables are ideal for braising. Put the vegetables into a heavy pan or flameproof casserole, add a small amount of water or stock (150–300ml/5–10fl oz of liquid per 450g/1lb of prepared vegetables), and bring to the boil. Season with salt and pepper and add a knob of butter. Cover with a tight-fitting lid and cook gently until just tender. Remove the vegetables, reduce the juices by rapid boiling, then pour over the vegetables.

See also At-a-glance Guide to Cooking Vegetables, pp186–89

Mashed vegetables

Many vegetables (not just potatoes) can be boiled or steamed then mashed: celeriac, carrots, swede, squash, and parsnips all mash well. They can be served on their own, or in combination with other vegetables, and also make a good topping for pies. If mashing several vegetables, you may need to boil them separately, as some take longer to cook than others.

Boiling green beans, broccoli, and sugarsnap peas

Tenderstem Broccoli, Sugarsnap Pea, and Pancetta Stir-fry

This is a great combination that goes particularly well with grilled or fried meats. I find it better to boil the broccoli and peas briefly before stir-frying, to ensure the vegetables are tender.

 Serves 4    165 calories per serving

INGREDIENTS

- 225g (8oz) Tenderstem broccoli, ends trimmed
- 200g (7oz) sugarsnap peas
- 85g (3oz) diced pancetta
- 3 tbsp olive oil
- 200g (7oz) chestnut mushrooms, quartered
- 2 garlic cloves, thinly sliced
- salt and freshly ground black pepper

1 Put the broccoli and sugarsnap peas in a large pan of salted boiling water, bring back to the boil, and boil for 2 minutes. Drain thoroughly in a colander, rinse under cold running water, and drain well again. (See below, Blanch the vegetables.)

2 Heat a large, non-stick sauté pan, deep-sided frying pan, or wok over a low heat. Add the pancetta and stir-fry until crisp, for 4–5 minutes, increasing the heat as necessary (see below, Crispy pancetta). Transfer to kitchen paper to drain using a slotted spoon.

3 Leave 1 teaspoon of the pancetta fat in the pan (remove any excess), then add the olive oil and heat. Tip in the mushrooms and garlic, and stir-fry over a medium–high heat for 2–3 minutes. Add the drained broccoli and sugarsnap peas and stir-fry for about 2 minutes (see below, Stir-fry briefly).

4 Mix in the drained crispy pancetta, season with salt and pepper, and serve drizzled with the juices from the pan.

KEYS TO PERFECTION

Blanch the vegetables

Boiling these whole vegetables before stir-frying means they don't need to fry for as long, so retain their colour and nutrients. To prevent overcooking, quickly drain and cool them down under cold running water.

Crispy pancetta

For the pancetta to be crisp (not tough), fry the cubes over a low heat at first until they release some fat, then increase the heat to medium–high; they will quickly turn crisp. Keep moving them around for even cooking.

Stir-fry briefly

When the mushrooms are tinged brown and the juices are just starting to run, add the broccoli and sugarsnap peas, and stir-fry just long enough to heat them through. You want them to be tender but crisp (al dente).

Honey-roasted Winter Vegetables

A hearty mix of root vegetables goes well with most roast meats, poultry, and game. Here, the honey and orange mix that is added towards the end complements the flavours of the vegetables.

 Serves 4   238 calories per serving

INGREDIENTS

- 600g (1lb 5oz) butternut squash
- 350g (12oz) celeriac
- 3 medium parsnips
- 4 tbsp olive oil
- 5 sprigs of fresh thyme
- freshly ground black pepper
- 2 tbsp runny honey
- finely grated rind of ½ small orange
- 1 tbsp orange juice
- sea salt flakes

1 Preheat the oven to 220°C (fan 200°C/425°F/Gas 7). Peel the vegetables. Cut the squash and celeriac into chunks, about 2.5cm (1in). Cut the parsnips into quarters lengthways. (See below, Equal-sized vegetables.)

2 Put all the prepared vegetables in a large roasting tin, pour over the oil, and toss them together to coat well, spreading oil on the bottom of the tin too, so the vegetables won't stick. (See below, Don't overcrowd the pan.) Tuck in the thyme sprigs and season with pepper. Roast for about 30 minutes or until golden.

3 In a small bowl, mix together the honey and orange rind and juice. Remove the vegetables from the oven, pour over the honey and orange mix, and return to the oven for a further 5–8 minutes or until the vegetables are more golden and crispy around the edges. (See below, Flavour at the last minute.)

4 Spoon over any juices left in the roasting tin and sprinkle with sea salt flakes before serving.

KEYS TO PERFECTION

Equal-sized vegetables

Trim then peel the celeriac, squash, and parsnips. When peeling the celeriac, you'll need to cut off any knobbly parts first. It's important to cut all the vegetables to a similar thickness so they roast evenly.

Don't overcrowd the pan

Choose a roasting tin that's large enough to accommodate the vegetables in a single layer so they're not overcrowded and can turn a lovely golden colour all over. A good coating of oil also helps the vegetables brown.

Flavour at the last minute

Pour over the honey and orange mix only once the vegetables have browned and are almost done. If the mixture is left on for too long, it can burn and dry out, and there won't be any lovely sticky juices to spoon over.

How to Roast Vegetables

When vegetables are roasted in a high oven, their natural sugars caramelize and their flavours intensify. The dry heat of the oven also gives the vegetables an attractive golden brown exterior.

Equipment for roasting

Use a large roasting tin with relatively shallow rather than deep sides, and space the food well apart in the tin: you want the vegetables to roast rather than steam. A metal roasting tin is best, as it conducts heat better than other materials.

Estimating quantities

Vegetables shrink considerably when roasted, so you need to take account of this. As a rule of thumb, 900g (2lb) of vegetables generally serves six, and for this quantity of vegetables you'll need about 1½ tablespoons of oil.

Prepare the vegetables

Wash and trim off the ends, peel if appropriate, and cut the vegetables into pieces all the same size. Before roasting potatoes, par-boil them first. Make sure they're well drained, so they won't make the dish watery, and fluff them up by shaking the pan or colander before roasting.

Stuffed vegetables

Several vegetables, including aubergines, peppers, mushrooms, courgettes, tomatoes, and butternut squash, can be stuffed with a flavoursome mixture and baked, sometimes with cheese or breadcrumbs on top. You can serve stuffed vegetables as a first course or light lunch or, if filled with rice, couscous, or meat, they can make a satisfying main meal.

Arrange, oil, and season the vegetables

Heat some fat in the roasting tin until it's piping hot, then add the vegetables in a single layer. If they're overcrowded, they will sweat rather than roast. Toss the vegetables really well in hot fat. Olive oil, goose fat, and duck fat are usually used for roasting. Season the vegetables with salt and freshly ground black pepper. You may also like to add herbs and spices or another flavouring, such as lemon or garlic.

Oven temperatures

When roasting vegetables, oven temperatures should be on the high side, about 200°C (fan 180°C/400°F/Gas 6). Cooking timings vary depending on the vegetables and how they're cut, so sometimes you'll need to roast different vegetables separately, or add some to the tin later. About half- to two-thirds of the way through the cooking time, turn the vegetables. They are done when they are tender and starting to char around the edges.

See also At-a-glance Guide to Cooking Vegetables, pp186–89

Drizzle olive oil over the vegetables and toss to coat.

Roasting parsnips, celeriac, and butternut squash

Buttered Peas with Spring Greens and Mint

This is my take on the French recipe "petits pois à la française", in which lettuce is cooked with peas. As a change from lettuce, I like to use spring greens. These peas go really well with roast lamb.

🍽 Serves 4   🥧 182 calories per serving

INGREDIENTS

- 1 bunch of spring onions, trimmed and thickly sliced on the diagonal
- 2 tsp mint jelly
- 1 bunch of spring greens, about 150g (5½oz)
- 300g (10oz) frozen peas
- 50g (1¾oz) butter
- salt and freshly ground black pepper
- 2 tbsp chopped fresh mint, to garnish

1 Put the spring onions into a large, wide pan or sauté pan. Add the mint jelly and pour over 250ml (9fl oz) of cold water. Bring to the boil over a high heat, stirring to break up the jelly, then cover and simmer over a medium heat for 10 minutes or until the spring onions are tender and the liquid begins to look slightly syrupy. Meanwhile, finely shred the leaves of the spring greens (see below, Tender spring greens).

2 Add the peas, half the butter, and ½ teaspoon of salt to the pan. Increase the heat to high and stir until the liquid is bubbling, then cover the pan again. Reduce the heat to medium and sweat the peas for 3 minutes or until they are just tender. (See below, Sweet-tasting peas.)

3 Tip in the shredded spring greens and stir to mix with the peas. Increase the heat to high to reduce the liquid, and cook, uncovered, for 2–3 minutes or until the greens are tender. To serve, sprinkle with the mint and a grinding of pepper, and top with the remaining butter.

KEYS TO PERFECTION

Tender spring greens

1 Separate the leaves by pulling them from the hard stalk at the base of the bunch. Cut away and discard the tough stalks and thick mid-ribs. Retain the soft parts of the leaves only, as they will be tender and sweet.

2 Stack a few leaves on top of each other and roll them up like a cigar. Cut across the roll into very fine shreds; the spring green leaves need to be this thinly sliced in order to cook as quickly as possible with the peas.

Sweet-tasting peas

Cooking the peas gently with butter and a little liquid (rather than fast boiling in lots of water) retains their sweet flavour. Shake the pan occasionally, to distribute the butter and to help the peas cook evenly.

Cook simple food well

Healthy, everyday meals can taste every bit as good as more elaborate dishes. It's important to use fresh ingredients whenever possible, prepare and cook them properly, and season them well to enhance their flavour.

How to Grill and Chargrill Vegetables

Many vegetables can be cooked under the grill or in a ridged cast-iron chargrill pan. It's a quick, easy, and healthy way to cook, requiring little fat, and gives vegetables a lovely smoky flavour.

Suitable vegetables

The most suitable vegetables for grilling and chargrilling tend to be relatively robust and reasonably fast-cooking: peppers, aubergines, courgettes, onions, fennel, asparagus, tomatoes, and mushrooms are all ideal.

Prepare the vegetables

Halve the vegetables or cut the larger ones into slices. Brush or toss the vegetables with olive oil before cooking, otherwise they will dry out and burn. You need only a light coating – too much can result in flare-ups under the grill. Skewers are useful for threading through small vegetables or vegetable chunks before grilling. If using wooden skewers, make sure you soak them in a dish of water for 6 hours to prevent burning.

Grilling and chargrilling temperatures

The chargrill pan or grill must be piping hot, so preheat for 5–10 minutes before use. Do not oil the chargrill pan, or it will smoke. Set the heat to medium–high when you add the vegetables, and turn them at least once for even cooking. You don't want the temperature to be too high, or they will burn on the outside without being cooked through.

Threading vegetables onto skewers makes grilling easier.

Cooking times

The grilling and chargrilling times of different vegetables vary, so consider this if you're planning to serve several vegetables together. Onions and aubergines take the longest time, followed by peppers, courgettes, asparagus, and mushrooms.

Don't overcrowd the chargrill pan

You may need to cook the vegetables in batches so as not to overcrowd the chargrill pan. The vegetables should be in a single layer for even cooking, and to ensure they grill rather than steam in their juices.

Attractive ridged markings

When chargrilling, try to leave the vegetables in one place as much as possible before you turn them, rather than moving them around in the pan. You want to encourage charred stripes from the ridges, as they're attractive and boost the smoky flavour. If you move the food around, the lines will not be distinct.

See also At-a-glance Guide to Cooking Vegetables, pp186–89

Marinades

For added flavour, soak vegetables in a marinade for at least 1 hour before grilling or chargrilling. Combine 250ml (9fl oz) of olive oil with 2 finely chopped garlic cloves, 1 tablespoon of chopped fresh herbs (such as rosemary, thyme, or oregano), and salt and pepper. Before cooking, shake off any excess marinade.

Chargrilling tomatoes, courgettes, aubergines, and peppers

Brussels Sprouts with Hazelnuts

I always cut my Brussels sprouts in half, as I find they cook much more quickly and look more attractive, too. They're traditional for Christmas, but this recipe is good all through the winter.

Serves 4   247 calories per serving

INGREDIENTS

- 450g (1lb) Brussels sprouts
- 1 large orange (preferably unwaxed)
- 45g (1½oz) butter
- 60g (2oz) blanched hazelnuts, coarsely chopped
- 4 tbsp snipped fresh chives
- salt and freshly ground black pepper

1 Prepare the sprouts: cut off the tough ends of the stalks and peel away any dirty, dark green, or yellowed outer leaves. Wash the sprouts in a colander under cold running water, then cut them in half lengthways through the stem. Finely grate the orange rind (see below, Finely grate the orange rind).

2 Melt the butter in a small, non-stick frying pan over a medium heat until foaming. Add the hazelnuts and stir to coat in the butter, then continue cooking for 2 minutes, stirring constantly (see below, Gently fry the hazelnuts). Remove the pan from the heat and stir in the orange rind. The sauce will bubble furiously and then subside. Set aside and keep warm.

3 Plunge the sprouts into a large pan of salted boiling water. Bring the water back to the boil and simmer, uncovered, for 3 minutes or until the sprouts are just tender (see below, Briefly cook the sprouts).

4 Drain the sprouts well, shaking them in a colander to get rid of as much water as possible, then tip them into a warmed serving dish. Pour the hazelnut butter over the sprouts, add the chives and some salt and pepper, and toss quickly to combine. Serve immediately.

KEYS TO PERFECTION

Finely grate the orange rind

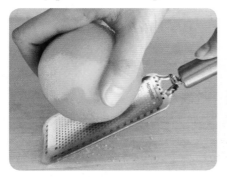

Ideally use an unwaxed orange (or wash and dry the fruit first). Rub it lightly over a fine microplane grater, making sure you grate the coloured rind only, not the bitter-tasting white pith beneath. Brush the rind out of the holes.

Gently fry the hazelnuts

Stir the hazelnuts in the foaming butter for 2 minutes, without taking your eyes off the contents of the frying pan. The moment the butter turns golden brown and the nuts smell toasted, remove the pan from the heat.

Briefly cook the sprouts

It's vital to cook sprouts for the shortest possible time and serve them as soon as they're cooked, or they will smell and taste unpleasant. To test, pierce a sprout with a fork; if it's just tender, it's done.

Pan-fried Courgettes with Crispy Shallots

Fried shallots give great flavour to this dish. However, they can sometimes be difficult to peel. If you put them in boiling water for about 5 minutes, the skins will soften and peeling will be easy.

 Serves 4  75 calories per serving

INGREDIENTS

- 3 small courgettes, about 450g (1lb) in total
- 115g (4oz) small shallots
- 2 tbsp olive oil
- 1 garlic clove, finely chopped
- salt and freshly ground black pepper
- ½ tsp finely chopped fresh rosemary

1 Trim the courgettes and halve them lengthways. Scoop out and discard the central seeds (see below, Deseed the courgettes). Slice the courgettes across into 1cm (½in) thick pieces.

2 Cut the shallots into small wedges. Heat 1 tablespoon of the oil in a large, non-stick frying pan or sauté pan. Add the shallots and fry over a medium–high heat for about 4 minutes, stirring occasionally. (See below, Make crispy shallots.)

3 Stir in the garlic with the remaining tablespoon of oil, then tip in the courgettes and fry for 6–8 minutes or until golden all over and just tender, stirring occasionally. Remove the pan from the heat, season with salt and pepper, and sprinkle over the rosemary.

KEYS TO PERFECTION

Deseed the courgettes

Run a teaspoon down the centre of each courgette half and scoop out the seeds, leaving the flesh intact. This prevents the courgettes from becoming watery and creates an interesting shape when sliced.

Make crispy shallots

1 Cut the shallots into small wedges, so that they will cook and brown evenly with the courgettes. Halve the shallots lengthways, lay them cut-side down, and slice each half into about 3 wedges.

2 The shallots should be slightly brown when you add the garlic and courgettes. Reduce the heat if the shallots are browning too fast. At the end of the cooking time they should be crispy, but not burnt.

How to Sauté Vegetables

Vegetables that are sautéed, or pan-fried, are crisp and golden on the outside, and soft and tender inside. Being partially caramelized, they're full of flavour and look appetizing, too.

Suitable vegetables

The best vegetables for sautéing are those that are tender, such as courgettes, onions, mushrooms, and aubergines. Other, harder vegetables (such as root vegetables) will have to be pre-cooked, for instance par-boiled (and then drained) before frying.

Equipment for sautéing

Use a large, wide-based, non-stick sauté pan or frying pan. The wide base and low sides allow steam to evaporate, so the vegetables will brown rather than steam in their juices and turn soggy. Sauté pans tend to be straight-sided, a little deeper than frying pans, and have a lid, so are more versatile.

Prepare the vegetables

Cut the vegetables into thin slices or small pieces, so they cook quickly without needing much oil. Don't use vegetables straight from the fridge; if cold, vegetables won't cook as well or brown properly. They must also be completely dry before sautéing.

Types of fat for sautéing

Use a good-quality oil or a mixture of oil with butter. Butter gives good flavour, but if it gets too hot it will

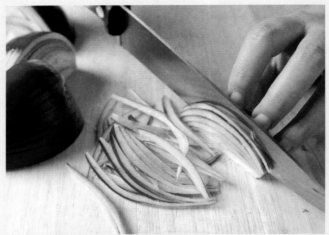

Slice onions thinly for sautéing, so they cook quickly.

burn. Don't use much fat; so long as the pan is hot enough, it won't be necessary.

Sauté in batches

Ensure the pan is big enough to take the vegetables easily, without overcrowding; if the pan is too full, the vegetables won't brown. Sauté in batches if the pan isn't large enough.

Heat and movement

To begin with, sauté the vegetables over a high heat, stirring and turning constantly, until they start to brown. Reduce the heat and continue cooking, stirring occasionally, until tender. Keep the vegetables moving to ensure that they cook evenly. Use a wooden spoon or spatula to move them around, or shake the pan.

See also At-a-glance Guide to Cooking Vegetables, pp186–89

Pan-fried potato cakes

Potato cakes make a great accompaniment to grilled meats, especially steak. Use leftover mash, or cook potatoes in a pan of salted boiling water for 15–20 minutes until soft, then drain and mash. Mix with chopped fresh herbs, for instance parsley or chives, and chopped spring onion or shredded par-boiled savoy cabbage, then add an egg yolk and salt and pepper. Shape into round cakes, chill for about an hour, then fry for 2–3 minutes on each side until golden.

Sautéing mushrooms

Roast New Potatoes with Garlic and Rosemary

I like to roast new potatoes in slices, combining them with garlic and fresh herbs. Make sure you use a large enough roasting tin, so the potatoes can spread out and their tops become brown and crisp.

 Serves 4    214 calories per serving   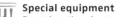 **Special equipment**
Roasting tin, about 35 x 28cm (14 x 11in) and 3.5cm (1½in) deep

INGREDIENTS

- 800g (1¾lb) new potatoes, such as Charlotte, scrubbed
- 4 tbsp olive oil
- 3 garlic cloves, thinly sliced
- 5 sprigs of fresh rosemary
- freshly ground black pepper and sea salt flakes

1 Preheat the oven to 200°C (fan 180°C/400°F/Gas 6). Slice the potatoes lengthways to a thickness of about 3mm (⅛in). There is no need to peel them first. Pat the slices dry with kitchen paper. (See below, Crisp, tender potatoes, steps 1 and 2.)

2 Spoon 1 tablespoon of the oil into the roasting tin and brush it all over the bottom of the tin using a pastry brush.

3 Scatter the potato and garlic slices into the tin, pour over the remaining 3 tablespoons of oil, and toss everything together so the slices are all thoroughly coated with the oil. Spread the potatoes out evenly in the tin and tuck in the rosemary sprigs, rubbing a little of the oil from the potatoes over them so they don't burn, then season with pepper. (See below, Crisp, tender potatoes, step 3.)

4 Roast for 35–40 minutes or until the potatoes are tender and golden. Put them in a serving dish and scatter over the sea salt flakes.

KEYS TO PERFECTION

Crisp, tender potatoes

1 Slice the potatoes thinly and evenly along their length using a sharp knife. This ensures that they roast evenly and become crisp once they're cooked.

2 Pat the sliced potatoes dry with kitchen paper to remove excess moisture from the cut surfaces. Again, this will help them to become crisp in the oven.

3 When the potatoes and garlic are in the roasting tin, drizzle over the rest of the oil and use your hands to mix so they're well coated. Spread them out for even cooking.

Rösti with Onions

I've added caramelized onions to bring extra flavour to a classic Swiss rösti. Serve it as a potato side dish, or put a fried egg and some crisp bacon on top for an indulgent, informal supper.

 Serves 8 |  227 calories per serving | **Special equipment** 26cm (10½in) non-stick frying pan

INGREDIENTS

- 4 tbsp olive oil
- 2 medium onions, halved lengthways and thinly sliced lengthways
- 1.35kg (3lb) smooth potatoes, such as Desirée, peeled
- salt and freshly ground black pepper
- 25g (scant 1oz) butter, plus a knob, about 15g (½oz)

1 Heat 2 tablespoons of the oil in the frying pan. Add the onions and fry over a medium heat for 15–20 minutes, stirring only occasionally, until golden, softened, and reduced down. Set aside.

2 Coarsely grate the potatoes. Put half of them in a clean tea towel and squeeze out the excess water (see below, Crispy outside, soft centre, steps 1 and 2). Tip into a large bowl. Repeat with the remaining potatoes. Stir in the onion, forking it through to combine. Season with salt and pepper.

3 Heat another tablespoon of oil in the same pan with the 25g (scant 1oz) of butter. Once the butter has melted, tip in the potatoes and onions. Spread them out and flatten with a fish slice. Dot knobs of the remaining 15g (½oz) of butter over the top. Fry over a medium heat for 18–20 minutes or until the base is golden and crisp. (See below, Crispy outside, soft centre, step 3.)

4 Put a large plate over the top of the pan and carefully invert the rösti onto it. Pour the last tablespoon of oil into the pan and when hot slide the rösti back into the pan. Tuck the edges under using a small, round-bladed knife, then cook for 10 minutes until the other side is golden and the potatoes are cooked.

5 Remove the rösti from the heat and leave to rest for 2 minutes, then slide it onto a large board or plate and cut into 8 wedges.

KEYS TO PERFECTION

Crispy outside, soft centre

1 After peeling the potatoes, grate them on the coarse side of a box grater. If you use one of the finer sides of the grater, too much starch will be released from the potatoes, which will spoil their flavour.

2 Put half the grated potatoes in a clean tea towel, tighten it up like a pouch, and squeeze well to get as much excess moisture out as you can. This will ensure the potatoes are not wet and the rösti will not be soggy.

3 When frying, reduce the heat slightly if you think the potatoes are browning too quickly. You don't want them to burn before they're cooked through. The total frying time for the rösti is about 30 minutes.

How to Stir-fry Vegetables

Stir-frying is one of the fastest and healthiest ways of cooking. It involves very fast cooking over an intense heat, which ensures the texture, flavour, and nutrients of the vegetables are retained.

Prepare the vegetables

Prepare all the vegetables before you start cooking, because once you start stir-frying speed is essential for success. Chop the vegetables into thin, equal-sized strips, dice, or shreds, so they cook quickly and evenly. Spring onions are best sliced on the diagonal. Remove any tough stems.

Equipment for stir-frying

A wok is ideal for stir-frying, as it's made of thin metal and has a rounded shape. However, a large, deep-sided, non-stick frying pan or sauté pan is fine, too. Buy the largest wok you can, as you want the food to fit in with plenty of room for tossing. The wok should never be more than one-third full, and the food should have room to touch the hot sides of the pan. You will also need a wok shovel, or a wooden spoon or spatula (or two if you find it easier), for tossing the food.

Temperature and timing

The wok or pan must be really hot before you add the oil, then the oil must be really hot before you

Slice carrots into fine matchsticks for stir-frying.

add the vegetables. To test the temperature, add a drop of oil; it will sizzle when the wok is ready. Add the vegetables in sequence according to their cooking times (see below, box). Retain a high heat throughout; it's vital to cook the vegetables quickly. They should take just a few minutes, until they are tender but still crisp, and should not require long cooking.

Toss the food

As you stir-fry the vegetables, keep tossing and stirring them around in the wok or pan using the shovel, wooden spoon, or spatula – the food must always be on the move.

Fry in batches

If you're using a frying pan or sauté pan instead of a wok, you may need to stir-fry the vegetables in two batches to ensure the pan isn't overcrowded.

See also At-a-glance Guide to Cooking Vegetables, pp186–89

Order of work

With stir-frying, the order of work is crucial. The aromatics are added to the wok or pan first (these include fresh ginger, chillies, and spring onions), then the vegetables in order of their cooking times, with those that require the longest times first – for instance, carrots require longer cooking so should go in the pan first, followed by broccoli and peppers, then mushrooms, then finally green leafy vegetables such as spinach. Any liquid for a sauce is added at the end of cooking.

Stir-frying peppers, spring onions, and broccoli

Aubergine and Goat's Cheese Crumble

This is a substantial and delicious vegetarian main course, consisting of layers of grilled vegetables, tomato sauce, fresh basil, Parmesan, and goat's cheese finished with a crispy topping.

 Serves 4

 497 calories per serving

Special equipment
1.4–1.5 litre (2½–2¾ pint) baking dish, about 25 x 20cm (10 x 8in) and 5cm (2in) deep

INGREDIENTS

- 7 tbsp olive oil, plus extra for greasing
- 2 aubergines, halved widthways and cut lengthways into slices just under 1cm (½in) thick
- 1 courgette, halved widthways and cut lengthways into slices about 3mm (⅛in) thick
- 1 onion, coarsely chopped
- 2 garlic cloves, crushed
- 400g can chopped tomatoes
- 1 tbsp tomato purée
- 1 tbsp chopped fresh basil, plus 12 whole basil leaves and a few extra small ones for garnish
- salt and freshly ground black pepper
- 50g (1¾oz) coarsely grated Parmesan cheese for the layers, plus 30g (1oz) for the topping
- 175g (6oz) firm goat's cheese (from a log), sliced into rounds about 5mm (¼in) thick
- 60g (2oz) fresh white breadcrumbs

1 Preheat the grill to its highest setting. Put 5 tablespoons of the oil in a small bowl. Brush a little of it onto a large, non-stick baking sheet, lay on as many of the aubergine and courgette slices as will fit in a single layer, and brush the tops generously with some of the oil. Grill for 7–8 minutes, then turn, brush with more oil, and grill for 4–5 minutes (see below, Tender vegetables). Set aside and repeat for the remaining vegetables, grilling in batches. Preheat the oven to 200°C (fan 180°C/400°F/Gas 6).

2 Grease the baking dish. Make the sauce: heat 1 tablespoon of the remaining oil in a pan. Add the onion and garlic and fry over a medium heat for 5–6 minutes. Stir in the tomatoes, tomato purée, and chopped basil. Season. Simmer for about 15 minutes, stirring occasionally, until quite thick.

3 Spread 3 tablespoons of the sauce in the dish. Lay the courgette on top, then sprinkle over one-third of the Parmesan. Put half the aubergines on top, then another third of Parmesan, and half the remaining sauce, seasoning each layer as you go. Finish with the remaining aubergines, Parmesan, and sauce. Scatter over the 12 basil leaves and cover with the goat's cheese. Mix the breadcrumbs with the final tablespoon of oil, rub together, stir in the 30g (1oz) of Parmesan, and sprinkle over the goat's cheese. (See below, Neat layers.) Bake for 25 minutes or until golden. Garnish with basil leaves.

KEYS TO PERFECTION

Tender vegetables

Grill the vegetables until golden and tender, oiling and turning once they soften and start to brown. Watch carefully, and remove any before they become too brown and crisp.

Neat layers

1 Spread a little sauce in the dish to stop the courgettes sticking and keep them moist, then add the Parmesan and aubergine in neat layers so they bake evenly.

2 Add more Parmesan, then a layer of sauce and seasoning. Repeat the layers, then lay the goat's cheese rounds on top of the sauce and basil leaves. Sprinkle over the topping.

Cauliflower and Sweet Potato Curry

Cauliflower and potatoes are a classic curry combination, and sweet potatoes work well in curries, too. This dish can accompany a meat curry or make a vegetarian main meal with rice or naan.

 Serves 4 (main course) or 6 (side dish)

 276 calories (main course) or 184 calories (side dish) per serving

INGREDIENTS

- 1 small cauliflower, about 400g (14oz) trimmed weight
- 2 tbsp sunflower oil
- 1 onion, halved lengthways and thinly sliced lengthways
- 2 garlic cloves, crushed
- 1 tsp finely grated fresh root ginger
- ½ tsp black mustard seeds
- ½ tsp cumin seeds
- 1 fresh, mild red chilli, deseeded and chopped
- 2 tomatoes, roughly chopped
- 1 sweet potato, about 250g (9oz), peeled and cut into 3.5cm (1½in) chunks
- 115g (4oz) fine green beans, stem ends trimmed and cut across into 3 pieces
- 1½ tsp garam masala
- ¼ tsp turmeric
- 115g (4oz) frozen peas
- salt
- 3 tbsp chopped fresh coriander
- 60g (2oz) roasted cashews
- plain, full-fat yogurt, to serve

1 Cut the cauliflower into small florets (see below, Tender vegetables, step 1). Heat 1 tablespoon of the oil in a large pan. Add the onion, garlic, ginger, mustard seeds, and cumin seeds and fry over a medium–high heat for 6–8 minutes or until the onion is golden brown, stirring often and adjusting the heat as necessary.

2 Stir in the chilli and tomatoes and fry for 1 minute or until the tomatoes start to soften. Add the remaining tablespoon of oil, then when hot add the cauliflower florets and fry for 3 minutes. Stir in the sweet potato, green beans, garam masala, and turmeric, stirring to deglaze the bottom of the pan. Pour in 250ml (9fl oz) of water and bring to the boil.

3 Reduce the heat, cover the pan, and simmer for 15–20 minutes, stirring occasionally, until tender (see below, Tender vegetables, step 2). Add 1–2 more tablespoons of water, if necessary, just to keep things moist and to give a little more sauce.

4 Tip in the peas and simmer for a further 3 minutes. Season with salt. Just before serving, stir in the coriander and cashews. Serve with plain yogurt.

KEYS TO PERFECTION
Tender vegetables

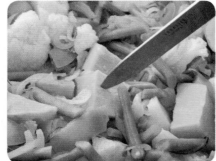

1 Slice the cauliflower in half lengthways, then cut out the hard, tough central core in a V-shape. This, combined with cutting the florets into smaller, same-sized pieces, ensures the cauliflower will cook evenly.

2 Towards the end of the cooking time, insert the tip of a sharp knife into the vegetables. If it goes in easily, the vegetables are done. You don't want them to overcook, or they will lose their shape, texture, and flavour.

Vegetable and Lentil Cottage Pie

This vegetarian pie is just as satisfying as the meaty version. You can make the filling ahead and chill it in its dish, which will give a really stable base for the mash; bake it for 5–10 minutes longer.

 Serves 6   431 calories per serving

Special equipment
1.7–2 litre (3–3½ pint) baking dish, about 25 x 18cm (10 x 7in) and 7.5cm (3in) deep

INGREDIENTS

- 3 tbsp olive oil
- 2 onions, coarsely chopped
- 2 garlic cloves, finely chopped
- 2 carrots, chopped into about 1cm (½in) cubes
- 200g (7oz) piece of swede, chopped into about 1cm (½in) cubes
- 125g (4½oz) dried red lentils
- 400g can plum tomatoes
- 1 tbsp sun-dried tomato paste
- 350ml (12fl oz) vegetable stock
- salt and freshly ground black pepper
- 85g (3oz) fresh spinach, chopped
- 900g (2lb) smooth potatoes, such as Desirée or Estima, peeled and cut into large chunks, about 5cm (2in)
- 30g (1oz) butter
- 5 tbsp full-fat or semi-skimmed milk
- 140g (5oz) mature Cheddar cheese, coarsely grated

1 Heat 2 tablespoons of the oil in a large, non-stick sauté pan. Add the onions and garlic and fry for 8–10 minutes over a medium–high heat or until starting to turn golden, stirring occasionally. Pour the remaining tablespoon of oil into the pan, tip in the carrots and swede, and fry for 3 minutes.

2 Reduce the heat to medium. Stir in the lentils, tomatoes, sun-dried tomato paste, and stock. Season and simmer, covered, for 35–40 minutes over a low heat, until the carrots and swede are tender and the lentils have softened.

3 Remove from the heat, stir in the spinach, and let it wilt. Check the sauce's consistency (see below, Moist, juicy filling). Pour the mixture into the baking dish. Leave to cool. Preheat the oven to 200°C (fan 180°C/400°F/Gas 6).

4 Put the potatoes into a large pan and cover with cold water. Bring to the boil, add salt, and simmer for 15–20 minutes or until tender. Drain well. Put the butter and milk in the pan and warm through over a low heat. Remove from the heat, return the potatoes to the pan, and mash with the milk and butter, then whisk until smooth (see below, Smooth, creamy mash). Season, then stir in the cheese.

5 Spread the mash over the filling (see below, Decorative topping). Bake for 30–40 minutes until golden and bubbling.

KEYS TO PERFECTION

Moist, juicy filling

The filling should be moist with plenty of sauce, but not sloppy. Add 2–3 tablespoons of water if it's too dry. Leave the filling to cool before adding the topping, as it will support the mash better.

Smooth, creamy mash

The potatoes are ready for mashing when a knife goes in easily. If undercooked, the mash will be lumpy; if overcooked, it will be sloppy. Mash the potatoes with hot milk and butter off the heat, then whisk with a balloon whisk.

Decorative topping

Spoon the cheesy, seasoned mash over the cooled vegetable and lentil layer. Spread it evenly over the surface, making patterns like furrows with a round-bladed knife to create an attractive, textured effect.

Salads

Vine Tomato and Shaved Fennel Salad with Balsamic Glaze

The combination of tomatoes and fennel is lovely for a summer buffet. Balsamic glaze – balsamic vinegar that has been reduced and sweetened – is perfect for drizzling and adds a tangy flavour.

 Serves 4   131 calories per serving   **Special equipment**
Mandolin

INGREDIENTS

- 1 fennel bulb, about 225g (8oz), trimmed
- 1 celery stick
- 4 medium tomatoes on the vine
- 175g (6oz) cherry tomatoes
- 2 tbsp extra virgin olive oil
- 2 tsp lemon juice
- sea salt flakes and freshly ground black pepper
- balsamic glaze, to drizzle

1 Slice the fennel very thinly on the mandolin. Cut the celery stick in half widthways and slice that thinly on the mandolin, too. Slice the vine tomatoes and halve the cherry tomatoes using a sharp knife. (See below, Create contrasting shapes and textures.)

2 In a small bowl, mix together the oil and lemon juice. Lay the tomato slices and halves on a serving plate or platter. Sit the fennel and celery on top in a loose, casual pile. Season with salt and pepper.

3 Drizzle over the oil and lemon juice, then a little balsamic glaze to finish (see below, Drizzle over the glaze). Serve immediately.

KEYS TO PERFECTION

Create contrasting shapes and textures

Drizzle over the glaze

1 Using a mandolin on its finest setting will give you ultra-thin shavings. By slicing the vegetables very finely, you're sure to get the flavour of the dressing into them. The blade is very sharp, so be careful of your fingers.

2 Slice the vine tomatoes relatively thickly using a sharp knife (ideally serrated), so they and the halved cherry tomatoes will provide a striking contrast in shape, as well as texture, with the crunchy fennel and celery shavings.

Pour over just enough of the balsamic glaze to add visual interest and flavour contrast, but be careful not to use too much, as it's quite strong. You can use balsamic vinegar if you can't source glaze.

Lentil and Chilli Bean Salad

Harissa paste, made with chilli peppers and a lively blend of spices, brings a special heat and flavour to this salad, which goes well with cold cuts. I've used three different pulses for variety.

 Serves 6  188 calories per serving

INGREDIENTS

- 400g can borlotti beans
- 400g can cannellini beans
- 400g can brown lentils
- ½ small red onion
- 1 fresh, mild red chilli
- 100g (3½oz) piece cucumber

FOR THE DRESSING

- 1 tbsp harissa paste
- 4 tbsp extra virgin olive oil
- 2 tbsp lime juice
- salt and freshly ground black pepper

1 Make the dressing: put the harissa paste in a small bowl, then stir in the oil and lime juice. Season with salt and pepper and set aside.

2 Drain and rinse each of the cans of beans and the lentils separately. Allow to drain thoroughly, then tip them into a serving bowl. (See below, Rinse the beans and lentils.)

3 Slice the onion lengthways into very thin slices. Deseed the chilli and slice it lengthways into long, thin strips. Add the onion and chilli to the serving bowl with the beans.

4 Halve the piece of cucumber lengthways and deseed (see below, Deseed the cucumber). Cut each cucumber half across into slices 5mm (¼in) thick, then chop each slice into small pieces. Tip them into the bowl with the rest of the vegetables.

5 Just before serving, mix in the harissa dressing (see below, Dress at the last minute). Taste and add more seasoning if needed.

KEYS TO PERFECTION

Rinse the beans and lentils

Rinse the beans and lentils to remove the thick, starchy liquid that clings to them. Tip them into a sieve to drain, rinse under cold running water, and drain really well. Leave to dry completely before making the salad.

Deseed the cucumber

Cut the cucumber in half lengthways. Using a teaspoon, scoop out the seeds and discard; if the seeds are left in, the salad will be too wet. Keep the skin on, to help the pieces retain their shape.

Dress at the last minute

Pour the dressing over the salad and gently toss everything together. Do this just before serving; if added too early, the onion and cucumber will lose their crunch and the beans will become too soft.

Mediterranean Pasta Salad

This multi-purpose salad is good for buffet parties, picnics, and packed lunches, as it holds up well and can be made ahead to the end of step 3. Simply add the other ingredients just before serving.

 Serves 4    811 calories per serving

INGREDIENTS

- 2 red peppers
- 250g (9oz) pasta shells (*conchiglie*) (see below, box)
- 75ml (2½fl oz) extra virgin olive oil
- finely grated rind and juice of 1 lemon
- salt and freshly ground black pepper
- 1 tbsp mayonnaise
- 75g (2½oz) semi-dried tomatoes, roughly chopped
- 8 cherry tomatoes, halved or quartered
- 60g (2oz) black olives, pitted and roughly chopped
- 125g (4½oz) piece of salami, cut into bite-sized chunks
- 1 small red onion, finely sliced
- 4 tbsp chopped fresh flat-leaf parsley
- 60g (2oz) pine nuts
- 200g packet feta cheese, drained and cubed
- 4 tbsp chopped fresh mint

1 Preheat the oven to 220°C (fan 200°C/425°F/Gas 7). Line a baking sheet with foil. Halve the peppers and remove the cores and seeds. Place them, cut-side down, on the baking sheet. Roast for 30 minutes until the skins are blistered. Transfer the hot peppers to a plastic food bag, seal, and leave to cool.

2 Meanwhile, plunge the pasta into a large pan of salted boiling water. Bring back to the boil, stir, and cook over a medium–high heat for 7–8 minutes (or according to the packet instructions) until al dente. Drain the pasta and mix it in a large bowl with the olive oil, lemon rind and juice, and seasoning (see below, Boost the flavour). Set aside to cool, stirring occasionally.

3 Remove the cooled peppers from the bag and peel off the skin. Roughly chop the flesh. Add it to the pasta with the mayonnaise, semi-dried and fresh tomatoes, olives, salami, onion, and most of the parsley. Toss well to mix, then check the seasoning.

4 Heat a small, non-stick frying pan until hot. Add the pine nuts and dry-fry over a medium–low heat for a few minutes (see below, Toast the pine nuts). Gently fold the feta into the salad, then scatter the remaining parsley, mint, and toasted pine nuts on top. Serve the salad at room temperature.

Choosing and using pasta shells

Italian pasta shells are good for salads, because their shape helps trap the dressing. They come in many different sizes, from tiny ones (*conchigliette*) for soup to the jumbo *conchiglioni*, which are used for stuffing. For this recipe, you need to use small to medium-sized shells (*conchiglie*).

KEYS TO PERFECTION

Boost the flavour

Cold pasta has a bland taste, so you need to dress the shells while they're still hot. The pasta will soak up the dressing, and the shapes will stay separate. Toss the pasta with the oil, lemon, and seasoning until glossy all over.

Toast the pine nuts

Toasting pine nuts enhances their flavour. They can burn easily, so stir and shake the pan constantly to prevent them from turning too dark. As soon as they're golden, tip them out of the pan or they will continue to colour.

Spinach, Green Bean, and Little Gem Salad

Choose a good-quality olive oil and vinegar for this light summer side salad. I also like to serve it at the end of a meal, with slim slices of Camembert or Dolcelatte instead of Parmesan for variety.

INGREDIENTS

- 140g (5oz) fine green beans, stem ends trimmed
- 30g (1oz) Parmesan cheese
- 100g (3½oz) fresh baby spinach leaves
- 2 Little Gem lettuces

FOR THE DRESSING

- 1 tbsp white wine vinegar
- 1 tsp Dijon mustard
- 1 tsp caster sugar
- salt and freshly ground black pepper
- 3 tbsp extra virgin olive oil
- 1 tbsp chopped fresh tarragon

1 Make the dressing: put the vinegar, mustard, sugar, and some salt and pepper in a small bowl. Whisk together with a hand whisk. Gradually add the oil, whisking vigorously as you go, until it is all incorporated. (See below, Make a classic French dressing.) Taste and add more seasoning and sugar, if you wish. Set aside.

2 Slice the green beans in half lengthways. Cook them in salted, boiling water for 2–3 minutes or until just tender. Drain and rinse under cold running water (so they retain their crunch), then drain again really well. Set aside. Make shavings of Parmesan using a vegetable peeler.

3 Tear any larger spinach leaves into manageable pieces, and leave the smaller ones whole. Tear the Little Gem lettuces into similar-sized pieces. Place the leaves in a large salad bowl and lay the beans on top of the leaves. Season with salt and pepper.

4 Stir the tarragon into the dressing, pour it over the leaves and beans, and gently toss together. Scatter the Parmesan shavings over the top.

Prepare the salad ahead

You can prepare the dressing (without the tarragon) up to 1 week ahead: store it in the fridge, then re-mix before using. The beans and leaves can be prepared 3–4 hours ahead, then covered and refrigerated until needed. However, it's vital not to put the dressing on the leaves and beans ahead of time, as they will quickly lose their crisp freshness. Do this just before you're ready to serve.

KEYS TO PERFECTION

Make a classic French dressing

1 Whisk the vinegar, mustard, sugar, and seasoning until combined, then whisk more vigorously until thick and cloudy. The mustard will form an emulsion that will help to stop the dressing from separating.

2 Pour in the olive oil slowly in a thin, steady stream, whisking well, until the dressing looks creamy. If you pour in the oil too quickly, the dressing may separate. Add the tarragon at the last minute, or it will discolour.

Quinoa Salad with Feta, Pomegranate, and Fresh Herbs

Using the tiny quinoa seed in a salad makes a great change from rice or couscous. It has many health benefits, and goes perfectly with dominant flavours, such as Peppadew peppers.

 Serves 4    288 calories per serving

INGREDIENTS

- 175g (6oz) quinoa
- 400ml (14fl oz) vegetable stock
- 4 spring onions, trimmed, halved lengthways, and thinly sliced
- 50g (1¾oz) mild Peppadew peppers from a jar, roughly chopped
- 1 tbsp lemon juice
- 2 tbsp extra virgin olive oil
- 3 tbsp chopped fresh coriander
- 2 tbsp chopped fresh mint
- 2 tbsp chopped fresh flat-leaf parsley
- 100g (3½oz) pomegranate seeds or ½–1 fresh pomegranate
- salt and freshly ground black pepper
- 125g (4½oz) feta cheese

1 Rinse the quinoa (see below, Make dry, fluffy quinoa, step 1). Put it in a medium pan and pour over the stock, then bring to the boil and stir. Reduce the heat to medium–low and simmer, covered, for 20 minutes or until the water is absorbed. Once cooked, the grains will look plumper and almost translucent, and should still have a bit of bite.

2 Drain the quinoa in a fine-meshed sieve, then put it back in the pan. Leave it off the heat, covered, for 10 minutes. (See below, Make dry, fluffy quinoa, step 2.) Spread out the quinoa in a large shallow serving dish. Leave to cool.

3 Mix in the spring onions and peppers, then stir in the lemon juice and oil. Gently stir in the coriander, mint, parsley, and half the pomegranate seeds with their juice (see below, Deseed the pomegranate). Season liberally with salt and pepper.

4 Crumble the feta over the salad. Scatter over the remaining pomegranate seeds and add an extra grinding of pepper.

KEYS TO PERFECTION

Make dry, fluffy quinoa

Deseed the pomegranate

1 You must rinse quinoa in cold running water before cooking, as it has a bitter coating that can spoil its taste. Use a fine-meshed sieve for rinsing, as the quinoa grains are so tiny.

2 After cooking, drain the quinoa thoroughly to ensure the salad isn't watery. To make the quinoa dry and fluffy, return it to the hot pan, off the heat, cover with a lid, and leave it to dry off in the steam inside the pan.

If using fresh pomegranate, release the seeds by holding the halved fruit over a bowl and hitting the skin hard with a rolling pin. Spoon out any remaining seeds if necessary. Save any juice, as it adds a tangy flavour.

Measure accurately

Treat yourself to a good set of digital scales and weigh accurately: use either metric or imperial measures; never mix the two. Measuring spoons are essential for baking, and check the capacity and dimensions of tins and baking dishes.

Roasted Pepper and Broad Bean Salad with Parma Ham

With its vibrant colours, this salad will enhance any table for a summer's lunch or light supper. Serve it at room temperature, with rustic bread on the side for dipping into the juicy dressing.

 Serves 4    161 calories per serving

INGREDIENTS

- 2 red peppers, halved, cored, and deseeded
- 2 yellow peppers, halved, cored, and deseeded
- 225g (8oz) frozen baby broad beans
- 3 slices of Parma ham

FOR THE DRESSING

- 2 tbsp extra virgin olive oil, plus 1 tsp for frying
- 2 tsp lemon juice
- 1 garlic clove, finely chopped
- 1 tbsp chopped fresh flat-leaf parsley
- salt and freshly ground black pepper

1 Preheat the oven to 220°C (fan 200°C/425°F/Gas 7). Roast the peppers for 30 minutes or until well charred. Transfer them to a large plastic food bag, seal, and leave to cool. (See below, Roast and skin the peppers, steps 1 and 2.) While the peppers are cooling, cook the broad beans in a small pan of simmering water for 3 minutes. Drain and rinse under cold running water. Skin the beans by squeezing one end of each bean so it pops out of its skin.

2 Make the dressing: mix together the 2 tablespoons of oil with the lemon juice, garlic, and parsley. Season with salt and pepper. Pour 1 tablespoon of the dressing over the beans and toss together. Set aside.

3 Heat 1 teaspoon of the oil in a non-stick frying pan. Add the Parma ham and fry for 2–3 minutes or until crisp, turning often. Remove and drain on kitchen paper. Remove the peppers from the bag and peel off the skins (see below, Roast and skin the peppers, step 3). Slice the flesh into long strips.

4 Crumble the Parma ham into small pieces. Scatter the broad beans onto 4 large plates. Loosely arrange the pepper strips on top, drizzle over the remaining dressing, and scatter some of the crumbled ham over each salad.

KEYS TO PERFECTION

Roast and skin the peppers

1 Roasting brings out the natural sweetness of a pepper. Place the pepper halves, cut-side down, on a baking sheet lined with foil and roast in a high oven until the skins are blackened and blistered.

2 While the peppers are still hot, place them in a large plastic food bag and seal the end tightly. This traps steam, which will help loosen the skin from the flesh, making the peppers easier to peel.

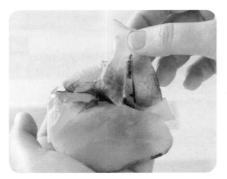

3 The peppers have a better texture and taste if the skin is removed. When the peppers are cool, pinch a little of the blistered skin and lift upwards. The skin should come away easily from the flesh.

Asian-style Coleslaw

This is a great crunchy winter salad that is best made ahead, so the dressing can flavour the vegetables. It keeps really well for a few days. Its bold taste goes well with simple chicken or pork dishes.

 Serves 10    166 calories per serving

INGREDIENTS

- 500g (1lb 2oz) hard white cabbage
- 2 large carrots
- 200g (7oz) large pink radishes
- 200g (7oz) mangetout
- handful of fresh mint
- handful of fresh coriander
- handful of fresh basil
- 100g (3½oz) roasted cashew nuts, chopped

FOR THE DRESSING

- 1 fresh, medium-hot red chilli, deseeded and finely chopped
- finely grated rind and juice of 2 limes
- 6 tbsp sesame oil
- 4 tbsp fish sauce (*nam pla*)
- 3 tbsp rice vinegar
- 2 tbsp caster sugar

1 Finely shred the cabbage, carrots, radishes, and mangetout (see below, Shred the vegetables finely). Toss all the vegetables together in a large serving bowl until evenly mixed.

2 Coarsely chop the mint and coriander, reserving a few whole leaves for the garnish. Add the chopped herbs to the vegetables in the serving bowl and toss thoroughly to combine.

3 Make the dressing by whisking all the ingredients together in a jug. Pour the dressing over the vegetables and, again, toss well to mix. Cover and chill for at least 1 hour, preferably longer – up to 12 hours.

4 Before serving, toss the salad well to bring up the dressing that has sunk to the bottom. Finely shred the basil and fold the shredded leaves into the salad with most of the chopped nuts.

5 To serve, scatter the remaining nuts and the reserved whole mint and coriander leaves on top. Serve the coleslaw at room temperature.

KEYS TO PERFECTION

Shred the vegetables finely

1 Shred the vegetables as finely as possible using a very sharp knife. Peel off the outer cabbage leaves and cut the cabbage into wedges. Remove the core. Lay each wedge cut-side down and slice into fine shreds.

2 Cut the carrots in half crossways, then lengthways into very thin slices. Stack a few of the slices on top of each other, then slice the stack lengthways into thin shreds. Cut the radishes into thin shreds.

3 Stack a few mangetout on top of each other and cut them on the diagonal into thin shreds. They look decorative sliced this way and are easier to eat in small pieces rather than when they're whole.

SALADS • Asian-style Coleslaw

Warm Chicken Salad with Avocado Salsa

This main meal salad is perfect for al fresco eating. Chargrilling the chicken and spring onions gives them extra flavour, best highlighted when they're served warm on the dressed leaves.

 Serves 4    405 calories per serving    **Special equipment**
Ridged cast-iron chargrill pan

INGREDIENTS

- 3 tbsp extra virgin olive oil
- 1 tbsp white wine vinegar
- salt and freshly ground black pepper
- about 1 tbsp olive oil, for brushing
- 4 skinless, boneless chicken breasts, about 140g (5oz) each
- 8 spring onions, trimmed and halved lengthways
- 1 tsp chopped fresh tarragon
- 30g (1oz) rocket leaves
- 45g (1½oz) lamb's lettuce leaves

FOR THE AVOCADO SALSA

- 2 medium, ripe avocados, halved, stoned, and peeled
- 1½ tbsp lime juice
- 2 spring onions, trimmed and finely chopped
- ¼ tsp Tabasco
- 2 tsp chopped fresh tarragon

1 Put the extra virgin olive oil and vinegar in a small bowl, mix together, and season with salt and pepper; set aside. Make the salsa: cut the avocado into chunky pieces, put in a bowl, then gently stir in the lime juice, chopped spring onions, Tabasco, and the 2 teaspoons of tarragon. Season with salt and pepper and set aside. (See below, Make a fresh green salsa.)

2 Preheat the chargrill pan over a high heat. Brush a little of the olive oil over both sides of the chicken breasts and season with salt and pepper. Lower the heat to medium–high and lay the chicken on the pan, with the plump, smooth-side down. Cook for 5 minutes or until the chicken is golden with charred grill marks, then turn and cook for a further 5 minutes. Transfer the chicken to a board, cover loosely with foil, and set aside to rest.

3 Brush the halved spring onions all over with the rest of the olive oil and season with salt and pepper. Lay them on the pan and cook for 2–3 minutes, so they get lightly charred all over (see below, Chargrill effectively).

4 To serve, stir the 1 teaspoon of tarragon into the oil and vinegar mix and toss the rocket and lamb's lettuce leaves with this dressing (see below, Keep the leaves crisp). Cut each warm chicken breast into 5 or 6 chunky slices. Serve the chicken on a pile of the leaves with the chargrilled spring onions, and the avocado salsa on the side.

KEYS TO PERFECTION

Make a fresh green salsa

Mix the salsa very gently, as the avocado pieces can quickly become mushy if over-stirred. Don't make it too far ahead, as the avocado will turn brown, although the lime juice will slow down the discolouring process.

Chargrill effectively

When chargrilling, turn the spring onions a few times so they soften quickly and don't burn. However, turn the chicken only once, so the grill markings don't get distorted. Serve them both warm.

Keep the leaves crisp

Toss the salad leaves with the dressing just before serving, otherwise they will wilt. The oil and vinegar can be mixed ahead of time, but add the tarragon right at the end or it will lose its colour.

Puddings

Apricot and Ginger Syrup Sponge with Creamy Custard

This pudding is moist and sticky, and to spice up the flavour I've mixed in some ginger. A jug of hot pouring custard is the perfect accompaniment. Comfort food doesn't get much better than this.

 Serves 6    903 calories per serving    **Special equipment**
1–1.2 litre (1¾–2 pint) pudding basin; parchment-lined foil (see p64)

INGREDIENTS

- 175g (6oz) butter (room temperature), plus extra for greasing
- 4 tbsp golden syrup
- 1 tbsp stem ginger syrup
- 175g (6oz) dark muscovado sugar
- 3 large eggs
- 175g (6oz) self-raising flour
- 1 tsp baking powder
- ½ tsp ground ginger
- 115g (4oz) ready-to-eat dried apricots, finely chopped
- 2 pieces of stem ginger, chopped
- 1 tbsp milk

FOR THE CUSTARD

- 2 large eggs
- 1 large egg yolk
- 25g (scant 1oz) caster sugar
- 1¼ tsp cornflour
- 2 tsp vanilla extract
- 300ml (10fl oz) milk
- 300ml (10fl oz) double cream

KEYS TO PERFECTION (*see overleaf*)
Wrap the pudding securely; Gently steam and serve the pudding; Make silky-smooth custard

1 Generously grease the inside of the pudding basin. Put 3 tablespoons of golden syrup and the stem ginger syrup in the bottom of the basin and mix them together with a spoon.

2 Put the butter, muscovado sugar, eggs, flour, baking powder, and ground ginger into a large bowl and beat using an electric hand whisk or wooden spoon until the ingredients are evenly blended. Gently fold in the apricots and stem ginger, then the milk and remaining tablespoon of golden syrup. Spoon the batter into the basin and level the surface.

3 Cut a 30cm (12in) square of parchment-lined foil, grease the parchment side with butter, and make a pleat in the centre. Place the square, buttered-side down, over the basin and tie securely with string. Use excess string to create a carrying handle. (See p250, Wrap the pudding securely.)

4 Place an upturned saucer in the bottom of a large, deep pan (this protects the base of the pudding from the pan's heat and prevents it from overcooking). Sit the basin on top of the saucer and pour boiling water into the pan until it comes one-third of the way up the basin. Bring the water back to the boil over a medium–high heat, then reduce the heat to a gentle simmer. Cover the pan and steam the pudding for 2¼ hours. (See p250, Gently steam and serve the pudding, step 1.)

5 Make the custard: whisk the eggs, egg yolk, caster sugar, cornflour, and vanilla extract in a heatproof bowl. Gently warm the milk and cream in a medium pan over a low heat, then gradually whisk it into the egg mixture. Strain the mixture into the cleaned pan and heat gently, whisking constantly, until the custard thickens. (See p251, Make silky-smooth custard.) If you are not serving the custard immediately, prevent a skin from forming by pressing a sheet of cling film directly onto the surface of the custard as soon as it is made; before serving, return it to the pan and reheat while whisking.

6 When the pudding is cooked, carefully lift the basin out of the pan, cut the string from the basin, and discard the parchment-lined foil. Invert the pudding onto a plate and let it stand for 5–10 minutes before cutting into wedges. (See p250, Gently steam and serve the pudding, step 2.) Serve with the hot custard in a jug.

KEYS TO PERFECTION

Wrap the pudding securely

1 Brush butter over the parchment side of the parchment-lined foil and make a pleat in it by folding over 2.5cm (1in) in the centre. The pleat will allow the sponge to rise and expand during steaming; the butter will prevent the sponge from sticking to the paper as it rises.

2 Place the parchment, foil-side up, over the basin and press it firmly around and under the rim. Tie string tightly under the rim. This will prevent water from seeping into the basin during steaming, which would make the sponge soggy. Make a handle over the top of the pudding with a double length of string, knotting it securely to the string under the rim. Trim off the corners of the parchment-lined foil.

Gently steam and serve the pudding

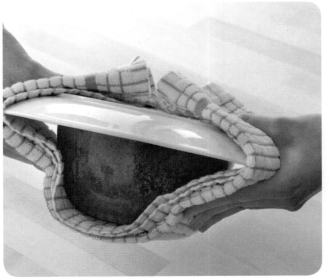

1 As the pudding steams, keep the water at a gentle simmer – you may need to increase or reduce the heat. Check the water level every so often and top up the pan with more boiling water if the level drops below one-third of the way up the basin. If there is not enough water the pudding won't steam properly, too much and it will bubble up beneath the foil and make the pudding soggy.

2 Remove the basin very carefully from the pan using the handle you made with the double length of string; take care, as the basin will be very hot. Remove the foil lid. Run a palette knife between the sponge and the basin to loosen the sides. Place an upturned, warmed plate over the pudding, then carefully turn them over together, holding firmly with a folded tea towel. Gently ease off the basin.

Make silky-smooth custard

1 Use a balloon whisk to whisk the eggs, egg yolk, caster sugar, cornflour, and vanilla together until evenly blended and no lumps of cornflour remain. The extra egg yolk acts as a thickening agent and makes the custard a little richer, and the addition of a small amount of cornflour to the mixture helps to stabilize the eggs and prevent them from curdling.

2 When mixing the warmed milk and cream with the eggs, the liquid must not be too hot, or the eggs may curdle. It should feel lukewarm when you dip your finger into it. After you've emptied the milk pan, rinse it before making the custard; you need to start with a clean pan, as any residue left from heating the milk and cream may catch or burn while the custard is cooking.

3 Strain the egg and milk mixture into the pan using a fine-mesh sieve. Straining is important, as it removes the stringy parts of the egg, which would spoil the texture of the custard if left in.

4 When cooking the custard, keep the heat low under the pan and be patient as you wait for the custard to thicken. It should be thick enough to coat the back of a wooden spoon. This stage can take as long as 10 minutes and you should watch it very carefully, whisking frequently. If you try to rush it by increasing the heat, the custard may split and curdle.

Treacle and Pecan Tart

I've combined the best characteristics of a dark treacle tart and a North American pecan pie, to create a tart with a soft and slightly sticky filling made crunchy with a pecan nut topping.

 Serves 8

 431 calories per serving

Special equipment
Loose-bottomed, round, small-fluted tart tin, 23cm (9in) diameter and 2.5cm (1in) deep; baking beans

INGREDIENTS

- 275g (9½oz) golden syrup
- 1 tbsp black treacle
- finely grated rind of 1 orange
- 85g (3oz) desiccated coconut
- 2 large eggs, beaten
- 2 tbsp orange juice
- 75g (2½oz) pecans
- clotted cream or crème fraîche, to serve

FOR THE PASTRY

- 175g (6oz) plain flour, plus extra for dusting
- 85g (3oz) cold butter, diced
- 15g (½oz) icing sugar
- 1 large egg yolk

1 Make the pastry: put the flour, butter, and icing sugar in a food processor. Process briefly until the mixture looks like breadcrumbs, then add the egg yolk and 1 tablespoon of cold water. Process again until the mixture sticks together in clumps. Tip onto the work surface, then gather into a ball with your hands. Knead the pastry just 2 or 3 times to make it smooth.

2 Roll out the pastry on a lightly floured surface and use it to line the tart tin. Trim the pastry. Prick the base with a fork and chill for 30 minutes. Preheat the oven to 200°C (fan 180°C/400°F/Gas 6). Place the lined tart tin on a baking sheet and bake blind for 15 minutes. Remove the paper and beans and bake for 5 more minutes. (See below, Bake the pastry case blind.)

3 Reduce the oven temperature to 180°C (fan 160°C/350°F/Gas 4). Make the filling: mix the syrup and treacle together in a medium bowl. Stir in the orange rind and coconut, then the eggs and orange juice. Pour the syrupy mixture into the baked pastry case.

4 Break a few of the pecans into smaller pieces and leave the rest whole. Scatter the nuts all over the top of the filling. Bake for 25–30 minutes or until the filling is golden and set. Leave to cool in the tin before removing. Serve with clotted cream or crème fraîche.

KEYS TO PERFECTION

Bake the pastry case blind

1 Once you've lined the tart tin with the pastry, prick the base all over with a fork to prevent air bubbles from forming during baking. Chilling the pastry case will help to reduce shrinkage in the oven.

2 Line the bottom and sides of the pastry case with baking parchment, and weigh it down with baking beans. This ensures the sides don't collapse and the base doesn't puff up, keeping a good shape while the case bakes.

3 After 15 minutes' baking, remove the paper and beans and bake the empty case for a further 5 minutes. You now have a case that is ready to be filled and baked again to give a crisp rather than soggy base.

Autumn Fruit Pie

Two classic autumn fruits are combined in this generously filled pie. It produces a fruity sauce, which thickens itself and coats the fruit as it bakes. The pastry cooks best if you use a metal pie tin.

 Serves 6

 564 calories per serving

 Special equipment
900ml–1 litre (1½–1¾ pint) metal pie tin, about 23cm (9in) diameter and 3.5cm (1½in) deep

INGREDIENTS

- 800g (1¾lb) cooking apples, such as Bramley
- 1 tbsp lemon juice
- 100g (3½oz) caster sugar
- 2 tbsp cornflour
- ½ tsp ground cinnamon
- 225g (8oz) blackberries
- fresh cream, custard, or vanilla ice cream, to serve

FOR THE PASTRY

- 350g (12oz) plain flour, plus extra for dusting
- 175g (6oz) cold butter, cut into small cubes
- about 1 tbsp milk, to glaze
- 2 tsp caster sugar, to glaze

KEYS TO PERFECTION *(see overleaf)*
Make a light pastry crust; Line the tin without stretching; Fill, cover, and seal the pie securely

1 Make the pastry: put the flour in a large bowl with the butter. Rub together with your fingertips until you have incorporated all the butter. Add about 6 tablespoons of cold water until the mixture holds together. Gently gather up, then pat into a ball. Wrap in cling film and refrigerate for 30 minutes. Cut off just over half the pastry and leave the rest wrapped. Lightly flour the work surface and rolling pin. Roll out the pastry into a circle about 35cm (14in) across. (See p256, Make a light pastry crust.)

2 Carefully line the pie tin with the pastry (see p257, Line the tin without stretching). Place a baking sheet in the oven and preheat the oven to 220°C (fan 200°C/425°F/Gas 7).

3 Quarter, peel, and core the apples, then cut them into slices about 5mm (¼in) thick. Put them in a large bowl and toss with the lemon juice. Mix the sugar with the cornflour and cinnamon in a bowl, then toss with the apples. Tip in the blackberries and briefly toss everything together. Be gentle when tossing, or the fruit will break up. Tip the fruit into the pastry-lined tin. (See p257, Fill, cover, and seal the pie securely, step 1.)

4 Make the pie lid: roll out the remaining piece of pastry as before, into a 30cm (12in) circle. Brush the rim of the pastry lining the tin with a little milk. Sit the folded pastry circle on the apples and unfold to cover the pie. Press the pastry edges down to seal, and trim off the excess with a small, sharp knife. Holding the knife horizontally and with its back to the cut edge of the pie, tap all around to secure the seal. Crimp the pie edge using your fingers. (See p257, Fill, cover, and seal the pie securely, step 2.) Cut a small slit in the centre, about 2cm (¾in) long, to release steam.

5 Re-roll the pastry trimmings and cut out pastry leaves. Brush the pie lid with milk. Arrange the leaves in a circle around the steam hole. Brush the leaves with milk and sprinkle the top of the pie with the 2 teaspoons of sugar.

6 Put the pie tin on the heated baking sheet and bake for 15 minutes, then reduce the temperature to 180°C (fan 160°C/350°F/Gas 4) and bake for a further 30–35 minutes. Remove and let the pie sit for 5–10 minutes to allow the juices to settle before serving. Serve with cream, custard, or ice cream.

KEYS TO PERFECTION

Make a light pastry crust

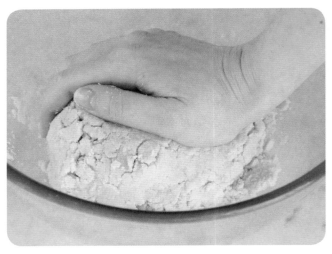

1 It's important to keep utensils, hands, and ingredients cool for pastry. Use chilled butter straight from the fridge, otherwise it will be too soft to handle. Lightly rub the flour and butter together until it looks like fine breadcrumbs, lifting the mixture up as you rub in, which will aerate it, too.

2 Add just enough water to bind the mixture together. Start with the 6 tablespoons, adding only a few drops more if needed to bring it together, since too much water can cause the pastry to be tough. Work gently with your hands to bring together into a rough ball. To keep the pastry light, do not over-handle it.

Go easy on the sugar for the filling

Fruit baked in a pie with sugar can create a lot of liquid, so I combine some cornflour with the sugar and cinnamon and toss the apples in the mixture, which helps to thicken the fruit juices that are released as the pie bakes. It's important not to add too much sugar, as this draws out juice from the fruit, and if there's too much it will overflow during baking. You can always offer extra sugar at the table if diners have a very sweet tooth.

3 Roll out just over half the chilled dough, flouring the work surface and the rolling pin first to prevent sticking. Don't use too much flour, or it will make the pastry dry. To prevent shrinkage later, roll the dough on one side only (so don't turn it over as you roll) and use short, sharp strokes in one direction only, giving a quarter turn between rollings so it rolls out evenly.

Line the tin without stretching

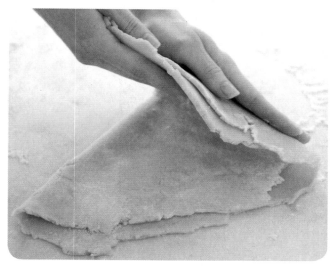

1 When lining the tin, it's easy to stretch the pastry, which will cause it to shrink back in the oven. The best way I find to minimize stretching is to fold the rolled-out pastry in half, then in half again, to resemble a fan shape. I then carefully lay it in the tin with the point in the centre. Use floured hands to prevent sticking.

2 Now unfold the pastry and ease it into the tin without stretching or pulling, so it fits snugly into the base and up the side. It's fine to have some pastry hanging over the edge, as it will get trimmed off later. Do not grease the pie tin before putting in the pastry. It is unnecessary and can cause the pastry to stick.

Fill, cover, and seal the pie securely

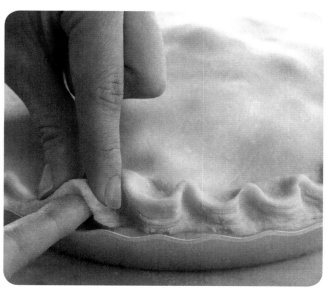

1 Fill the pie tin with the fruit mixture, mounding it up slightly in the centre. Mounding the mixture keeps the fruit away from the pastry edge, so you can seal that easily when the lid goes on. Also, it gives the pie a good shape. The fruit will settle as it softens, so without mounding the pie could end up with a dip in the centre.

2 After you've sealed and trimmed the pie edge, and tapped around it with the back of a knife, crimp (or flute) the edge. Use your thumb and index finger of one hand to pinch the outer edge of the pastry while pushing the index finger of your other hand between them and upwards slightly. Continue all around the pie edge at even intervals.

Pink Rhubarb and Orange Compote

Young, slender, forced pink rhubarb gives this simple dessert a rosy colour and fresh flavour. Being more tender than the seasonal, thicker-stemmed rhubarb, it just needs brief simmering.

 Serves 4    126 calories per serving

INGREDIENTS

- 2 large oranges (preferably unwaxed)
- 60g (2oz) caster sugar
- 4 thin slices peeled, fresh root ginger
- 700g (1lb 9oz) pink (forced) rhubarb, sliced into pieces 6cm (2½in) long
- 2 tbsp redcurrant jelly
- plain yogurt or crème fraîche, to serve

1 Peel 3 strips of rind from one of the oranges using a vegetable peeler and set aside, then squeeze the juice from the fruit. You should have about 5–6 tablespoons of juice. Pour the squeezed juice into a sauté pan or large frying pan, tip in the sugar, and stir over a medium–low heat until it has dissolved. Add the ginger slices and reserved orange rind.

2 Tip the rhubarb into the pan and simmer for 2 minutes. Once the undersides start to soften, gently turn the rhubarb, then cover and simmer for a further 5 minutes or until almost tender but still holding its shape, carefully pressing it down into the liquid. Remove it from the heat and let it sit in the liquid for 15 minutes, with the lid on. (See below, Gently cook the rhubarb, steps 1 and 2.) Discard the ginger and orange rind.

3 Peel the rind and white pith from the remaining orange using a small, sharp knife, then cut out the segments, reserving any juice. Transfer the rhubarb using a slotted spoon to a wide, shallow bowl. Add the orange segments.

4 Pour any reserved orange juice into the pan, then add the redcurrant jelly and stir over a medium heat until it has melted. Increase the heat to medium–high and let the liquid bubble quite rapidly for 2–3 minutes. (See below, Gently cook the rhubarb, step 3.) Cool for 10 minutes, then pour over the fruit and leave to cool completely. Serve with yogurt or crème fraîche.

KEYS TO PERFECTION

Gently cook the rhubarb

1 Rhubarb can quickly collapse and lose its shape when cooking. Use a wide-based pan, so you can spread out the pieces, and don't stir, or they will break up; instead, turn them carefully using a slotted spoon.

2 Test the rhubarb with the tip of a knife. As soon as it's almost (but not quite) tender, remove it from the heat and let it sit for 15 minutes, covered. It will finish cooking in the hot liquid while retaining its shape.

3 Remove the rhubarb and reduce the liquid in the pan to create a light, shiny syrup. If you were to cook the rhubarb and the syrup together at this stage, the rhubarb would overcook and turn mushy.

Plum and Apple Crumble with a Super-crunchy Topping

My shortbread mix makes a buttery crumble topping with extra crunch. If preparation time is short, you can assemble the crumble without poaching the fruit and bake it for 10 minutes longer.

 Serves 6   437 calories per serving

Special equipment
1.7–2 litre (3–3½ pint) baking dish, about 30 x 23cm (12 x 9in) and 5cm (2in) deep

INGREDIENTS

- 750g (1lb 10oz) ripe red plums (see p262, box)
- 2 large cooking apples, about 500g (1lb 2oz) in total (see p262, box)
- 2 cinnamon sticks (see p262, box)
- 75g (2½oz) caster sugar
- fresh cream, to serve

FOR THE TOPPING

- 150g (5½oz) plain flour
- 75g (2½oz) semolina
- 100g (3½oz) cold butter, cut into cubes
- 60g (2oz) caster sugar
- 2 tbsp demerara sugar

1 Preheat the oven to 180°C (fan 160°C/350°F/Gas 4). Halve and stone the plums and quarter, peel, core, and thickly slice the apples. Put the fruit in a large, wide pan with the cinnamon sticks and caster sugar and 2 tablespoons of water. Place the pan over a medium heat and bring the liquid to a simmer, stirring gently. Cover and poach the fruits for about 10 minutes, stirring occasionally. (See p262, Poach the fruits before baking.)

2 Remove the cinnamon sticks. Tip the poached fruit mixture into the baking dish. Spread out the mixture evenly, then set aside.

3 Make the topping: place the flour and semolina in a bowl and add the butter. Rub in the butter until the mixture has the consistency of breadcrumbs. Mix in the caster sugar. Spoon the topping over the fruit in the dish, then sprinkle the demerara sugar evenly over the top. (See p263, Make a crunchy crumble topping.)

4 Bake the crumble for 40 minutes, or until the topping is golden and the fruit juices are bubbling up around the edges. Allow to settle for 5–10 minutes before serving with fresh cream.

KEYS TO PERFECTION (*see overleaf*)
Poach the fruits before baking; Make a crunchy crumble topping

KEYS TO PERFECTION

Poach the fruits before baking

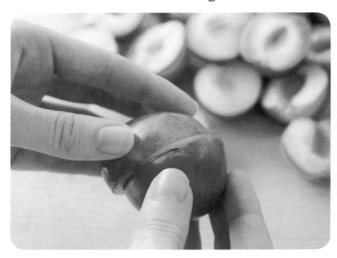

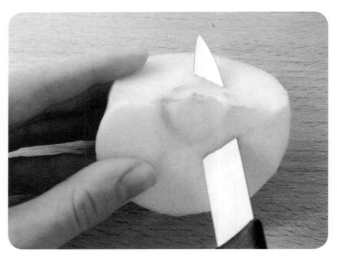

1 Poaching the fruits before covering with the topping makes a particularly juicy crumble. To halve the plums, run a small, sharp knife around the groove in each fruit, then twist the halves in opposite directions until they come apart. Push out the stone with your fingertips, or use the tip of the knife.

2 Cut the apples into quarters lengthways, then peel off the skin and cut out the cores with a small, sharp knife. Cut each quarter into 4 thick slices.

Fruit and flavourings

Victoria plums are my favourite for cooking, because I like their lovely red colour and sweet juiciness. Bramleys are the most famous of English cooking apples, and they're the perfect variety for a crumble. They soften down beautifully during baking and are just tart enough to balance the sweetness of the plums and sugar.

Cinnamon gives the poached fruit a sweet, woody flavour and aroma. Cinnamon sticks vary in size. For this recipe, mine were about 7.5cm (3in) in length, but if yours are the very long ones, simply snap one in half.

3 A large, wide pan is best for poaching, as it enables the fruit to cook evenly without the need to stir too frequently. During poaching, the apples will start to break up. This is as it should be, and it helps to thicken the juices. As soon as the plums have started to soften, remove the pan from the heat.

Make a crunchy crumble topping

1 Stir the flour and semolina together in a large mixing bowl until they're evenly combined. Using half semolina to flour is a simple way to add texture and crunch to the baked crumble topping.

2 Using your fingertips, rub the cubes of butter into the flour and semolina. Do this very gently; never mash it with your fingers. The final texture should resemble breadcrumbs; don't make it too fine, or the topping will be stodgy. Cold butter and cold fingertips are vital to prevent the mixture from becoming sticky. If necessary, hold your hands under cold running water to cool them, then quickly dry them.

3 Stir in the caster sugar until it is evenly distributed. When making crumble, always add the sugar after working in the butter. If you add the sugar beforehand, the mixture will become too sticky to handle.

4 Spoon the crumble topping over the fruit in the dish, so that it forms an even layer, then top with demerara sugar. Make sure that all the fruit is covered, especially around the edges. It's good to have a little juice bubbling up around the edges during baking, but too much juice will overflow and make the topping soggy.

Mary's TOP TIPS

9

Stress-free entertaining

Take the stress out of entertaining by planning your menu carefully and preparing and cooking ahead. If serving a hot main course, provide a first course or pudding that you can make at least a day before. Use your freezer, too.

Vanilla Panna Cotta with Raspberry Coulis

Traditionally, this dessert is set in moulds and turned out, but for a change I have served it in glasses. I use double cream, as I find it gives a smoother texture than single or whipping cream.

 Serves 4    873 calories per serving   **Special equipment**
4 glasses, about 200ml (7fl oz) capacity

INGREDIENTS

- 600ml (1 pint) double cream
- 3 tbsp full-fat milk
- 60g (2oz) caster sugar
- 1 vanilla pod
- 3 small leaves of fine leaf gelatine, each 11 x 6cm (4½ x 2½in) (see p269, box)

FOR THE COULIS

- 175g (6oz) raspberries, plus 140g (5oz) extra to serve
- 1 tbsp icing sugar
- 1 tsp crème de cassis

1 Pour the cream and milk into a medium pan and stir in the caster sugar. Split the vanilla pod and scrape out the seeds into the cream, then drop in the pod. Heat the cream and milk over a low heat, stirring until the sugar has dissolved. Remove from the heat and leave to infuse for 5 minutes. (See p268, Make a rich, creamy vanilla mixture.)

2 Meanwhile, soak the gelatine in cold water for 4–5 minutes, then squeeze well to remove any excess moisture. Stir the leaves into the hot cream until melted, then let the mixture sit for 5 more minutes to cool slightly. Remove the vanilla pod from the cream. (See p268, Use gelatine for setting.)

3 Carefully pour the cream mixture into the glasses. Leave to cool. Cover with cling film and chill for about 6 hours or, preferably, overnight. (See p269, Cover and chill the mixture.)

4 Make the coulis: crush the raspberries with the icing sugar in a bowl, using a fork. Put a nylon sieve over a bowl and press the mixture through the sieve using a wooden spoon, then stir in the crème de cassis. (See p269, Make a vibrant, smooth coulis.)

5 To serve, spoon a little of the coulis on top of each panna cotta so that it covers the surface, then sit 5 or 6 raspberries on top (the number will depend on the size of your glasses). Put the rest of the coulis in a small jug and hand it round separately.

KEYS TO PERFECTION *(see overleaf)*
Make a rich, creamy vanilla mixture; Use gelatine for setting; Cover and chill the mixture; Make a vibrant, smooth coulis

KEYS TO PERFECTION

Make a rich, creamy vanilla mixture

1 There are several ways of adding vanilla flavour to a dish, but for this dessert a vanilla pod gives the most fragrant taste. To extract the tiny black seeds, lay the pod flat on a board. Slice it in half through the centre, sliding a small, sharp knife down the pod's length. Scrape out the seeds, then carefully add them to the cream and milk. Drop the pod in, too, for added flavour.

2 Warm the cream and milk just until tiny bubbles start to appear around the edge of the pan. Boiling too rapidly, or for too long, will reduce the volume in the pan and spoil the flavour. Allowing the cream to just get hot enough to warm up the vanilla, then letting it infuse will bring out the vanilla flavour. Leave the mixture to infuse for 5 minutes before adding the gelatine.

Use gelatine for setting

1 To soften the gelatine leaves so they will melt completely, you need to soak them briefly in cold water before adding them to the hot liquid. Lay the gelatine leaves in a small, shallow dish and pour over enough cold water to cover them. Leave the gelatine in the liquid for 4–5 minutes only, no longer.

2 When the leaves are ready, they will look wrinkled and will be more pliable. Squeeze out excess water before dropping them into the hot cream. Keep stirring, so they melt evenly and completely. This is all done off the heat, as gelatine put into boiling liquid may not set later. Leave for 5 minutes, then remove the vanilla pod.

Cover and chill the mixture

Covering the panna cottas before chilling will protect their subtle vanilla flavour. Make sure they're cold first, then stretch a piece of cling film over the top of each glass. If the desserts are covered while they're still warm, condensation will collect under the cling film and will drop onto the surface of the panna cottas. Chill for 6 hours, or overnight if possible.

Make a vibrant, smooth coulis

1 For the best flavour and colour, choose raspberries that are just ripe – not too soft, not too firm. Put them in a bowl and crush them using a fork. Crushing the raspberries with the icing sugar helps to break them down and release their juices, making them easier to push through the sieve.

2 Press the raspberries firmly through a fine-mesh sieve set over a bowl, using the back of a wooden spoon to extract all their juices and as much pulp as will go through. A nylon sieve is best, as the acid in the fruit can react with metal. The coulis should be a thin, smooth purée. The crème de cassis, added at the end, gives depth of flavour.

Cappuccino Crème Brûlée

The addition of a little coffee makes this rich, creamy dessert rather special. Measure the coffee carefully, as the flavour should be subtle. Any shape of ramekin will set these brûlées off perfectly.

 Serves 6

 447 calories per serving

Special equipment
Six 150ml (5fl oz) ramekins; cook's mini-blowtorch (see p273, box)

INGREDIENTS

- butter, for greasing
- 4 large egg yolks
- 45g (1½oz) caster sugar
- ½ tsp vanilla extract
- 300ml (10fl oz) single cream
- 300ml (10fl oz) double cream
- 2½ tsp instant coffee granules
- about 50g (1¾oz) demerara sugar

1 Preheat the oven to 160°C (fan 140°C/325°F/Gas 3). Lightly grease the ramekins with butter. Break the egg yolks into a large bowl, tip in the caster sugar and vanilla, and beat with a wire whisk to combine.

2 Put both the creams in a medium pan and heat until scalding. Remove from the heat and stir in the coffee until it dissolves, then leave the mixture to cool slightly for about 2 minutes. Pour the cream mixture into the egg yolk mixture and stir thoroughly to combine. Strain the custard and pour it into the prepared ramekins. (See p272, Make a silky-smooth custard.)

3 Stand the ramekins in a roasting tin and pour hot water into the tin until it comes halfway up the sides of the ramekins. Bake for 25–30 minutes, then remove the ramekins from the roasting tin and leave to cool. Cover and chill in the fridge overnight (or up to 2 days ahead). (See p272, Gently cook and chill the custards.)

4 Sprinkle the demerara sugar evenly over the tops of the custards. Use the blowtorch to caramelize the sugar, being careful not to burn it. (See p273, Make a crunchy brûlée topping.) Serve as soon as the caramel has cooled and become brittle.

KEYS TO PERFECTION (see overleaf)
Make a silky-smooth custard; Gently cook and chill the custards; Make a crunchy brûlée topping

KEYS TO PERFECTION

Make a silky-smooth custard

1 When heating the cream, make sure you take it off the heat just before it comes to the boil, so at the point when you can see small bubbles appearing around the edge of the pan. Add the slightly cooled cream and coffee mixture to the egg yolks in a steady stream, beating all the time with a wire whisk.

2 For an ultra-smooth texture, strain the custard into a heatproof jug before carefully pouring it into the greased ramekins, distributing the mixture equally.

Gently cook and chill the custards

1 Pour enough hot water into the roasting tin so it comes halfway up the sides of the dishes. The water bath ensures that the egg mixture cooks gently and is less likely to curdle.

2 The custards should have a slight wobble when removed from the oven. If overcooked, they will become too firm and air bubbles will develop, which will spoil the texture. Cool the custards completely before covering and putting in the fridge. If still warm when covered, the tops will get speckled with drops of condensation.

Make a crunchy brûlée topping

1 Sprinkle demerara sugar over the custards, to a thickness of about 3mm (⅛ inch). Make sure that you cover the custard evenly, using the back of a teaspoon to pat the sugar down over the surface. I prefer to use demerara sugar for the topping, as I find that it gives a much tastier, crunchier caramel topping than white sugar.

2 Light the blowtorch and, holding it a few inches above the sugar, keep it moving continuously in a circular motion. As soon as the sugar melts and turns golden brown in one area, move it to another immediately. Do not leave the blowtorch over one particular area for too long, or the sugar will burn.

How to make the topping using a grill

It's best to use a blowtorch to caramelize the sugar, as grilling is slightly slower and can start to overcook the softly set custard. However, if you don't have a blowtorch, you can use a preheated, very hot grill instead. Put the heatproof ramekins as close to the grill as possible and grill for about 5 minutes. After grilling, chill the brûlées for 2–3 hours before serving, so the caramel can soften slightly: this makes it easier to crack when eating (it is not necessary if you've used a blowtorch).

3 The melted sugar cools quite quickly and becomes brittle. Serve soon after being caramelized. If left to stand for too long after using the blowtorch, the caramel begins to dissolve to the point where it will start to turn to liquid. The brûlée can be cracked open with a teaspoon.

Lemon and Limoncello Posset

The Italian liqueur, limoncello, brings a unique taste and added zest to a wonderfully simple, traditional British pudding. Serve with thin pieces of shortbread or amaretti biscuits.

 Serves 4  645 calories per serving 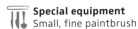 **Special equipment**
Small, fine paintbrush

INGREDIENTS

- 400ml (14fl oz) double cream
- 100g (3½oz) caster sugar, plus extra for frosting
- finely grated rind of ½ lemon
- 4 tbsp lemon juice
- 3 tbsp limoncello
- 4–8 fresh mint leaves
- egg white, for brushing
- 4 tsp full-fat crème fraîche

1 Pour the cream into a medium pan and add the sugar and lemon rind. Heat slowly over a low heat, stirring, until the sugar has dissolved completely. Increase the heat slightly and simmer gently for 3 minutes, stirring occasionally. Remove the pan from the heat and stir in the lemon juice and limoncello. Strain into a jug. (See below, Super-smooth mixture.)

2 Pour the mixture into 4 small glasses or coffee cups and leave to cool completely. Cover and chill for a few hours, or overnight, until set.

3 Meanwhile, sugar-frost the mint leaves. Lightly beat the egg white with a fork until very slightly foamy, then brush it over both sides of the leaves (see below, Crisp, frosted leaves). Sprinkle with caster sugar, gently shaking off any excess. Lay the leaves on a board and set aside for at least 1 hour or until dry and crisp.

4 To decorate and serve each chilled posset, scoop some crème fraîche into a teaspoon. Gently scrape the bowl of a second teaspoon inside the bowl of the first, pressing as you go, so you scoop the contents from the first spoon to the second. Transfer the crème fraîche back to the first spoon in the same way. Repeat, scooping back and forth until you have a smooth oval "quenelle" shape. Place it on top of a posset and top with 1 or 2 frosted mint leaves.

KEYS TO PERFECTION

Super-smooth mixture

1 Keep the heat low at first, so the sugar dissolves rather than crystallizes, and stir; when you no longer hear the sugar "crunch" on the bottom of the pan, increase the heat.

2 For a really smooth, silky texture, pour the mixture through a fine-mesh sieve into a measuring jug. This will make it easier to pour into the serving glasses or cups.

Crisp, frosted leaves

Make sure the mint leaves are dry before you start and use a clean, fine paintbrush to apply the egg white. Use the egg white sparingly; if too heavily coated, the leaves will droop.

Chocolate and Irish Cream Roulade

This is one of my all-time favourite, make-ahead party desserts. It freezes beautifully (un-iced), then you simply thaw it in the fridge overnight and drizzle over the icing just before serving.

 Serves 8  534 calories per serving

Special equipment
Swiss roll tin, 30 x 23cm (12 x 9in) and 2cm (¾in) deep; small piping bag (optional)

INGREDIENTS

- butter, for greasing
- 175g (6oz) plain dark chocolate (about 50% cocoa solids)
- 6 large eggs, separated
- 175g (6oz) caster sugar
- 2 tbsp cocoa powder
- 300ml (10fl oz) double cream
- 4 tbsp Baileys Irish Cream liqueur
- icing sugar, sifted, for dusting

FOR THE ICING
- 50g (1¾oz) icing sugar, sifted
- 2 tsp double cream
- 2–3 tsp Baileys Irish Cream liqueur

KEYS TO PERFECTION (see overleaf)
Make a light cake; Roll a neat roulade

1 Preheat the oven to 180°C (fan 160°C/350°F/Gas 4). Lightly grease the Swiss roll tin with butter and line with baking parchment. It helps to make a small diagonal snip in each corner of the baking parchment, about 3cm (1¼in) long, so the paper fits snugly into the corners of the tin.

2 Break the chocolate into pieces and place in a heatproof bowl set over a pan of gently simmering water. The base of the bowl must not touch the water. Leave until just melted, then remove from the heat, stir, and leave the chocolate to cool slightly (see p278, Make a light cake, step 1).

3 Meanwhile, place the egg whites in a large bowl and whisk using an electric hand whisk on high speed until fluffy and stiff, but not dry.

4 Tip the caster sugar and egg yolks into another large bowl and whisk on high speed until light, thick, and creamy, for about 1½ minutes. Pour in the cooled chocolate and stir until blended. Add two large spoonfuls of the egg whites to the chocolate mixture and mix gently, then fold in the remaining egg whites. Sift the cocoa and fold it into the mixture. Pour the mixture into the prepared tin and level the surface (see p278, Make a light cake, step 2).

5 Bake for 20–25 minutes or until the cake is well risen and firm on top. Remove the cake from the oven and set aside, leaving it in its tin, until cold (expect it to dip and crack a little).

6 Place the cream in a bowl with the Baileys Irish Cream liqueur and whip until thick enough to just hold its shape. If insufficiently whipped it will be too runny to spread; if over-whipped, it will become too thick to spread evenly.

7 Lightly dust a large piece of baking parchment with icing sugar. Turn the cake out onto the parchment and carefully peel off the lining paper. Spread the surface of the cake with the whipped cream, leaving a bare rim of about 2cm (¾in) all the way around the edges. With one of the short ends near you, make a score mark 2cm (¾in) in from this edge, being careful not to cut right through. Starting at this point, tightly roll up the roulade. Transfer the roulade to a serving platter or board. (See pp278–79, Roll a neat roulade.)

8 Make the icing: put the icing sugar in a bowl, then mix in the cream and enough Baileys Irish Cream liqueur to give a smooth consistency. Drizzle the icing over the top of the roulade, or pipe it using the small piping bag.

KEYS TO PERFECTION

Make a light cake

1 As soon as the chocolate has melted, take the pan off the heat so the chocolate doesn't overheat, or it will become too stiff; it needs to be a pourable consistency. Stir, lift the bowl off the pan, and leave the chocolate to cool until it feels tepid. If the chocolate is too hot when stirred into the egg yolks, it will start to cook them.

2 Pour the cake mixture into the buttered and lined Swiss roll tin. The mixture should be light and airy now that the egg whites have been added. Ease it into the corners and smooth the surface level using a spatula. Do this very gently, so that you don't squash out the air you have just whisked in.

Roll a neat roulade

1 Leave the roulade cake to cool completely before you tip it out of the tin. Run a small palette knife around the inside of the baking parchment in the tin to loosen the cake, so you can turn it out easily without it breaking.

2 Gently turn the cake out onto a large sheet of baking parchment that has been lightly dusted with icing sugar. Carefully loosen the parchment that surrounds the cake and peel it off, making sure you don't take the cake with it.

Roll a neat roulade (continued)

3 Using a palette knife, spread the cream evenly over the roulade, so you will get a uniform spiral of cream in each slice. Rather than spread the cream right up to the edges, leave a gap of about 2cm (¾in) all round, or the cream will start to ooze out as you start rolling.

4 Use a sharp knife to make a score mark 2cm (¾in) in from a short edge, and cut about halfway through the cake on the score line. This will be a useful starting point when you start rolling and will give you a tighter, neater roulade.

5 Roll the cut edge over tightly to start with, using the baking parchment to help keep it all tight by gently pulling it up and over the roll. Don't worry if the cake cracks – that is quite normal and will be part of the roulade's charm.

6 Keep rolling, again using the parchment to help by pulling it up and over as you roll. After rolling, ensure the join is underneath, as this will keep the roll secure, then transfer the roulade to a serving platter using a large, wide spatula or two fish slices.

Raspberry Crush Mini Meringues

These are perfect little mouthfuls for a dessert treat. You can make the mini meringues up to two weeks ahead, store them in an airtight tin, and fill them just before serving.

 Makes about 20 filled meringues

 74 calories per serving

Special equipment
Large piping bag; 10mm (½in) plain piping nozzle

INGREDIENTS

- 3 large egg whites
- 175g (6oz) caster sugar (preferably golden)

FOR THE FILLING

- 20 raspberries, about 115g (4oz) in total
- about 10 tsp lemon curd
- about 10 tbsp full-fat crème fraîche

1 Preheat the oven to 130°C (fan 110°C/250°F/Gas ½). Cut out 2 pieces of baking parchment to fit 2 large baking sheets. Draw about 20 circles, approximately 4.5cm (1¾in) diameter, on each sheet of parchment. (See p282, Pipe even rounds, step 1.)

2 Put the egg whites in a large bowl and whisk using an electric hand whisk on full speed until stiff and resembling a cloud. Start to add the sugar a tablespoon at a time, whisking well between each addition, until it has all been mixed in. The finished meringue mixture should look stiff and glossy. (See p282, Make a smooth, glossy meringue mixture.)

3 Dab a small bit of the meringue mixture on each corner of the baking sheets and gently press the parchment on top, face down (so the pencil marks are underneath). Fit the piping bag with the piping nozzle. Spoon the rest of the meringue mixture into the bag (pipe half at a time if your bag is not big enough for all the mixture). Pipe about 40 small meringues onto the lined baking sheets. (See p282–83, Pipe even rounds, steps 2–4.)

4 Bake for 1 hour. Turn the oven off, open the oven door so it is slightly ajar, and leave the meringues in the oven until they are completely cold, for about another 1 hour. (See p283, Bake crispy meringues.)

5 To fill each pair of meringues, crush a raspberry on a small plate using a fork. Spread one flat side of a meringue with about ½ teaspoon of the lemon curd. Carefully spoon the crushed raspberry over the curd. Spread the flat side of another meringue with about ½ tablespoon of crème fraîche and sandwich the two together. (See p283, Make neat meringue sandwiches.) Repeat with the remaining meringues and filling. Do this no more than about 1 hour before serving, or the meringues will go soft.

KEYS TO PERFECTION (*see overleaf*)
Make a smooth, glossy meringue mixture; Pipe even rounds; Bake crispy meringues; Make neat meringue sandwiches

KEYS TO PERFECTION

Make a smooth, glossy meringue mixture

1 Take the eggs out of the fridge about 30 minutes before you need them, as you'll get more volume from the whites if they're at room temperature. Make sure you separate the eggs really carefully to prevent any yolk from mixing with the whites. Whisk the egg whites in a large, clean bowl, using the electric hand whisk on full speed. The mixture will become stiff and create soft peaks if the beater is lifted.

2 Immediately start to whisk in the sugar, 1 tablespoon at a time. Whisk well between each addition, so the sugar is incorporated fully, otherwise the meringue may collapse during baking, or "weep" beads of sugar. When all the sugar has been added, the meringue will look smoother and very glossy and will stand in taller, stiffer peaks. Pipe the mixture straightaway, or the mixture will start to deflate.

Pipe even rounds

1 To ensure the meringues are of an equal size when piped, draw about 40 circles in total, about 4.5cm (1¾in) in diameter and 2–2.5cm (¾–1in) apart, in pencil on the sheets of baking parchment. Use a round shape as a guide, such as a pastry cutter or small pot. Do this before you make the meringue mixture, or it may deflate.

2 Before piping, dab a little of the raw meringue mixture in the corners of the baking sheets, then press the baking parchment onto them. Lay the parchment face down, so the pencilled circles are underneath but still visible. The parchment will stick to the baking sheets and be kept firmly in place for piping onto.

Pipe even rounds (continued)

3 To fill the piping bag more easily, sit it in a measuring jug and fold the ends of the bag over the top of the jug. Spoon in the meringue, without overfilling the bag. Lay the bag on the worktop, and tap it down very gently with the side of your hand to remove any air bubbles. Twist the end of the bag to seal.

4 Hold the bag vertically, about 2.5cm (1in) above the baking sheet, and pipe rounds just inside the pencil lines, gently squeezing the mixture out into a smooth round with an even pressure as you lift the bag up. To finish, lightly push the nozzle down into the meringues, then quickly lift it off to give a small peak.

Bake crispy meringues

Make neat meringue sandwiches

It's important to allow the meringues long enough in the oven, so they can cook to the perfect texture. When done, they should be pale and crisp if tapped with a finger. They will also come away easily and cleanly from the baking parchment. If they're still sticking, keep them in the oven a bit longer. Leaving them in the turned-off oven with the door slightly ajar enables them to dry out without overcooking.

When spreading the lemon curd, crushed raspberry, and crème fraîche on each meringue, go almost but not right to the edge, otherwise the mixture will ooze out when you sandwich the meringues together. It's important to use full-fat crème fraîche rather than a low-fat variety, as full-fat will retain its thick, creamy consistency better after the meringues have been filled.

American-style Cheesecake with Blueberry Topping

You can't beat a simple, rich cheesecake with a crumb base and a classic soured cream topping. To make this one extra special, I've included a lightly cooked, fresh blueberry sauce for spooning over.

 Serves 8   705 calories per serving

Special equipment
Round springform tin or loose-bottomed cake tin, 20cm (8in) diameter and 5.5cm (2¼in) deep

INGREDIENTS

- 700g (1lb 9oz) full-fat cream cheese (room temperature)
- 125g (4½oz) caster sugar
- 1 tbsp plain flour
- 1 tsp vanilla extract
- 1 tsp finely grated lemon rind
- 1 tsp lemon juice
- 2 large eggs
- 100ml (3½fl oz) full-fat soured cream

FOR THE BASE

- 60g (2oz) butter, plus extra for greasing
- 8 digestive biscuits, about 115–125g (4–4½oz), broken into large pieces

FOR THE TOPPING

- 50g (1¾oz) caster sugar, plus 1 tsp to serve
- 300g (10oz) blueberries
- 100ml (3½fl oz) full-fat soured cream

KEYS TO PERFECTION *(see overleaf)*
Make a crispy base; Make a smooth, creamy filling; Chill the baked cheesecake; Make a syrupy blueberry topping

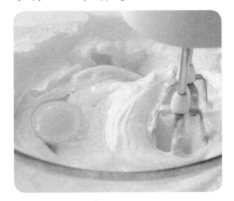

1 Preheat the oven to 160°C (fan 140°C/325°F/Gas 3). Lightly grease the springform or cake tin with butter. Line the bottom with baking parchment.

2 Make the base: put the biscuits in a plastic food bag, seal the bag, and crush the biscuits with a rolling pin. Melt the butter in a medium pan. Remove from the heat and stir in the crumbs. Tip the buttery crumbs into the tin and press the mixture evenly over the bottom. Sit the tin on a baking sheet and set aside. (See p286, Make a crispy base.)

3 Make the filling: put the cream cheese in a large bowl and beat using an electric hand whisk on low speed until creamy. Gradually beat in the sugar, then the flour. Next, beat in the vanilla and lemon rind and juice, then the eggs, one at a time. Briefly beat in the soured cream. Pour the filling over the base. (See p286, Make a smooth, creamy filling.)

4 Bake the cheesecake for 40 minutes, then turn off the oven and leave the tin in the oven (with the door closed) for 2 hours. Remove from the oven, then loosen the cheesecake from the side of the tin using a palette knife. When completely cold, chill the cheesecake in its tin for at least 6 hours, preferably overnight. (See p287, Chill the baked cheesecake.)

5 Make the topping: put the sugar in a medium, heavy-based pan with 1 tablespoon of water. Heat over a low heat for several minutes until the sugar has dissolved. Increase the heat and let it bubble for less than a minute, without stirring, until syrupy and a very pale gold colour. Remove the pan from the heat and stir in half the blueberries, then return to the heat and let the berries cook briefly in the syrup for 1–1½ minutes to release their juices. Take the pan off the heat and stir in the rest of the blueberries. Leave to cool. (See p287, Make a syrupy blueberry topping.)

6 To serve, mix the teaspoon of sugar into the soured cream. Remove the cheesecake from the tin, then slide it onto a serving plate, removing the lining paper as you do. Spread the soured cream smoothly over the top, as near to the edge as you can. Chill for 20–30 minutes. Use a large, sharp knife to slice, then place a spoonful of the blueberries on top of each slice and hand round the rest separately.

KEYS TO PERFECTION

Make a crispy base

1 Lay the bag of digestive biscuits on a flat work surface and pound them with a rolling pin, or run a rolling pin over the biscuits until crushed – or a combination of both. You're aiming for fine crumbs, as this will give the cheesecake base a better texture than if it consisted of large lumps, and makes the cheesecake easier to slice.

2 After combining the crumbs with melted butter, press them down firmly onto the bottom of the tin using the back of a metal spoon, or use your fingers to smooth and pat it down – whichever you find easiest. Try to make the crust the same thickness all over, so you have a firm, even base for the filling.

Make a smooth, creamy filling

1 Take the cream cheese out of the fridge at least 2 hours before making the cheesecake, so you can mix it quickly and smoothly without over-beating. Use an electric hand whisk on a low speed throughout the mixing. Beat the ingredients together to remove lumps, but be careful not to over-beat, or you'll mix in too much air and create bubbles in the mixture.

2 After you've filled the tin with the mixture, jiggle it gently to settle the filling evenly, and then burst any air bubbles that rise to the surface with the back of a teaspoon.

Chill the baked cheesecake

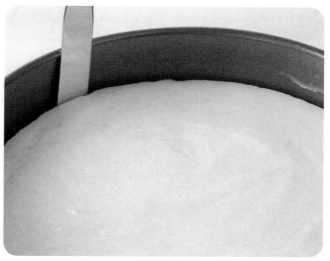

1 After baking, the cheesecake will appear to be very soft and wobbly in the centre and slightly puffy at the side. So it doesn't overcook, finish the cooking slowly by leaving it in the switched-off oven. As the cheesecake cools, a small crack or two may appear on the surface, but don't worry if this happens – it will be covered with the soured cream topping later.

2 Loosen the cheesecake from the tin by running a small palette knife around the inside of the tin. Releasing the side of the cheesecake from the tin (but keeping it in its tin while it continues to cool) makes it easier to remove and helps to stop it cracking across the middle. When completely cool, put the cheesecake in the fridge, in its tin, to chill. This improves the texture.

Make a syrupy blueberry topping

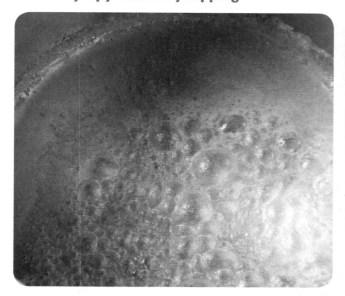

1 When making the syrupy base for the fruit topping, keep the heat low to start with, or the sugar will crystallize (you don't want it to bubble at this stage). Once the sugar has dissolved, increase the heat to medium–high, so the mixture can bubble and become syrupy; don't stir. It will take 35–40 seconds to reach a syrupy consistency; if you cook it for too long, the syrup will turn to caramel.

2 As soon as the bubbles start to turn a very pale golden colour, remove the pan from the heat and stir in half the blueberries. The syrup may stiffen, but don't worry – it will loosen again when it is reheated. Return the pan to the hob and cook gently, stirring, until the blueberries are just starting to burst and release their juices. Take the pan off the heat again and stir in the remaining blueberries.

Blackberry and Elderflower Sorbet

For a light end to a meal, a sorbet is ideal, and it keeps for up to a month in the freezer. Fresh blackberries give an intense flavour and colour, and the elderflower adds a refreshing note.

 Serves 4

 237 calories per serving

Special equipment
2 freezerproof containers: large and shallow, about 2.8 litres (5 pints) capacity; smaller and deeper, 1–1.2 litres (1¾–2 pints) capacity

INGREDIENTS
- 175g (6oz) granulated sugar
- 600g (1lb 5oz) blackberries, plus a few extra to serve
- 3 tbsp elderflower cordial
- 1 tbsp lemon juice

1 Put the sugar and 300ml (10fl oz) of water into a large pan and heat gently over a low heat until the sugar dissolves, stirring occasionally with a wooden spoon. Increase the heat and bring to the boil. Boil fairly rapidly for 2 minutes over a medium heat.

2 Add the blackberries, and when the liquid gently bubbles reduce the heat and simmer for about 2 minutes to soften. Remove from the heat and leave to cool. Pour the mixture into a food processor and process to a thin purée. Sieve the mixture into a bowl. (See below, Make a smooth, fruity mixture.)

3 Stir in the elderflower cordial and strain the lemon juice into the bowl. Leave until completely cold. (The sorbet mixture can be made up to a day ahead and kept covered in the fridge.)

4 Pour the mixture into the large container, cover, and freeze for 2–3 hours. Spoon the partially frozen mixture into a food processor and process. Transfer the puréed mixture into the smaller container, cover, and freeze for about 8 hours or overnight. (See below, Check the consistency.)

5 About 30 minutes before serving, transfer the sorbet to the fridge to soften slightly. Serve in scoops topped with a few extra blackberries.

KEYS TO PERFECTION

Make a smooth, fruity mixture

Check the consistency

1 As soon as the blackberries have softened slightly, take the pan off the heat. They need to be soft enough to purée, but not so soft that they break up and start to lose their colour and flavour.

2 Sieving the base will give you a super-smooth texture. Place a small, fine-mesh sieve (ideally nylon) over a bowl and press the fruit through with the back of a wooden spoon. Discard the pips and pulp left in the sieve.

After the first freeze, the sorbet should be turning mushy. Processing the mixture will break down the ice crystals and the sorbet will be smooth, thick, and slushy. After the final freeze, it will be firm.

Clotted Cream and Strawberry Ripple Ice Cream

This luxurious ice cream, with ripples of fresh strawberry purée running through it, can be made easily without a machine. Both the ice cream and extra sauce can be frozen for up to a month.

 Serves 4   653 calories per serving    **Special equipment**
Freezerproof container, about 1–1.2 litres (1¾–2 pints) capacity

INGREDIENTS

- 4 large egg yolks
- 115g (4oz) caster sugar
- 300ml (10fl oz) full-fat milk
- 200ml (7fl oz) double cream
- 100g (3½oz) clotted cream
- 1 tsp vanilla extract
- 225g (8oz) strawberries, hulled and chopped
- 2 tbsp strawberry or raspberry jam or conserve

1 Make a rich custard: put the egg yolks and sugar in a large heatproof bowl and whisk using a balloon whisk until thick, light, and fluffy, and the mixture leaves a trail when the whisk is lifted. Gently warm the milk in a medium pan over a low heat until hand-hot, then gradually whisk the milk into the egg mixture.

2 Pour the mixture back into the pan (rinse it out first so the mixture doesn't burn) and heat gently over a low to medium–low heat, whisking all the time, until the mixture is thick enough to coat the back of a spoon (this can take about 10 minutes). Do not boil, or the eggs will curdle.

3 Pour the custard into a heatproof bowl and let it cool slightly, then cover the surface of the custard with cling film (to prevent a skin from forming). Refrigerate for several hours until completely cold, preferably overnight.

4 Pour the double cream into a large bowl and lightly whisk using a wire whisk. Stir 2 tablespoons of the custard into the clotted cream, to loosen. Slowly stir the chilled custard into the double cream, then the clotted cream/ custard mix and the vanilla extract. Pour into the freezerproof container and freeze for about 3 hours. (See p292, Make a smooth, creamy base.)

5 Meanwhile, put the strawberries in a large bowl with the jam and blend using a hand-held blender to a smooth purée. Press through a fine sieve into a bowl and chill until needed. (See p293, Add the fruity ripples, step 1.)

6 Once the ice cream is starting to freeze around the edges of the container, stir it well. Freeze again for a further 2–3 hours or until more thickly frozen. Stir, then transfer the ice cream to a food processor and process briefly. Put the ice cream back in the freezerproof container and freeze for 1–2 hours more. (See pp292–93, Freeze the ice cream.)

7 Stir the ice cream, then pour in just under half the purée (a little at a time) and gently swirl it into the ice cream so it ripples through rather than being completely mixed in (see p293, Add the fruity ripples, step 2.)

8 Freeze for a further 3 hours or until firm enough to scoop. If the ice cream becomes quite firm (that is, if it has been frozen for several days), take it out of the freezer and bring to room temperature for 10 minutes before serving, to make scooping easier. Serve with the rest of the sauce.

KEYS TO PERFECTION (see overleaf)
Make a smooth, creamy base; Freeze the ice cream; Add the fruity ripples

KEYS TO PERFECTION

Make a smooth, creamy base

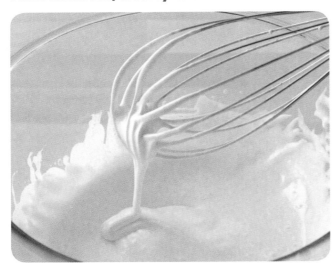

1 As this recipe is made by hand rather than in an ice-cream maker, I like to lightly whisk the double cream to create extra lightness. You don't want to whisk too stiffly, just briefly until it's light and floppy and holds a soft shape. Stir the chilled custard into the cream, then the clotted cream and vanilla. As the clotted cream is quite thick, it will blend in more easily if you mix a little of the custard into it first.

2 Pour the custard and cream mixture into a rigid freezerproof container with a capacity of about 1–1.2 litres (1¾–2 pints). You want the mixture to almost fill the container, leaving about 5mm (¼in) for expansion during freezing. If there is too much space between the lid and the surface of the ice cream, ice crystals will start to form.

Freeze the ice cream

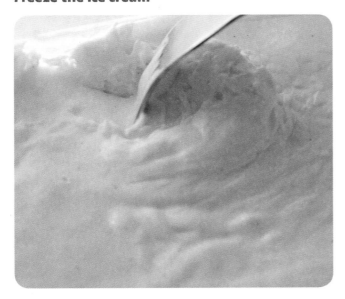

1 When the ice cream starts to freeze around the edges of the container, use a fork to scrape the partly frozen crystals from the edge and mix them in with the softer ice cream in the middle. Stir until the mixture is well blended and smooth.

2 When making ice cream by hand, I've found that processing it in a food processor after it has been in the freezer for a few hours gives it a really good texture. Stir the ice cream a couple of times before processing, and don't process it for long – just enough to make it smooth and so more of the ice crystals are broken down.

Freeze the ice cream (continued)

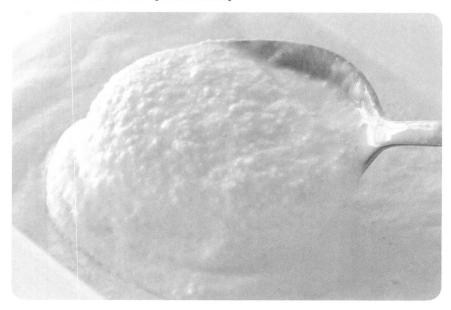

Using an ice-cream maker

If you prefer to use an ice-cream maker instead of making the ice cream by hand, there is no need to whisk the double cream. Simply stir it into the chilled custard with the clotted cream and vanilla. Once the ice cream has been churned, transfer it to a freezerproof container and ripple the sauce through as described below, before returning it to the freezer to finish freezing.

3 Since putting the ice cream in the processor softens it, return it to its container and freeze for a further hour or two, until it's thick enough to ripple the strawberry sauce through. The ice cream is ready to be rippled once it feels quite thick when stirred, but not too solidly frozen.

Add the fruity ripples

1 The strawberries must be dry before you purée them, or the sauce will be too runny. Use a hand-held blender, as this works best for a small amount. I've sweetened with jam rather than sugar, to deepen the colour and intensify the fruity flavour. After puréeing, press through a nylon sieve, using the back of a wooden spoon to extract as much of the pulp as you can; this will help thicken the sauce.

2 Use just under half the sauce for the ripples (the rest can be served with the ice cream), pouring or spooning it over the top in batches, then stirring gently through with a dessert spoon (in between pourings) to create swirls of sauce all through the ice cream. If you add too much too quickly and stir it in too vigorously, you will lose the effect of the ripples.

Cakes, Small Bakes, and Bread

Cheese and Poppy Seed Straws

These buttery, savoury biscuits are always popular. They're best eaten within a day or two, while still crisp, but if you keep any for longer they can be revived in a medium oven for 3–4 minutes.

 Makes 24    60 calories per serving

INGREDIENTS

- 115g (4oz) plain flour, plus extra for dusting
- 85g (3oz) butter (room temperature), cut into small pieces
- 50g (1¾oz) mature Cheddar cheese, finely grated
- 30g (1oz) Parmesan cheese, finely grated
- ¼ tsp paprika
- 1½ tsp poppy seeds
- 1 large egg yolk

1 Put the flour and butter in a large bowl and rub them together lightly with your fingertips until the mixture resembles breadcrumbs. Stir in the Cheddar, 1 tablespoon of the Parmesan, the paprika, and the poppy seeds.

2 Stir the egg yolk into the dry ingredients using a round-bladed knife. Work everything together with your hands to form a dough, but don't over-handle. Wrap the dough in cling film and chill for 10–15 minutes.

3 Meanwhile, preheat the oven to 190°C (fan 170°C/375°F/Gas 5). Line a large baking sheet with baking parchment.

4 Roll out the dough on a lightly floured surface to make a rectangle about 20 x 18cm (8 x 7in) and 5mm (¼in) thick. Scatter over the remaining Parmesan. Lay a piece of cling film over and press the cheese into the dough using a rolling pin. (See below, Shape neat straws, steps 1 and 2.)

5 Cut the dough rectangle in half across, then cut each half lengthways into 12 strips. Carefully lay the strips on the lined baking sheet. (See below, Shape neat straws, step 3.)

6 Bake for about 15 minutes or until golden. Remove and transfer the straws to a wire rack to cool completely.

KEYS TO PERFECTION

Shape neat straws

1 Roll out the chilled dough. Keep the sides of the rectangle as straight as you can as you roll, so you can get as many neat straws as possible. Lightly trim the edges after rolling, if necessary.

2 Scatter Parmesan over the dough. Cover with cling film to prevent sticking, then press and roll gently so the cheese is pressed in; don't let the rectangle get any bigger or the dough will be too thin. Remove the cling film.

3 Use a sharp knife to cut the dough into neat strips, then use a long palette knife to transfer the strips to the lined baking sheet. The parchment makes it easier to remove the baked straws without breaking them.

Raspberry and Apple Muffins

Fruity and lightly spiced, these muffins make a tempting mid-morning snack and go surprisingly well with cheese at lunchtime. They're best eaten fresh, but will keep for up to two days.

 Makes 12    236 calories per serving    **Special equipment**
12-hole muffin tin; 12 paper muffin cases

INGREDIENTS

- 85g (3oz) butter
- 250g (9oz) self-raising flour
- 1 tsp baking powder
- 45g (1½oz) ground almonds
- 1½ tsp ground cinnamon
- 115g (4oz) caster sugar
- 2 large eggs
- 250g (9oz) plain, full-fat yogurt
- 1 tbsp full-fat or semi-skimmed milk
- 175g (6oz) fresh raspberries
- 1 eating apple, such as Cox's, about 150g (5½oz), peeled and chopped into 1cm (½in) pieces

FOR THE GLAZE

- 2 tbsp caster sugar
- 1 tbsp orange juice

1 Preheat the oven to 200°C (fan 180°C/400°F/Gas 6). Line each hollow of the muffin tin with a paper muffin case. Warm the butter in a small pan over a low heat until it melts, then set aside to cool.

2 Tip the flour, baking powder, ground almonds, cinnamon, and sugar into a large bowl and stir to combine. In a medium bowl beat the eggs and stir in the yogurt, milk, and cooled melted butter. Stir this mixture into the flour mixture, then add the raspberries and apple and stir briefly. (See below, Make a light mixture.)

3 Spoon the mixture into the muffin cases. Bake for about 25 minutes or until well risen and firm to the touch.

4 Meanwhile, make the glaze: warm the sugar and orange juice in a small pan over a low heat, just until the sugar has dissolved, then increase the heat and let the mixture bubble for about 30 seconds so it turns a bit syrupy – not too long, or it will get too sticky.

5 Remove the muffins from the oven. Leave them in their tin for 1–2 minutes, then transfer them to a wire rack. While they are still warm, brush the top of each muffin with the glaze. Leave to cool.

KEYS TO PERFECTION

Make a light mixture

1 Stir the wet ingredients into the dry ones quickly, gently, and briefly; over-mixing will result in tough muffins. Stop stirring as soon as they are combined. The mixture should feel light and soft.

2 Tip in the fruit and stir 3 or 4 times only. If you add the raspberries too soon, or keep stirring after they've been added, they will start to break down, which will make the mixture too wet.

Coffee and Walnut Butterfly Cakes

The combination of coffee and walnut is always popular. For these small cakes I've used the all-in-one method, which really simplifies cake-making and, I think, makes it much more foolproof.

 Makes 12

 413 calories per serving

 Special equipment
12-hole shallow bun tin; 12 paper bun cases; large piping bag; medium star (size 8) nozzle

INGREDIENTS

- 2 tsp instant coffee granules
- 115g (4oz) butter (room temperature) or baking spread (at least 70% fat)
- 115g (4oz) caster sugar
- 115g (4oz) self-raising flour
- 1 tsp baking powder
- 2 large eggs
- 45g (1½oz) walnut halves, finely chopped

FOR THE ICING

- 2 tsp instant coffee granules
- 350g (12oz) icing sugar, plus extra for dusting
- 175g (6oz) butter (room temperature)
- 6 walnut halves, halved lengthways

1 Preheat the oven to 180°C (fan 160°C/350°F/Gas 4). Line each hollow of the bun tin with a paper case. Stir the coffee with 2 teaspoons of hot water in a small bowl until the granules have dissolved. Set aside to cool.

2 Place the butter, caster sugar, flour, and baking powder in a large bowl. Add the eggs and the cooled coffee mixture and beat well using an electric hand whisk or a wooden spoon until smooth. Stir in the walnuts. Divide the mixture equally among the paper bun cases. (See p302, Light, all-in-one mixture.) Bake for 15–20 minutes or until well risen and firm on top. Remove the cakes from the tin and leave to cool on a wire rack.

3 Make the icing: stir the coffee and 2 teaspoons of hot water in a small bowl until the granules have dissolved, then leave to cool. Sift the icing sugar into a large bowl, add the butter and the coffee mixture, and beat using an electric hand whisk or a wooden spoon until smooth and well blended (see p303, Smooth, swirled icing, step 1).

4 Cut a circle out of the top of each cake and cut each circle in half. Set aside. Spoon the icing into the piping bag fitted with the nozzle, and pipe the icing into the centre of each cake. (See p303, Smooth, swirled icing, steps 2–4.)

5 Place the reserved semi-circles on top of each cake to represent butterfly wings. Sit a walnut quarter between the "wings" and dust with icing sugar.

KEYS TO PERFECTION (*see overleaf*)
Light, all-in-one mixture; Smooth, swirled icing

KEYS TO PERFECTION

Light, all-in-one mixture

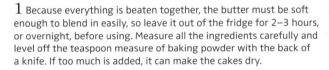

1 Because everything is beaten together, the butter must be soft enough to blend in easily, so leave it out of the fridge for 2–3 hours, or overnight, before using. Measure all the ingredients carefully and level off the teaspoon measure of baking powder with the back of a knife. If too much is added, it can make the cakes dry.

2 After adding the eggs and coffee mixture, beat using an electric hand whisk. Set it at a slow speed initially, then increase the speed once the flour has been absorbed. You can use a wooden spoon to beat the ingredients instead, but it will take a little longer (about 2 minutes with an electric whisk, or 3 minutes with a wooden spoon).

3 As you beat, keep turning the bowl around and scrape the sides with a flexible spatula to make sure that all the ingredients are beaten in evenly. The mixture will start to look paler, creamier, and slightly glossy. It will also be soft enough to drop off the beaters when you lift them up.

4 Use a teaspoon and a round-bladed knife to transfer the mixture to the paper bun cases. Put the same amount of mixture into each case, so the cakes bake evenly and end up the same size.

Smooth, swirled icing

1 Sift the icing sugar into a large bowl in order to remove any lumps. This will give the icing a more even texture, which will make it easier to pipe. After the butter and coffee mixture have been mixed in, the finished icing should have a smooth, fluffy consistency.

2 Using a small, sharp knife, cut a circle from the top of each cake, about 5cm (2in) in diameter and 2.5cm (1in) deep. Cut it at an angle, so you end up with a cone-shaped hole that is large enough for you to pipe the icing into. Cut each circle in half to make "butterfly wings" to decorate the tops of the cakes.

3 Before filling the piping bag with icing, insert the nozzle and fold back the top of the bag so it doesn't get messy as you fill. Carefully spoon the icing into the bag, twist the top tightly, and press the bag lightly to get rid of any trapped air bubbles.

4 To pipe, hold the bag upright over the hole in the centre of each cake, then gently squeeze the top of the bag to pipe the icing in a steady stream, guiding the nozzle around the hole to make neat swirls. Repeat for the other cakes.

Chocolate Chip Shortbread Cookies

Buttery and very moreish, few can resist these delicious cookies. Semolina brings a lovely crunch, and mixing in cocoa powder with chocolate chips makes the chocolate flavour all the more intense.

 Makes 16–18   161 calories per serving   **Special equipment**
7.5cm (3in) plain round cutter

INGREDIENTS

- 75g (2½oz) semolina or ground rice
- 140g (5oz) plain flour, plus extra for dusting
- 75g (2½oz) light muscovado sugar
- 25g (scant 1oz) cocoa powder
- 175g (6oz) butter (room temperature), cut into cubes
- 100g (3½oz) plain dark chocolate chips

1 Put the semolina in a large bowl with the flour, sugar, and cocoa powder. Add the butter and rub it in with your fingertips. Work the dough together with your hands, stir in the chocolate chips, then press the dough until it forms a smooth, round ball. (See below, Make a rich, buttery dough.)

2 Roll out the dough on a lightly floured surface to a 5mm (¼in) thickness (you can roll half at a time if you find it easier to handle). Using the cutter, cut the dough into cookies. (See below, Roll and cut carefully.) Gather up the trimmings, re-roll, and cut out more cookies.

3 Lay the cookies on 2 large baking sheets. Chill until firm, for about 30 minutes. Meanwhile, preheat the oven to 160°C (fan 140°C/325°F/Gas 3).

4 Bake for 20–25 minutes or until the cookies start to look very slightly darker at the edges. Remove from the oven and leave on the baking sheets for a few minutes, then transfer to a wire rack to cool completely.

KEYS TO PERFECTION

Make a rich, buttery dough

1 Bring the butter to room temperature before making the dough, for easy blending and rolling. Using your fingertips, rub the butter into the dry ingredients until the mixture resembles fine breadcrumbs.

2 Stir in the chocolate chips just as the dough mix is starting to come together. That way they won't melt from being over-handled. Press and knead the mixture until it forms a smooth ball.

Roll and cut carefully

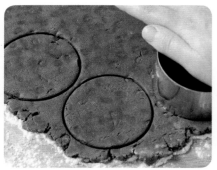

Before rolling, ensure the surface is lightly dusted with flour; too much will dry out the dough and make it over-crumbly. A plain cutter cuts through the chocolate chips more easily than a fluted one.

Fig and Nut Bars

These bars are wonderfully crisp on top and beautifully moist inside. As they hold together well, they're perfect for lunch boxes. They will keep for at least a week stored in an airtight container.

 Makes 24    173 calories per serving    **Special equipment**
Traybake tin, 30 x 23cm (12 x 9in) and 4cm (1½in) deep

INGREDIENTS

- 175g (6oz) butter, cut into large cubes, plus extra for greasing
- 275g (9½oz) porridge oats
- 100g (3½oz) roasted chopped hazelnuts
- 2 tsp ground cinnamon
- 200g (7oz) demerara sugar
- 75g (2½oz) golden syrup
- 125g (4½oz) ready-to-eat dried figs

1 Preheat the oven to 160°C (fan 140°C/325°F/Gas 3). Grease the traybake tin. Line the bottom with baking parchment. Put the oats, hazelnuts, and cinnamon into a large bowl and stir well using a wooden spoon until combined.

2 Put the butter, sugar, and golden syrup into a medium pan. Place the pan over a medium–low heat and stir until all the ingredients are melted together and smooth. Remove the pan from the heat.

3 Holding each fig by its stalk over the pan, snip the fruit into about 10 small pieces using kitchen scissors. Discard the stalks. Stir the figs into the melted mixture, then pour the melted mixture into the large bowl containing the dry ingredients and stir until everything is evenly combined.

4 Spoon the mixture into the prepared tin and level the surface (see below, Even baking). Bake for 35 minutes. At the end of this time, the top will be golden brown and just firm to the touch. Don't be tempted to cook for longer, as the bars will be too crisp – they continue to firm up as they cool.

5 Remove the tin from the oven and leave to rest for 10 minutes, then mark into bars. Leave to go cold before cutting completely and removing from the tin (they will break if taken out too soon). (See below, Neat bars.)

KEYS TO PERFECTION

Even baking

Spread the mixture over the bottom of the tin using the back of a metal spoon. Ease it into the corners and press down firmly to make it level for even baking.

Neat bars

While the mixture is warm, mark out 24 bars with a sharp knife. Run the tip around the edge of the tin, then cut about halfway through the mixture. Finish cutting when the bars are cold.

Chocolate and Amaretti Bars

These no-bake bars are lovely to have with coffee at the end of a meal. The edible gold-leaf decoration looks elegant, but you can top them with shavings of chocolate instead, if you prefer.

 Makes 18   250 calories per serving  **Special equipment**
20cm (8in) square cake tin, 5cm (2in) deep; small paintbrush

INGREDIENTS

- 115g (4oz) butter, plus extra for greasing
- 50g (1¾oz) whole, blanched almonds, coarsely chopped
- 50g (1¾oz) pine nuts
- 3 tbsp golden syrup
- 200g (7oz) plain dark chocolate, chopped into small pieces
- 2 tsp cocoa powder
- 100g (3½oz) ready-to-eat dried apricots, chopped
- 300g (10oz) soft amaretti biscuits
- edible gold leaf, to decorate

1 Grease the cake tin with butter and line the bottom with baking parchment. Heat a medium, non-stick frying pan, tip in the almonds and pine nuts, and dry-fry over a medium heat for about 3 minutes or until golden, turning often so they brown evenly. Tip into a small bowl and set aside.

2 Put the butter, syrup, and half the chocolate into a large heatproof bowl set over a pan of gently simmering water; the base of the bowl should not touch the water. As soon as the chocolate has melted, remove the bowl from the pan. Stir in the cocoa, then the apricots and dry-roasted almonds and pine nuts. Coarsely crumble in the amaretti biscuits (see below, Crunchy base). Stir just to combine.

3 Tip the mixture into the tin and press down with a palette knife to level the surface. Cover and put in the fridge to set for at least 3 hours, or overnight. Remove the tin from the fridge. Put the remaining half of chocolate into a heatproof bowl set over a pan of gently simmering water, and when melted remove the bowl from the pan. Pour the chocolate over the top of the biscuit base, spread it thinly over the surface, and leave to set for 30 minutes to 1 hour (see below, Even chocolate topping).

4 Cut into 18 bars using a sharp knife, remove from the tin, and decorate each bar with edible gold leaf (see below, Elegant finish).

KEYS TO PERFECTION

Crunchy base

When adding the amaretti to the chocolate mixture, crumble the biscuits quite coarsely, and try to have a mixture of sizes and textures – crumbly and chunky – for variety. Stir them in gently so they don't break up.

Even chocolate topping

Smooth the melted chocolate topping evenly over the biscuit base using a palette knife, then let the topping set so it will cut cleanly when sliced. Don't return the bars to the fridge, or the chocolate will lose its sheen.

Elegant finish

Edible gold leaf is paper-thin and extremely delicate. Use the tip of a small, sharp knife to cut a tiny piece away from the sheet, then use a small paintbrush to apply it from the knife's tip onto the chocolate once it has set.

Spiced Dorset Apple Traybake

As well as being a good coffee- or tea-time cake, this makes a comforting pudding, served warm with clotted cream or crème fraîche. I often make it in autumn, when I have a glut of apples.

 Serves 12    341 calories per serving   **Special equipment**
Traybake tin, 30 x 23cm (12 x 9in) and 4cm (1½in) deep

INGREDIENTS

- 225g (8oz) butter (room temperature), plus extra for greasing
- 550g (1¼lb) cooking apples, such as Bramley
- juice of ½ lemon
- 225g (8oz) light muscovado sugar
- 300g (10oz) self-raising flour
- 2 tsp baking powder
- 1 tsp ground cinnamon
- 4 large eggs
- 1 tbsp full-fat or semi-skimmed milk
- icing sugar, to dust

1 Preheat the oven to 180°C (fan 160°C/350°F/Gas 4). Grease the traybake tin with butter and line with baking parchment. Quarter, peel, core, and thinly slice the apples, and put them in a shallow dish. Pour over the lemon juice and toss gently together. (See below, Soft, juicy apples.)

2 Put the butter, muscovado sugar, flour, baking powder, ½ teaspoon of the cinnamon, the eggs, and milk in a large bowl. Beat thoroughly using an electric hand whisk for about 2 minutes (or use a wooden spoon for about 3 minutes) until smooth and light.

3 Spoon half the mixture into the prepared tin and spread it out evenly. Lay half the apple slices on top and sprinkle over the remaining ½ teaspoon of cinnamon. Spoon the remaining cake mixture on top and carefully level the surface. Scatter the rest of the apple slices over the cake mixture and press them lightly into the surface. (See below, Defined layers.)

4 Bake for 40 minutes or until well risen and golden brown on top. The cake will feel spongy but firm, and will be starting to come away slightly from the edges of the tin. Also, the apples should be soft. Leave the cake to cool in the tin for 10 minutes, then loosen the sides with a small palette knife and turn out the cake, peel off the parchment paper, and leave to cool on a wire rack. Sift icing sugar over the top of the cake.

KEYS TO PERFECTION

Soft, juicy apples

It's important to slice the apples very thinly. If they're too thick, they won't soften enough when baked. Tossing them in lemon juice helps stop them from turning too brown, as well as giving flavour and extra juiciness.

Defined layers

1 When spreading the second half of the cake mixture over the apples and cinnamon, do so gently using a palette knife to ensure the apple slices beneath aren't disturbed, thus retaining the layered effect.

2 Spread the apples evenly over the cake mixture and lightly press them in. You don't need to be too neat when layering the apples; in fact, the top looks more interesting if you scatter over the apples in a random pattern.

Mary's TOP TIPS
10

Get the timing right

Timing is crucial, particularly when baking, so it's worth investing in a timer (preferably digital) and always preheat the oven when specified. All ovens vary, so be vigilant and make a note of timings for next time.

My Favourite Fruit Cake

Rich, dark, and temptingly moist, this is based on a Victorian recipe and makes the perfect Christmas, birthday, or christening cake. You can either decorate it or enjoy it just as it is.

 Serves 20

 430 calories per serving

Special equipment
Loose-bottomed, round cake tin, 20cm (8in) diameter and 7.5cm (3in) deep; fine skewer

INGREDIENTS

- 200g (7oz) natural glacé cherries, rinsed, thoroughly dried, and quartered
- 175g (6oz) raisins
- 400g (14oz) currants
- 350g (12oz) sultanas
- 150g (5½oz) dried cranberries
- 100g (3½oz) dried apricots, chopped to the same size as the cherries
- 150ml (5fl oz) sherry, plus extra for "feeding"
- finely grated rind of 2 oranges
- 250g (9oz) butter (room temperature), plus extra for greasing
- 250g (9oz) light muscovado sugar
- 4 large eggs
- 1 tbsp black treacle
- 75g (2½oz) self-raising flour
- 175g (6oz) plain flour
- 1½ tsp mixed ground spice
- 50g (1¾oz) blanched almonds, chopped
- 50g (1¾oz) Brazil nuts, chopped

KEYS TO PERFECTION (*see overleaf*)
Grease and line the cake tin; Moist, rich, golden brown cake

1 Place all the dried fruit in a large container with a tight-fitting lid, pour over the sherry, and add the orange rind. Stir well. Cover and leave the fruit to soak for 3 days, stirring every day. (See p317, Moist, rich, golden brown cake, step 1.)

2 Grease the bottom and side of the cake tin and line with a double layer of greased baking parchment (see p316, Grease and line the cake tin). Preheat the oven to 140°C (fan 120°C/275°F/Gas 1).

3 Put the butter, sugar, eggs, and treacle in a very large bowl and beat well using an electric hand whisk to combine. Don't worry if the mixture looks curdled at this stage. Add both the flours and the mixed ground spice, and stir thoroughly using a large metal spoon until blended. Stir in the soaked fruit (half at a time if it is easier), then the nuts. Spoon the mixture into the prepared cake tin and level the surface with the back of the spoon.

4 Bake in the centre of the oven for 4–4½ hours (checking the colour after 2 hours) or until the cake feels firm and is a rich golden brown colour. Remove and leave the cake to cool in the tin. When cold, pierce the top of the cake at intervals with the skewer and "feed" with 2 tablespoons of sherry. (See Moist, rich, golden brown cake, steps 2–4).

5 Remove the cake from the tin but keep the lining paper on (to keep the cake moist). Wrap the cake in a double layer of baking parchment and again in foil. Store in a cool place for up to 3 months, skewering and "feeding" once a week with sherry.

KEYS TO PERFECTION

Grease and line the cake tin

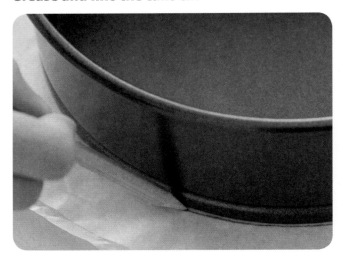

1 As this fruit cake bakes for several hours, you need to line the cake tin with a double layer of baking parchment, or the cake may burn around the edges. To make a lining for the bottom of the tin, sit the base on a double thickness of parchment and draw around the circumference onto the paper in pencil. Cut just inside the pencil line.

2 To line the side, cut a strip of double thickness parchment that is long and deep enough to go all around the tin, allowing a small overlap for the ends. Make a fold, about 2.5cm (1in) wide, along one of the long sides. Cut slightly slanting lines into the folded strip at about 2.5cm (1in) intervals.

3 Fit the lining paper for the side inside the greased tin, so the snipped strips sit snugly on the base. Lay the parchment circles for the bottom of the tin over the snipped part of the side strip, then grease all the parchment paper well using a pastry brush and a little butter. Make sure the butter is at room temperature, so it is soft enough to spread easily.

Make the fruit cake well ahead

This cake is best made 2 months before you want to serve it, although you can make it up to 3 months or as little as 3 weeks ahead. If it's eaten too early, it will be crumbly. Wrap it in a double layer of parchment, then in foil; never put foil directly in contact with a fruit cake, as the acid in the fruit can cause the foil to corrode, impairing the flavour of the cake. Store the cake in a cool place, such as a fridge or cool cupboard, as it may turn mouldy in a warm kitchen.

Moist, rich, golden brown cake

1 You must allow 3 days before making the cake for marinating the dried fruit in sherry. This is essential to plump up and flavour the fruit. If you reduce the soaking time, there will be a surplus of liquid, which will alter the texture of the finished cake. Leave to marinate at room temperature, and turn the fruit in the liquid every day.

2 Inspect the cake after it has been in the oven for 2 hours: it may be the desired colour by then, but the cake will not yet be cooked. If it's already a rich golden brown at this stage, lay a piece of foil loosely over the top. This will protect the top of the cake as it finishes cooking and prevent it from getting too dark.

3 After 4 hours, the cake may be done. To test if it's cooked, insert a fine skewer into the centre of the cake. When withdrawn, the skewer should be clean and dry, not wet and sticky. If it's still sticky, return the cake to the oven to bake for a bit longer.

4 When the cake has cooled, pierce the top at intervals with the skewer and drizzle over 2 tablespoons of sherry. To ensure a wonderfully moist cake with lots of flavour, I repeat this "feeding" process about once a week.

Banana Loaf with Honey Icing

This is a great way to use up ripe bananas, including black-skinned ones. The riper they are, the better the flavour of this loaf. You can keep very ripe bananas in the freezer until you're ready to bake.

 Serves 12    287 calories per serving

Special equipment
900g (2lb) loaf tin, about 21.5 x 11cm (8½ x 4½in) and 6cm (2½in) deep, 1.2 litres (2 pints) capacity

INGREDIENTS

- 115g (4oz) butter (room temperature) or baking spread (at least 70% fat), plus extra for greasing
- 2 very ripe bananas, about 200g (7oz) total peeled weight
- 150g (5½oz) light muscovado sugar
- 2 large eggs
- 225g (8oz) self-raising flour
- 1 tsp baking powder
- 2 tbsp full-fat or semi-skimmed milk
- 75g (2½oz) pecans, chopped

FOR THE ICING AND DECORATION

- 25g (scant 1oz) icing sugar
- 2 tsp clear honey
- 10–12 pecan halves, about 20g (¾oz)

1 Preheat the oven to 180°C (fan 160°C/350°F/Gas 4). Grease the loaf tin and line with baking parchment (see below, Line the loaf tin).

2 Mash the bananas (see below, Optimum flavour and texture). Put the butter, muscovado sugar, eggs, flour, baking powder, and milk in a large bowl and beat using an electric hand whisk for 1 minute (or 2 minutes with a wooden spoon) until blended. Add the banana and beat for 30 seconds or until mixed in. Stir in the chopped pecans. Spoon the mixture into the prepared tin. Level the top.

3 Bake for about 1 hour or until well risen and golden brown. Check after 45 minutes. If the top is browning too much, lay a piece of foil over it. To see if the loaf is done, insert a fine skewer in the middle; it should come out clean.

4 Leave the loaf to cool in the tin for a few minutes. Run a palette knife around the edge of the tin, turn out the loaf, peel off the lining paper, and finish cooling on a wire rack. When the loaf is cold, sift the icing sugar into a bowl and stir in the honey and ½ teaspoon of cold water to make a runny icing. Drizzle this over the cake and lay the pecan halves down the middle.

Loaf tin sizes and capacity

900g (2lb) loaf tins can vary in size and be thinner, fatter, or deeper than the one I have used for this recipe. Provided your tin has the same volume capacity (1.2 litres/2 pints), you will have the right amount of mixture for the loaf. However, if the dimensions are different you may have to adjust the cooking time. For instance, if your tin is slightly shallower but longer than the one I've recommended, the loaf may bake a bit more quickly. Conversely, if it is shorter and deeper, it may take longer.

KEYS TO PERFECTION

Line the loaf tin

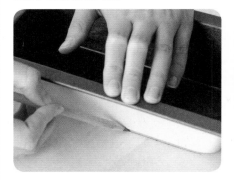

To prevent the loaf from sticking, grease and line the tin: sit the tin on baking parchment and draw around the base, then cut just inside the lines. Lay the paper in the bottom of the tin. You don't need to line the sides.

Optimum flavour and texture

Use very ripe bananas and mash them with a fork until broken down and pulpy. Check you have about 200g (7oz) of mashed banana. Too little will result in lack of flavour, too much and the cake may have a heavy texture.

Pastel Rainbow Cake

There are many versions of the multi-layered rainbow cake. This is my simple one, which is perfect for all sorts of occasions. I like subtle colours, but you can make it as bright as you like.

 Serves 15   525 calories per serving

Special equipment
2 loose-bottomed, round sandwich tins, 20cm (8in) diameter and 4.5cm (1¾in) deep

INGREDIENTS

- 225g (8oz) butter (room temperature) or baking spread (at least 70% fat), plus extra for greasing
- 225g (8oz) caster sugar
- 225g (8oz) self-raising flour
- 2 tsp baking powder
- 4 large eggs
- edible red food paste

FOR THE FILLING

- 350g (12oz) icing sugar
- 175g (6oz) butter (room temperature)
- ¼ tsp vanilla extract
- 4 tsp full-fat or semi-skimmed milk
- 6 tbsp lemon curd

FOR THE GLACÉ ICING AND DECORATION

- 275g (9½oz) icing sugar
- edible coloured food pastes: red, mint green, and yellow
- 15 Smarties (5 pink, 5 green, 5 yellow)

KEYS TO PERFECTION (*see overleaf*)
*Evenly layered, beautifully baked cakes;
Smooth icing and pastel decoration*

1 Preheat the oven to 180°C (fan 160°C/350°F/Gas 4). Grease the sandwich tins and line the bottoms with baking parchment. Put the butter, caster sugar, flour, and baking powder in a large bowl. Add the eggs and beat well using an electric hand whisk for about 2 minutes (or use a wooden spoon for about 3 minutes) until smooth and light.

2 Divide the mixture equally in half. Spoon one half of the mixture into one of the prepared tins. Colour the other half pale pink with the red food paste (add it bit by bit until you're happy with the shade) and spoon it into the other tin. Level the surfaces. Bake both cakes for about 25 minutes. Cool for 2 minutes, then loosen the sides and leave for 10 minutes. Turn the cakes out, carefully remove the tin bases and lining paper, and leave to cool on a wire rack. (See p322, Evenly layered, beautifully baked cakes, steps 1 and 2.)

3 Make the filling: sift the icing sugar into a large bowl, add the butter, vanilla, and milk, and beat together using an electric hand whisk (or wooden spoon) until soft, smooth, and well blended.

4 When the cakes are cold, cut them in half. Place a white sponge layer, cut-side uppermost, on a flat serving plate or a cake stand. Spread with 2 tablespoons of the lemon curd, then with one-third of the filling. Lay a pink sponge layer on top and, again, spread with 2 tablespoons of lemon curd and one-third of the filling. Repeat with another white layer of sponge and the remaining lemon curd and filling. Finish with a pink layer of sponge on top, with the base uppermost to give a flat top. (See p322, Evenly layered, beautifully baked cakes, steps 3 and 4.)

5 Make the glacé icing: sift the icing sugar into a bowl. Stir in 7 teaspoons of cold water, then adjust if necessary with a few more drops of water to make a thickish, spreadable icing. Make 3 small piping bags from baking parchment. Set out 3 small bowls and put 1 tablespoon of the icing into each. Using the coloured food pastes, colour one batch pink, one pale green, and one yellow. Spoon each batch of icing into separate piping bags and fold over the tops to seal. (See p323, Smooth icing and pastel decoration, steps 1–3.)

6 Check the consistency of the remaining white icing and add a drop more water if needed. Spread it evenly over the top of the cake. While it is still soft, quickly pipe squiggly lines over using each of the coloured icings. (See p323, Smooth icing and pastel decoration, step 4.) Stick alternate coloured Smarties upright all around the top edge. Leave the icing to set before slicing.

KEYS TO PERFECTION

Evenly layered, beautifully baked cakes

1 To ensure you have an equal amount of cake batter for each tin, weigh each half of the mixture before you add the edible red food paste. If they weigh exactly the same, the cakes will be of the same depth, giving you attractive, even layers when cut. Gradually add the food paste to half the batter until you get the shade you like.

2 After dividing the mixture equally between the prepared tins, smooth over the surfaces with a palette knife to level, so the cakes cook evenly. Bake the cakes side by side in the oven for even cooking. Don't be tempted to open the oven door before 20 minutes, or the cakes will sink. When done, the cakes will shrink away from the sides of the tins and the tops will spring back if pressed.

3 The cakes need to be halved evenly for the layering to look its best. Let the baked cakes become completely cold before slicing, as they will be more crumbly and difficult to cut if warm. Mark a guide-line in the centre of the side of each cake with a large serrated knife, then continue working your way around the cake. Carefully slice through the cake on the guideline to give two even halves.

4 When spreading the buttercream filling over the surface of the cakes, make sure you do so evenly using a palette knife or round-bladed knife. If it's spread unevenly, the cake layers will be uneven, too. As you spread the filling, try not to disturb the lemon curd layer underneath; you don't want it to get mixed in with the icing.

Smooth icing and pastel decoration

1 Adding just the right amount of water to the icing is key. You want just enough so the icing is smooth and runny, but not so runny that it will run down the sides of the cake. If you lift the spoon out of the bowl, the icing should fall in a slow, steady stream. When piping, the icing needs to be firm enough to hold its shape (if it's too runny, the lines will not be well defined) but soft enough so it flows easily.

2 When adding colouring to the icing (and the batter), it's best to add it cautiously, as if too much is added the colours can quickly become very vivid. Dip a wooden cocktail stick into the food paste and dab in just a little to start with. More can be added to deepen the colour, but it's hard to take it away if too much is used. Stir so it blends in well, otherwise you'll have streaks of colour in the icing.

3 For perfect lines, use a piping bag. For each bag, cut out a piece of baking parchment 20cm (8in) square. Fold it in half to make a triangle. With the long, folded edge near you, take one corner up to the tip of the triangle, then bring the other corner across and wrap it around the back to make a pointed bag. Fold over tightly to seal. Snip off the tip to make a small piping hole.

4 After spooning the icing into the piping bags, fold the top of each bag over the icing so it can't leak out. Taking one filled bag at a time, hold it upright between your fingers and use your thumbs to press the icing out in a steady trail, moving the bag around over the top of the cake so the icing falls in squiggly lines. Repeat with the other icing bags so the lines overlap all over the cake to give a colourful pattern.

Lime and Blueberry Ring Drizzle

Fresh limes and juicy blueberries add a lovely flavour, colour, and texture to this sponge. To get maximum juice from the limes, microwave them all together for 30–60 seconds before squeezing.

 Serves 24

 200 calories per serving

Special equipment
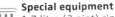 1.7 litre (3 pint) ring mould, 23cm (9in) diameter and 7.5cm (3in) deep; fine skewer

INGREDIENTS

- 225g (8oz) butter (room temperature) or baking spread (at least 70% fat), plus extra for greasing
- 225g (8oz) caster sugar
- 275g (9½oz) self-raising flour
- 1 tsp baking powder
- 4 large eggs
- 2 tbsp full-fat or semi-skimmed milk
- finely grated rind of 3 limes
- 100g (3½oz) blueberries

FOR THE GLAZE
- 6 tbsp lime juice (from 3–4 limes)
- 175g (6oz) granulated sugar

1 Preheat the oven to 180°C (fan 160°C/350°F/Gas 4). Grease the ring mould. Cut about 8–10 strips of baking parchment, each 15 x 2.5cm (6 x 1in), and use them to line the mould (see below, Line the ring mould).

2 Place the butter, caster sugar, flour, and baking powder in a large bowl. Add the eggs, milk, and lime rind and beat using an electric hand whisk for about 2 minutes (or 3 minutes with a wooden spoon) until smooth.

3 Spoon half the mixture into the ring mould and level it, then scatter the blueberries over the top, keeping them away from the edge of the mould (this makes them less likely to stick). Spoon the rest of the mixture over the blueberries, and spread it evenly with a palette knife to cover the fruit.

4 Bake for 35–40 minutes or until well risen and the top springs back when lightly pressed. While the cake bakes, make the glaze: mix the lime juice with the granulated sugar and set aside. Leave the cake to cool in its tin for a few minutes, then loosen the side with a palette knife. Turn it out onto a wire rack set over a baking tray, and peel off the lining strips.

5 While the cake is still warm, prick all over with the skewer. Stir the glaze, then spoon it over the warm cake. Leave to cool completely. (See below, Glaze the warm cake.)

KEYS TO PERFECTION

Line the ring mould

To prevent the cake from sticking to the ring mould, line it with 8–10 parchment strips. Lay the strips at equal intervals, starting from the top of the inner funnel, down to the bottom of the mould, and up the side.

Glaze the warm cake

1 As the ring mould is quite deep, it's best to skewer very small holes all over the warm cake before glazing, so the glaze can soak in. Use a fine skewer (sometimes called a "cake tester") so the holes aren't too big.

2 Spoon the glaze over the cake slowly (or it will run off) and let it drizzle down and soak in before spooning over more. Rub it down the sides with the spoon. Glaze while the cake is still warm; if cool, the glaze will not soak in.

Gorgeous Ginger and Chocolate Cake

Mixing chocolate and a hint of ginger together creates an intriguing blend of flavours in this moist, rich cake. To make sure the ginger doesn't sink, it's important to chop it finely.

 Serves 10 488 calories per serving

Special equipment
2 loose-bottomed, round sandwich tins, 20cm (8in) diameter and 4.5cm (1¾in) deep

INGREDIENTS

- 200g (7oz) butter (room temperature) or baking spread (at least 70% fat), plus extra for greasing
- 50g (1¾oz) cocoa powder
- 4 tbsp full-fat or semi-skimmed milk
- 3 eggs
- 175g (6oz) self-raising flour
- 1 tsp baking powder
- 1 tsp ground ginger
- 250g (9oz) caster sugar
- 2 pieces of stem ginger, finely chopped

FOR THE FILLING AND TOPPING

- 225g (8oz) icing sugar
- 115g (4oz) butter (room temperature)
- 2 tbsp stem ginger syrup
- 1 tbsp full-fat or semi-skimmed milk
- 2 pieces of stem ginger, finely shredded

1 Preheat the oven to 180°C (fan 160°C/350°F/Gas 4). Grease the sandwich tins and line the bottom of each with baking parchment. Put the cocoa powder into a large, heatproof bowl. Stir in 6 tablespoons of boiling water, then add the milk. Mix to make a smooth paste (see below, Smooth mixture).

2 Add the remaining cake ingredients and combine using an electric hand whisk for 1–2 minutes only (or 3 minutes with a wooden spoon); do not over-mix, or the cake may not rise.

3 Divide the cake mixture equally between the prepared tins and level the tops. Bake for 25–30 minutes or until the cakes shrink away from the side of the tin and spring back when lightly pressed in the centre. Let the cakes cool for a few minutes in their tins, then turn them out and peel off the paper. Turn the cakes the right way up and leave to cool on a wire rack.

4 Make the filling and topping: sift the icing sugar into a large bowl. Add the butter, stem ginger syrup, and milk, and beat together using an electric hand whisk (or wooden spoon) until well blended. Transfer one of the cakes to a serving plate and spread half the icing over the top. Place the second cake over the filling and cover the top with the remaining icing. (See below, Evenly iced cakes.) Use the palette knife to draw large "S" shapes to give a swirl effect, then decorate the edge with the shredded stem ginger.

KEYS TO PERFECTION

Buying and using cocoa powder

This cake looks and tastes very chocolatey, but it doesn't actually contain any chocolate – it's made with cocoa powder. Buy a good-quality cocoa powder, preferably an organic one. This will be darker than the less expensive varieties, and will ensure that your cake has a deep, rich chocolate colour and flavour.

Smooth mixture

Cocoa powder can be lumpy, so mix it to a smooth paste with boiling water, then milk before adding the remaining ingredients. Use a wooden spoon to break up any lumps.

Evenly iced cakes

Make sure the butter for the icing is at room temperature, so it will spread easily. Use equal amounts of icing between the layers and on top of the cake, and cover right to the edges.

Hot Cross Bun Loaf

For this recipe the fruit and flavourings are similar to those in traditional hot cross buns, but I've made one large loaf instead, which is quicker. Try it fresh or toasted – it's utterly delicious.

 Makes 1 loaf   2826 calories per loaf

Special equipment
900g (2lb) loaf tin, about 21.5 x 11cm (8½ x 4½in) and 6cm (2½in) deep, 1.2 litres (2 pints) capacity (see p318, box)

INGREDIENTS

- 50g (1¾oz) butter
- 85g (3oz) raisins
- 50g (1¾oz) natural glacé cherries, rinsed, dried, and chopped
- 30g (1oz) currants
- 450g (1lb) strong white flour, plus extra for dusting
- 7g sachet easy-blend (fast-action) dried yeast
- 1 tsp salt
- 1½ tsp ground mixed spice
- 1 tsp ground cinnamon
- 50g (1¾oz) light muscovado sugar
- 150ml (5fl oz) full-fat or semi-skimmed milk
- 1 large egg, beaten
- sunflower oil, for greasing

FOR THE CROSSES AND GLAZE
- 2 tbsp plain flour
- 2 tsp granulated sugar

KEYS TO PERFECTION (*see overleaf*)
Make a rich, fruity dough; Get the best shape; Decorate the loaf

1 Melt the butter and let it cool. Mix the raisins, cherries, and currants in a large bowl and set aside. Combine the strong white flour, yeast, salt, spices, and sugar in a separate large bowl. Heat the milk with 5 tablespoons of water until hand-warm. Make a dip in the flour mixture and pour in the cooled butter and beaten egg. Add the warm milk and water in a steady stream, while mixing everything together with a round-bladed knife. Gather the dough into a ball. (See p330, Make a rich, fruity dough, step 1.)

2 Turn out the dough onto a lightly floured surface and knead for 8–10 minutes or until smooth and elastic. Lay the dough on top of the dried fruit mix in the bowl and knead together to combine. To finish working in the fruit, tip the dough onto the work surface again and knead for 1–2 minutes. Shape the dough into a round and place it in a large, lightly oiled bowl. Cover with cling film and leave in a warm place for about 1½ hours or until doubled in size. (See p330, Make a rich, fruity dough, steps 2–4.) Lightly grease the loaf tin and line the bottom with baking parchment.

3 Tip the risen dough out onto the work surface and knead it just 3 or 4 times. Divide the dough into 4 equal pieces. Shape each one into an oval. Place each piece in the tin in a line. (See p331, Get the best shape.) Cover with a clean tea towel and leave in a warm place to rise for about 50 minutes to 1 hour or until the dough reaches about 5cm (2in) above the top of the tin. Preheat the oven to 230°C (fan 210°C/450°F/Gas 8).

4 For the crosses, make a small piping bag out of baking parchment (see p323, step 3). Mix the plain flour with 4½ teaspoons of cold water in a small bowl to make a smooth paste, then spoon it into the piping bag. When the dough has risen, pipe a cross on top of each piece. (See p331, Decorate the loaf, step 1.)

5 Bake for 5 minutes, then reduce the temperature to 220°C (fan 200°C/425°F/Gas 7) and bake for a further 15 minutes, covering the top loosely with foil when the top is golden brown. Bake for 5–10 minutes more. The loaf is done when it feels firm.

6 Make the glaze: mix the granulated sugar with 1 teaspoon of cold water. Loosen the sides of the loaf with a small, round-bladed knife, then turn out of the tin. Peel off the baking parchment and place the loaf on a wire rack. Brush the glaze over the top of the loaf while it is still warm. (See p331, Decorate the loaf, step 2.) Slice when the loaf is cold.

KEYS TO PERFECTION

Make a rich, fruity dough

1 The dough for this loaf is enriched with butter, milk, and egg. Add the milk and water to the flour, butter, and egg in a slow, steady stream, and as you pour stir the mixture to combine well using a round-bladed knife. The dough is ready when it comes together to form a ball; it should feel quite soft and slightly sticky.

2 To make the dough elastic, knead it for 8–10 minutes on a lightly floured work surface. Push down with the heel of your hand into the ball of dough and stretch it out away from your body, then bring the end of the dough back over the top and press it down in the middle. Give a quarter turn and repeat.

3 To incorporate the fruit into the kneaded dough, lay the dough on top of the fruit in the bowl. Knead from the outside into the centre, so everything starts to get evenly mixed in. Once you've worked in as much of the fruit as you can, tip the dough out and finish kneading in any stray bits of fruit for 1–2 minutes more. To keep the dough light and the fruit intact, don't knead too much at this stage.

4 Leave the dough to rise until it has doubled in size. Generally, if the dough is left in a warm place, this will take about 1½ hours, but the timing can vary depending on the temperature of the room, so keep checking. Bread will rise at its best pace in a warm environment – about 25°C (77°F) (typically found in an airing cupboard) is ideal – rather than one that is too hot or too cold.

Get the best shape

1 Divide the risen dough into 4 equal-sized pieces by cutting it with a sharp knife. Weigh each piece of dough to make sure they're all of equal weight. Weighing will give a more accurate result than dividing by eye, and will give you the best shape for the finished loaf.

2 Form each piece of dough into a plump oval shape by rolling it on the work surface with your hands so it's the width of the tin, checking that each piece is the same length. Again, this will give the best shape to your loaf. Position the ovals in the tin so they fit snugly next to each other in a line.

Decorate the loaf

1 When mixing the paste for the crosses, add enough water so the mixture is liquid enough to pipe yet is able to hold its shape. If too much water is added, the crosses will be less defined. So that the crosses cover the whole of each domed piece of the loaf, start to pipe each line where the dough meets the rim of the tin and take it over the top of the dough until it touches the rim on the other side.

2 For a perfect finish, brush the sugar glaze over the top of the loaf while it is still warm. The warmth of the dough will help the glaze to set and give the loaf a glossy sheen.

Irish Soda Bread

This traditional bread is made without yeast, so it's perfect for days when you want a loaf on the table quickly. The buttermilk provides a soft-textured dough with a unique flavour.

 Makes 1 loaf    1762 calories per loaf

INGREDIENTS

- 20g (¾oz) butter (room temperature), plus extra for greasing
- 225g (8oz) plain white flour, plus extra for dusting and sprinkling
- 225g (8oz) plain wholemeal flour
- 1 tsp bicarbonate of soda
- 1 tsp salt
- 400ml (14fl oz) buttermilk

1 Preheat the oven to 200°C (fan 180°C/400°F/Gas 6). Lightly grease a baking sheet with a little butter.

2 Put both the flours in a large bowl. Add the butter and rub it in with your fingertips. Stir in the bicarbonate of soda and salt. Pour in the buttermilk and 2 tablespoons of hand-warm water. Briefly mix the ingredients (see below, Make a light-textured dough, step 1). The dough should be very soft and sticky, but still easy to shape. Add another tablespoon of water if needed.

3 Turn out the dough onto a lightly floured surface and gather into a neat round, about 20cm (8in) in diameter (it needn't be too smooth). Place the loaf on the baking sheet and cut a 1cm (½in) deep cross in the top. (See below, Make a light-textured dough, steps 2 and 3.) Sprinkle the top of the loaf with a little white flour.

4 Bake for 30–35 minutes or until risen and golden brown. Tap the base of the loaf to see if it is cooked: it should sound hollow. Transfer to a wire rack to cool. The soda bread is best eaten very fresh, but if wrapped well it will keep for 1 or 2 days.

KEYS TO PERFECTION

Make a light-textured dough

1 A few turns using your hands are all that is required to make sure the buttermilk and water are blended in. Throughout the process, don't over-handle the dough; the less you handle it, the lighter the bread will be.

2 Shape the dough into a round with your hands. Just lightly gather it together into a ball, then gently pat it out to a circle about 20cm (8in) across. As there is no yeast in this mixture, it doesn't require any kneading.

3 Using a sharp knife dipped in flour to prevent sticking, cut a cross on the loaf, about 1cm (½in) deep. As the loaf bakes, the cross will open out, enabling the bread to cook through to the centre.

Seeded Granary Twist

I've learnt from Paul Hollywood that when making bread it's good to have a slightly wet, sticky dough, as it produces better results. This loaf contains a mix of seeds for added texture and flavour.

 Makes 1 loaf   2308 calories per loaf

INGREDIENTS

- 300g (10oz) Granary flour
- 200g (7oz) strong white flour, plus extra for dusting
- 1½ tsp salt
- 7g sachet easy-blend (fast-action) dried yeast
- 30g (1oz) butter (room temperature), cut into small pieces
- 6 tbsp mixed seeds, such as sesame, sunflower, linseed, and pumpkin
- sunflower oil, for greasing

1 Mix both the flours, salt, and yeast together in a large bowl. Add the butter and rub it in with your fingertips. Stir in 5 tablespoons of the seeds. Make a well in the centre of the flour mixture and pour in 300ml (10fl oz) hand-warm water. Mix everything together to make a dough. Gather the dough into a ball. (See p336, Make a soft, pliable dough, step 1.)

2 Turn the dough out onto a lightly floured surface and knead for 8–10 minutes or until smooth and elastic. Put the dough in a large, lightly oiled bowl and cover with cling film. Leave to rise in a warm place for about 1½ hours or until the dough doubles in size. (See p336, Make a soft, pliable dough, steps 2–4.)

3 Line a large baking sheet with baking parchment. When the dough has risen, gently knead it on the lightly floured work surface 3 or 4 times (no more, as too much handling now will reduce the dough's lightness).

4 Cut the dough into 2 equal-sized portions and roll the pieces into "ropes" about 40cm (16in) long. Lay one on top of the other to make an "X", then twist them together tightly. Tuck the ends under and press to seal. (See p337, Create an evenly shaped twist.)

5 Lay the loaf on the prepared baking sheet and cover with a clean tea towel. Leave for 40–50 minutes or until doubled in size. Preheat the oven to 230°C (fan 210°C/450°F/Gas 8).

6 Uncover the loaf and brush the top with cold water. Sprinkle the remaining 1 tablespoon of seeds over the twists and gently press in. Bake the loaf for 10 minutes, then reduce the oven temperature to 220°C (fan 200°C/425°F/Gas 7) and bake for a further 20 minutes. (See p337, Bake a crisp crust.) Place on a wire rack to cool.

KEYS TO PERFECTION *(see overleaf)*
Make a soft, pliable dough; Create an evenly shaped twist; Bake a crisp crust

KEYS TO PERFECTION

Make a soft, pliable dough

1 Add the hand-warm water to the ingredients in the bowl in a steady stream, mixing as you do so with a round-bladed knife. It's crucial to measure the water accurately and add the full amount. If you don't add enough initially and the dough is too dry, it's harder to add more water later. Once all the water is added and the dough has come together, feel the texture: it should be soft, moist, and sticky.

2 Gather the dough into a ball, turn it out onto a lightly floured work surface, and begin to knead. The process of kneading makes the dough more elastic, and you need to do it for 8–10 minutes at this stage for a well-textured loaf. Use the weight of your body to push down with the heel of your hand into the ball of dough, then stretch it away from your body.

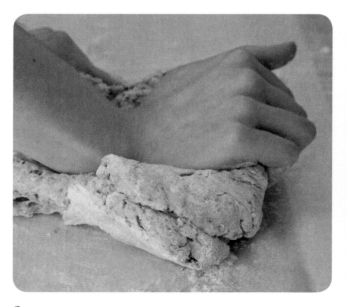

3 Bring the end of the stretched-out dough back over the top and press it down in the middle. Give a quarter turn and repeat. Get into a smooth rhythm. As you knead, the dough will start to feel less sticky but still soft and smooth. Add more flour to the work surface only if the dough is sticking to it; too much extra flour may dry out the dough. Put the dough into an oiled bowl (the oil will prevent sticking).

4 Leave the dough to rise in a warm place, but not too hot or it could dry out the dough – an airing cupboard or warm kitchen is ideal. Rising is important to improve the bread's structure and flavour. You want the dough to reach double its original size and look and feel very light and spongy. This will usually take about 1½ hours, but keep checking, as it depends on the temperature of the room.

Create an evenly shaped twist

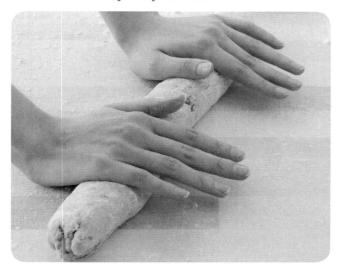

1 Weigh each half of dough to make sure they're the same weight, to give you an evenly shaped twist. Using the palms of your hands, roll each half to make two long "ropes". If the dough sticks and is difficult to roll, rub a tiny amount of olive oil onto the surface to help it grip.

2 Lay both dough strands to form an "X" on the work surface. Taking hold of the bottom two ends, twist them over each other 2 or 3 times to make a tight twist. Taking hold of the whole loaf from the middle, carefully turn it over and twist the other 2 ends in the same way. This will give you a plump rather than long, thin twist. Tuck both ends under very slightly and press down to seal.

Bake a crisp crust

1 Before putting the twist in the oven, make sure the oven has preheated to the correct temperature (otherwise the loaf may continue to rise and the sides may split) and that the dough has risen to twice its previous size (but no more, or it may collapse). Just before baking, brush the loaf lightly with water, to create a crisp crust, and scatter over the reserved seeds, pressing them in gently.

2 When the loaf is baked it should be golden brown and firm. I tap it on the base to check if it's ready. It should have a hollow drum-like sound. If it doesn't, return the loaf to the oven for a few more minutes.

Cheese and Chive Flowerpot Loaf

Using a terracotta flowerpot as a mould for this cheese loaf gives it an interesting and unusual shape. Buy a new, clean flowerpot, season it (see below, box), and keep it just for baking bread.

 Makes 1 loaf  1884 calories per loaf 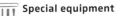 **Special equipment**
Terracotta flowerpot, 15cm (6in) diameter and 13cm (5¼in) deep

INGREDIENTS

- 375g (13oz) strong white flour, plus extra for dusting
- 1½ tsp easy-blend (fast-action) dried yeast
- 1 tsp salt
- 20g (¾oz) butter (room temperature), cut into small pieces
- 45g (1½oz) mature Cheddar cheese, coarsely grated
- 45g (1½oz) Parmesan cheese, coarsely grated
- 2 tbsp snipped fresh chives
- sunflower oil, for greasing
- 1 egg, beaten

1 Mix the flour, yeast, and salt in a large bowl. Rub in the butter with your fingertips. Combine the cheeses, reserving 15g (½oz) for the top. Add the rest to the bowl with the chives. Make a well and add 240ml (8fl oz) of hand-warm water in a steady stream, mixing with a round-bladed knife to make a soft dough, adding a little extra water if required. Gather the dough and knead on a lightly floured surface for 8–10 minutes or until smooth and elastic. Shape into a round, put it in a large, lightly oiled bowl, cover with cling film, and leave in a warm place for 1½ hours or so, until at least doubled in size.

2 Brush the seasoned flowerpot inside with oil and line (see below, Line the pot). Knead the dough 3 or 4 times, form it into a sausage shape about 18cm (7in) long and narrower at one end, and put it in the pot. Cover with a tea towel and leave for 45–55 minutes or until the dough has risen to about 4cm (1½in) above the pot. (See below, Let the dough rise.)

3 Move the oven shelf to its lowest position. Preheat the oven to 230°C (fan 210°C/450°F/Gas 8). Brush the loaf top with the egg and sprinkle with the reserved cheese. Sit the pot on a baking sheet and bake for 5 minutes, then reduce the oven temperature to 220°C (fan 200°C/425°F/Gas 7) and bake for a further 30 minutes. When the loaf is firm on top, remove it from the oven and let it sit in the pot for 2–3 minutes. Remove it from the pot, carefully peel off the baking parchment, and leave to cool on a wire rack.

Season the flowerpot

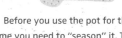

Before you use the pot for the first time you need to "season" it. To do this, wash it thoroughly and dry well, then brush it all over generously, inside and out, with sunflower or vegetable oil. Stand the pot on a baking sheet and put it in an oven preheated to 230°C (fan 210°C/450°F/Gas 8) for 1 hour. Be careful when you remove the pot, as it will be very hot. After baking the bread, just wipe the inside of the pot rather than wash it.

KEYS TO PERFECTION

Line the pot

Cut out a circle of baking parchment to fit the bottom of the pot and a strip to fit round with a slight overlap. Cut the strip in half. Line the bottom then sides. Oil where the strips overlap.

Let the dough rise

Put the dough in the flowerpot with the narrow end facing down and leave to rise. The dough should rise above the pot before you put the loaf in the oven.

Little Cottage Rolls

A large, cottage-style loaf is traditional, but here I've used the same shape to make daintier, individual rolls. They're the ideal size for serving with soup or cheese, and freeze really well, too.

 Makes 10    213 calories per serving

INGREDIENTS

- 500g (1lb 2oz) strong white flour, plus extra for dusting
- 7g sachet easy-blend (fast-action) dried yeast
- 1½ tsp salt
- 45g (1½oz) butter (room temperature), cut into small pieces
- sunflower oil, for greasing
- 1 egg, beaten
- about 1 tsp poppy seeds, for sprinkling

1 Combine the flour, yeast, and salt in a large bowl. Add the butter and rub it in with your fingertips. Make a well in the flour mixture and pour in about 300ml (10fl oz) of hand-warm water in a steady stream, while mixing together with a round-bladed knife. Gather the dough together, adding a few more drops of water, if needed. Turn the dough out onto a lightly floured surface and knead for 8–10 minutes or until smooth and elastic. Put it in a large, lightly oiled bowl, cover with cling film, and leave to rise for about 1½ hours or until doubled in size. Line 2 large baking trays with baking parchment.

2 Tip the dough out onto the work surface and knead 3 or 4 times. Cut the dough into 10 equal-sized pieces. For each piece of dough, cut off one-third with a sharp knife, then shape both the smaller and larger portions into balls. Put the larger balls on the baking sheets and sit the smaller balls on top. Flour the handle of a wooden spoon and push it through the centre of each stacked roll. (See below, Make neat rounds, steps 1 and 2.) Cover with a tea towel and leave to rise in a warm place until doubled in size, for 40–45 minutes.

3 Preheat the oven to 230°C (fan 210°C/450°F/Gas 8). Brush the rolls with the egg and sprinkle with poppy seeds (see below, Make neat rounds, step 3). Bake for 5 minutes, then reduce the temperature to 220°C (fan 200°C/425°F/Gas 7). Bake for a further 10 minutes or until the rolls are golden and firm and sound hollow when tapped on the underside. Cool on a wire rack.

KEYS TO PERFECTION
Make neat rounds

1 Sit the large balls well apart on the baking sheets, so they can rise without touching, otherwise they will lose their shape. Place the smaller balls on top of the larger ones.

2 To secure the top ball to the bottom one, and prevent it from toppling over in the oven, push a floured wooden spoon handle right through the centre of both balls.

3 When the rolls have doubled in size, for a glistening glaze brush them all over with beaten egg using a pastry brush, then add a light sprinkling of poppy seeds.

INDEX

ACKNOWLEDGMENTS

About the author

Mary Berry is one of the UK's most loved and respected cookery writers and bakers. She is also widely known as a judge on the hit BBC2 TV programme *The Great British Bake-off* and is the author of over 80 cookbooks, with 6 million sales worldwide, including the recent *Mary Berry's Cookery Course* (DK) and the bestselling *Mary Berry's Complete Cookbook* (DK), which has sold over a million copies. Mary shares her secrets to perfect home cooking in this book.

Mary Berry would like to thank

As ever, I have a wonderful team working with me on my book. Huge thank yous to Angela Nilsen and Jeni Wright, who worked with us to create perfect recipes with true dedication – thank you for your amazing hard work. My thanks also to Polly Boyd, who has edited this book with a fine-tooth comb, making sure every letter and photo is in place; Mary-Clare Jerram at DK for always being the most devoted commissioner; Peter Luff, Nicola Powling, and Karen Constanti for the design; and Dawn Henderson and Christine Keilty for overseeing the project. For the lovely food photography I would like to thank William Reavell and Stuart West, and home economists Jane Lawrie, Emma-Jane Frost, Nico Ghirlando, and Carol Tennant. Thanks are also due to lovely photographer Georgia Glynn Smith for the action photos of me – what a talent and delight to have on shoot.

Finally, and most important of all, to Lucy Young, who has been my assistant for 24 years and liaises with everyone above ... I now refer to *her* as the boss!

DK would like to thank

Angela Nilsen and Jeni Wright, who worked with Mary Berry to develop and perfect the recipes; Lucy Young for recipe consultation; Geoff Fennell and Penny Stock for art direction; Liz Hippisley for recipe styling; Laura Buscemi, Mandy Earey, Anne Fisher, and Vicky Read for design assistance; Steve Crozier and Karen Constanti for retouching; Isabel de Cordova for wardrobe styling; Jo Penford for hair and make-up; Elizabeth Clinton, Sarah Edwards, Kate Fenton, and Jenny Volich for hand modelling; Fiona Hunter for calorie counts; Norma MacMillan and Corinne Masciocchi for proofreading; Vanessa Bird for indexing.

A note about ingredients

Baileys is a trademark of R & A Bailey & Co in the UK and other countries; Dolcelatte is a trademark of S.P.A. Egidio Galbani in the UK and other countries; Granary is a trademark of Premier Foods Group Limited in the UK and other countries; Guinness is a trademark of Diageo Ireland in the UK and other countries; Peppadew is a trademark of Piquante Brands International (Proprietary) Limited in the UK and other countries; Smarties is a trademark of Société des Produits Nestlé S.A. in the UK and other countries; Tenderstem is a trademark of Marks and Spencer plc in the UK and Ireland.